Imaginative Moods
Aesthetics, Religion, Philosophy

Dorthe Jørgensen

Imaginative Moods

Aesthetics,
Religion,
Philosophy

In ever loving memory of my beloved Willy

Willy Aastrup (1948–2019)

Contents

Introduction 9

The Meaning of Art 17

The Significance of Sensitivity 21

Body and Prayer 35

The Receptivity to Faith 45

Protestantism and Its Aesthetic Discontents 57

The Metamorphosis of Beauty 73

Experience, Metaphysics, and Immanent Transcendence 91

Sensuousness and Transcendence 115

The Philosophy of Imagination 145

The Intermediate World 183

The Aesthetics of Prayer 201

Bibliography 219

Acknowledgments 233

Introduction

The word 'metaphysics' usually denotes philosophy about something static and ahistorical, but this notion of metaphysics is ripe for revision. Both traditional metaphysics and modern antimetaphysics have become dismissible, and many people appear to seek an alternative. In *Imaginative Moods*, I insist on reinterpreting metaphysics rather than rejecting all metaphysical thought. I explore what philosophical aesthetics and hermeneutic phenomenology can offer the attempt to develop a new view of metaphysics, and I exhibit the potential of this effort for the philosophy of religion. My *metaphysics of experience*, which innovatively treats the mind-opening and world-transformative experiences usually called 'aesthetic' or 'religious' experiences, including the sensitively expanded thinking related to such experiences, crosses and revitalizes philosophy and theology, and it introduces and applies new concepts such as the 'experience of immanent transcendence' and the 'intermediate world.' I explore the revelatory nature of sensitivity as well as its ethical value and epistemological significance, including its importance in both science and religious practice. I also explore the importance of imagination for any kind of transgressive experience, including the felt insight and appeal to action delivered by such experience.

Presenting the epistemological significance of aesthetic and religious experiences, the texts included in *Imaginative Moods* offer detailed explanations of the value of treating such experiences in the experience-metaphysical way performed here. For example, the book's various texts attest the potential consequences of the epistemological value of aesthetic experience for our understanding of the relation between sensation, faith, and comprehension, and thus also for philosophical and theological thought. They also make evident that the metaphysics of experience and its notions of 'immanent transcendence,' the 'experience of divinity,' the 'intermediate world,' and 'world poetry' contribute innovatively to the philosophy of religion. Similarly, they demonstrate how the metaphysics of experience can qualify our understanding and treatment of secular phenomena of both philosophical and theological relevance, for example, contemporary works of art or the question of what it means to be a human being.

In *Imaginative Moods*, I introduce and apply new interpretations of our concepts of, for example, truth, beauty, experience, sensation, metaphysics, transcendence, imagination, faith, and prayer. With reference to an unusual museum visit, the first chapter presents and highlights art's capacity to seize and change us as humans. The second chapter follows up on this by introducing the distinction developed by philosophical aesthetics between sense perception and sensitive experience, and the distinction coined by hermeneutic phenomenology between the body and the lived body. Moreover, this chapter describes the significance of sensitivity in relation to our understanding of not only art but also nature, science, and ethics. The third chapter consists of a meditation on the importance of being lived-bodily attentive in one's bodily presence, be it as pastor or stage performer. The fourth chapter further develops this reminder of the importance of lived-bodily attentiveness by discussing the human receptivity to faith regarded as a potential that is both innate and vulnerable. Consequentially, the fifth chapter challenges many Protestant thinkers' and hermeneutic phenomenologists' ambivalence toward aesthetics and emphasizes the ethical significance and theological relevance of aesthetic sensitivity.

The sixth chapter challenges the current tendency to favor the sublime at the expense of the beautiful. The criticism articulated here is based on a study of the historical metamorphoses of beauty since antiquity and a distinction between traditional and modern notions of beauty. Similarly, the seventh chapter challenges the current antimetaphysics by interpreting aesthetic and religious experiences as experiences of transcendence and by explaining the meaning of immanent transcendence, regarded as the most recent notion of transcendence and as a key concept in the metaphysics of experience. Describing the experience of beauty as the experience that something is valuable in itself—and thus as an experience of divinity, but not a religious experience of the divine—the eighth chapter follows up on the reflections on aesthetic experience articulated in the previous chapters. Likewise, the ninth chapter takes up references to the imagination made in the previous chapters, and paves the way for the following chapters by interpreting various historical and contemporary understandings of imagination and by presenting an experience-metaphysical understanding according to which imagination is essential for cognition, moral action, aesthetic experience, and aesthetic thinking. The tenth chapter describes the intermediate world, which was introduced in the second chapter, as the origin of all knowledge: it is a state related to attunement, mood, and atmosphere and characterized by feeling, sensation, and presentiment. It is in this state constituting the realm that houses 'basic experience,' which is characterized by sensation, faith, and comprehension, that imagination is at work and transcendence takes place. Through a contemplation on prayer interpreted as an aesthetic-sensitive phenomenon, the eleventh chapter studies what actually happens in the intermediate world. This chapter thus develops the approach to prayer introduced in the third chapter by integrating elements of aesthetic, hermeneutic, and phenomenological thought introduced in other chapters. The chapter shows that prayer both presupposes and constitutes *kenosis*, that is, an emptying of the rational subject in favor of emotional subjectivity and a suspension of instrumental thinking in favor of sensitive contemplation.

* * *

Imaginative Moods is part of a duology that also includes the book *Poetic Inclinations: Ethics, History, Philosophy*.[1] Together these books represent the first comprehensive presentation in English of what I term the metaphysics of experience, and which, owing to my monographs in Danish, is well known and widely used in the Nordic countries. Aesthetics plays an important role in both books, but each book has its own scope and can therefore be read as an individual work. As is evident from the description of *Imaginative Moods* presented in the previous paragraphs, this book includes a focus on aesthetics, religion, and philosophy (for example, the potential contribution of aesthetics to the understanding of prayer). *Poetic Inclinations*, on the other hand, includes a focus on ethics, history, and philosophy (for example, the ethical significance of aesthetic thinking, in the sense of its formative consequences). Nevertheless, the two books are interrelated due to their shared task as introductions to the metaphysics of experience and their mutual cross references. They genuinely supplement and complement each other.

Poetic Inclinations makes the metaphysics of experience available to beginners and introduces practitioners in various professions to the implications of this philosophy. It proves the relevance of the metaphysics of experience by emphasizing the significance of aesthetic thinking in fields such as education, politics, and social work. Besides appealing to scholars and students, this book may also appeal to practitioners such as teachers, pedagogues, and social workers. *Imaginative Moods*, on the other hand, provides further knowledge about and insight into the metaphysics of experience. This book is slightly more demanding, since it focuses on the aforementioned metaphysics as such and its theoretical implications in aesthetics and theology. *Imaginative Moods* may appeal to scholars, students, pastors, psychologists, and artists, as well as those who have read *Poetic Inclinations* and who are thus already familiar with the relevance of the metaphysics of experience.

---

1   Dorthe Jørgensen, *Poetic Inclinations: Ethics, History, Philosophy* (Aarhus: Aarhus University Press, 2021).

Poetic Inclinations and *Imaginative Moods* give an international readership access to innovative work that includes the reinterpretation of established concepts, the introduction of new notions, and the presentation of the practical and theoretical implications of both. They also offer new ways to conceive of and apply aesthetics, hermeneutics, and phenomenology, which includes groundbreaking theoretical work in the form of a unique integration of these disciplines as well as a unique integration of aesthetics and theology. Phenomenologists and hermeneutic philosophers generally reject or diminish aesthetics in favor of the philosophy of art. Traditionally, Protestant theologians also rejected aesthetics, and contemporary theological attempts to include aesthetics mostly confuse it with the study of art. Finally, *Poetic Inclinations* and *Imaginative Moods* present numerous practical (critical, ethical, pedagogical) as well as philosophical and theological perspectives for contemplating contemporary phenomena within the framework of the metaphysics of experience. They expose the importance of sensitive contemplation that has an eye for transgressive experience and acknowledges both the existential relevance of such experience and its significance for the production of knowledge, for contemporary culture, and for society in general.

Both books consist of collections of texts written in various contexts but revolving around the aforementioned topics. The texts I have selected for publication together constitute two monographs thanks to their thematic kinship, common terminology, and common introduction and application of the metaphysics of experience; I edited and organized them for their present release, in English and in book form. I was motivated to produce these monographs by my international colleagues, who have often lamented that the majority of my research, including my major presentation of the metaphysics of experience—that is, the 965-page monograph *Den skønne tænkning* (Beautiful Thinking)—is only available in Danish.[2] Many scholars and artists from various backgrounds have

---

2 Dorthe Jørgensen, *Den skønne tænkning: Veje til erfaringsmetafysik. Religionsfilosofisk udmøntet* (Beautiful Thinking: Pathways to the Metaphysics of Experience. Religio-Philosophically Implemented) (Aarhus: Aarhus University Press, 2014).

requested a comprehensive English introduction to the metaphysic of experience, including the research in which this philosophy originates, the way of thinking of which it is a product, and its practical and theoretical implications. It is my great hope that *Poetic Inclinations* and *Imaginative Moods* will fulfill this request, at least partly, and I am deeply grateful for the interest that has motivated their publication.

    The editing of the present material was guided by a wish to avoid unnecessary repetition but also to enable the reader to approach and understand each text and each book without prior knowledge of the others. A certain amount of repetition was thus unavoidable, but, as a teacher and knowledge disseminator, I have learned that repetition is far from harmful for educational purposes, especially when the content being mediated is philosophical and thus potentially difficult to access. Some of the texts presented in *Poetic Inclinations* and *Imaginative Moods* have been published previously, in various books or journals and in Danish or English, while others represent hitherto unpublished material produced with a foothold in my Danish monographs. Precise details can be found in the acknowledgments, where I also express my deep gratitude to the journal editors and publishers who have authorized me to reproduce previously published work. The editorial organization of the texts makes it possible, as mentioned, to favor an anarchistic way of reading in which one jumps between the texts and books or perhaps only reads a single text or book. However, it also entails that one benefits from reading the books from beginning to end, starting with *Poetic Inclinations* and finishing with *Imaginative Moods*. At the end of the day, reading with an open mind is the most important premise of the outcome, and such a mindset aligns perfectly with the moral implication of the metaphysics of experience and thus with the ethos of the books.

* * *

The texts included in the present publication were translated into American English by me, in close cooperation with various copy-editors and proofreaders, and edited following the Chicago Manual of Style. Each text constitutes a chapter. To make it easier to use the chapters on an individual basis, I provide full bibliographic information in a footnote about texts I refer to the first time they appear in a chapter. All quotations follow current translations into English; where there is no available translation, I have made one myself. Numbers and letters in references to Plato's texts refer to the Stephanus pagination, and in references to Aristotle's texts to the Bekker numbering. Citations and quotations from Kant's texts refer to page numbers in the Cambridge Edition of the Works of Kant followed by volume and page numbers in the Academy Edition, except for references to the *Critique of Pure Reason,* which is cited and quoted by page numbers in the original first (A) and second (B) editions.

The Meaning of Art

My husband disappears when we go to a museum. After a quarter of an hour, he has had enough and, after an hour, he has gone. Fortunately, I know where to find him—in the museum café. In this way, the presence of the experience economy in the museum world serves a purpose after all: the better the museum's coffee, the cleaner my conscience when I let my husband disappear.

Yet when we visited Pamuk's museum in Istanbul, my husband did not disappear. On the contrary, he was seized by enthusiasm.[3] That was fortunate, as there is no café in this museum. At the entrance door one is instructed to watch in silence, at most to whisper. Here, the experience economy has not made an entrance. Everything in this place is art: not only the exhibited objects, which were originally ordinary household items but are now used by Pamuk as ingredients in the total installation that his museum constitutes, but also the museum as such.

I am referring to the Turkish writer and Nobel laureate Orhan Pamuk's "The Museum of Innocence" in Istanbul. In 2008, Pamuk published the novel *The Museum of Innocence*, whose narrative is about the relationship between the wealthy businessman Kemal and his younger poor relative Füsun.[4] From a cultural-historical point of view, it is also about Turkish culture in the last decades of

---

3   The enthusiasm described in this chapter must not be confused with the *Schwärmerei* (fanaticism, also called enthusiasm) discussed in the chapter "The Philosophy of Imagination."

4   Orhan Pamuk, *The Museum of Innocence: A Novel*, trans. M. Freely (London: Faber and Faber, 2010).

the twentieth century. From an ideahistorical perspective, it deals with this period's conflicts between tradition and modernity, and, from a philosophical perspective, it is about memory, life, and narrative, especially the importance of things to us and to our understanding of ourselves and the world.

In the museum that shares its name with the novel, the visitor finds objects that he or she will recognize from reading the book; for example, Füsun's earring. As tableaus presented in showcases, these objects are exhibited along with others that are brought into the story through their exhibition—that is, brought into the novel's story and its afterlife in the reader's memory. Furthermore, Pamuk has also produced a catalogue titled *The Innocence of Objects*, in which the reader finds his reflections on the significance of things, in addition to pictures from the museum.[5] "If objects are not uprooted from their environs and their streets, but are situated with care and ingenuity in their natural homes, they will already portray their own stories."[6]

According to the novel's and the museum's presentations of their love story, Kemal and Füsun knew each other as children. Just two months before his planned engagement to Sibel, who is his age and, like him, is from the better bourgeoisie, adult Kemal coincidentally sees Füsun again and falls in love. Still, Kemal is engaged to Sibel, and Füsun marries Feridun. But Kemal's love for Füsun persists and he begins to gather things related to her. These things are the objects on display at the "Museum of Innocence," including a wall with 4213 cigarette butts and remains of lipstick. Under each butt, Pamuk, at Kemal's request, has meticulously written out Kemal's short note on that day.

The museum is housed in the building in which Füsun lived with her parents and her husband, and where Kemal later lived on his own for many years. According to the novel, as well as the museum and the catalogue, the exhibition consists of objects collected by Kemal, and the museum itself was his idea. It was Pamuk, the

---

5   Orhan Pamuk, *The Innocence of Objects*, trans. E. Oklap (New York: Abrams 2012).

6   Orhan Pamuk, *The Innocence of Objects*, 57.

writer of the novel, who built the museum, but at the request of Kemal. Apparently, the catalogue is the only thing that Pamuk produced on his own (in as far as this was actually the case).

"Kemal first told me what he had been through over the course of three hours in a restaurant," writes Pamuk in the catalogue. "When I decided to write a novel about his love for Füsun, we inevitably became friends. On many a night over the seven years between March 2000 and February 2007, I sat in the attic on the chair on the right and listened to his story."[7]

The attic mentioned by Pamuk is the top floor of the little building that houses the three small levels of the museum. I had read the novel in advance of our visit to the museum, but my husband had not. Just as he quickly tires of museums, he had already tired of novels as a young man, having read everything written by Danish authors since the Modern Breakthrough. Some days I am tempted to say that he perhaps did not approach literature with the right attitude—that the joy of novels last longer if one reads in a different way. However, there is still hope, as I learned at the museum in Istanbul.

When we reached the attic, my husband and I had not exchanged many words during the hour we had spent in the museum thus far. Not only were we instructed to watch in silence, but we had each in our own way been absorbed by the showcases and by the installation as a whole. In the attic, we found the bed in which Kemal slept after he moved in, and beside the bed was the chair in which Pamuk had been sitting when Kemal told him his story. What I later read in the catalogue, and what also appeared from a text on the wall, was that this was the place where Kemal passed his story on to Pamuk. Nearby, we saw a showcase with worldwide translations of Pamuk's novel, which appeared as an installation in itself.

For my husband, the illusion lasted to this very moment. "But isn't it true at all?" he asked in surprise. Pamuk had succeeded in gripping my husband to such a degree that he, moving from showcase to showcase, was convinced that it was Pamuk's love story he

---

7   Orhan Pamuk, *The Innocence of Objects*, 249.

was being told. "Isn't it about him at all?" asked my husband in disbelief. Yet the shattering of my husband's illusion did not damage the work! His enthusiasm did not disappear once he realized that it was not Pamuk's story, or that it is difficult to distinguish between life and narrative—that this itself is the point. Instead, this revelation simply added an intellectual dimension to his enthusiasm.

It may sound like my husband is what Pamuk, in the essay *The Naive and the Sentimental Novelist,* calls a 'naive' reader: one who simply has experiences. Or perhaps it sounds like my husband prefers to be such a reader after having been too 'sentimental' as a young man, which here means too intellectual—that he prefers to be seized by art when he visits a museum rather than to study it intellectually.[8] However, my husband is not at all naive, and, according to Pamuk, the point is not to be either naive or sentimental, but to be both, that is, both to surrender to art and to reflect on it, and especially to be able to reflect as though seized by it.

"The Museum of Innocence" in Istanbul is a successful work. Had I not been able to recognize this on my own, I would only have needed to watch my husband to know. With this museum, Pamuk succeeded in putting my husband in a state of enthusiasm characterized by both naivety and sentimentality, both feeling and reflection. Such an event requires a great artist as well as the willingness of the recipient to be influenced by the work, and that is the meaning of art: to open the mind, so that enthusiasm can find its way in and lift us out of the tyranny of mediocrity.

---

[8] Orhan Pamuk, *The Naive and the Sentimental Novelist,* trans. N. Dikbas (London: Faber and Faber, 2010). Pamuk's reflections are inspired by Friedrich Schiller's essay "Naive and Sentimental Poetry." See Friedrich Schiller, "Naive and Sentimental Poetry," in *Naive and Sentimental Poetry, and On the Sublime: Two Essays,* ed. and trans. J.A. Elias (New York: Frederick Ungar Publishing Company, 1975).

The Significance of Sensitivity

Sensitive Experience

Some people sense the world more intensely than others. A couple walks through the park, but only one of them notices the light. The other is concerned with how to get back at his boss. Three conference participants have a lively discussion before bedtime, after which two of them sleep soundly but the other relives the discussion all night in her mind. A class of students go to a museum with their teacher, but they all react differently. Some of them sit in a corner discussing the exercises they have been given, while others are concerned with the composition of the images or the poetic dimension of the texts included in the exhibition.

If we, as humans, could do nothing but perceive the world with our physical senses or process our sense impressions intellectually, we would not notice the special light on a given day, become so engrossed in a conversation that we are kept awake at night, or be attracted to poetry and visual art. This attention, intensity, and free interest presuppose that there is something other and more in us than pure physical perception and intellectual thought: that we also have feelings, sensations, and presentiments of what happens both inside and outside us.

Philosophical aesthetics is the philosophy of those experiences that are of a feeling, sensate, and presentimental nature. This philosophy was introduced at a time when it was a widespread belief that we experience nothing but sense perceptions and intellectual cognitions. The rationalists of the seventeenth and eighteenth centuries nourished this thought, which many people still share. Through his work on poetry, the German eighteenth-century philosopher Alexander Gottlieb Baumgarten became aware, however, that it is possible to achieve insight in a different way, which I, for convenience, here choose to term *sensitive experience*.[9] Baumgarten discovered the existence of a kind of experience that, whilst not identical to intellectual cognition, nevertheless has cognitive value. He discovered the existence of what we nowadays often term *aesthetic experience*, and which teaches us something about ourselves and the world, and the relationship between the two.

Aesthetics versus Aestheticism

In our time, words such as 'aesthetic' and 'aesthetics' are used with a meaning that differs from that used in the previous section. We live in a time often described as marked by an extensive aestheticization of everything, from everyday goods to the political debates in the media. It is misleading, however, when such phenomena are described as *aesthetic* phenomena just because they are results of this current aestheticization. As mentioned, aesthetics is about aesthetic experience understood as a particular sort of cognition, and the aesthetic quality of this kind of experience consists in it being sensitive by nature; phenomena such as the story telling by which today's goods are sold or the stylized staging of political exchanges in the media are nothing but sources of impressions. They are stimulating but deliver no insight; they are sensuous without being truly aesthetic.

However, even if we treat the concept of aesthetics with more philosophical rigor than is common in the discourse on current aesthetic trends, the term 'aesthetics' denotes something that is somewhat broader than the experience of beauty. Nevertheless, this is not due to what many of us might think, namely that the beautiful is identical to the pretty and that beauty therefore is passé, especially

---

9 See Alexander Gottlieb Baumgarten, *Ästhetik, Volume 1–2*, trans. D. Mirbach (Hamburg: Felix Meiner Verlag, 2007), § 1.

artistically considered. The reason is rather that the experience of beauty is the *epitome* of aesthetic experience.

In addition to being aesthetically impressive, a fine dinner at the Michelin-starred restaurant Noma may also result in aesthetic experience; rather than just entertaining, it can arouse reflection. Like experiences of beauty, aesthetic *experiences* distinguish themselves by reflexivity and by being educating, whereas aesthetic *impressions* are merely stimulating. However, compared with aesthetic experiences (in the broad sense), experiences of *beauty* distinguish themselves by the strength of the feeling of coherence and meaningfulness that accompanies them, and which results from the fact that, in such experiences, something appears as uniquely valuable and as part of a whole to which one experiences oneself as belonging, too. An experience of this kind can, in principle, come into being on a night at Noma but, regardless of how well presented the dinner is, the experience is not guaranteed. Beauty is not only absolute but also contingent: we cannot call it forth by will.

Potential Thought

Beauty is not a property of the object we perceive and call beautiful; it is not purely objective and does not exist in the world as something given. But nor is beauty purely subjective; it does not depend solely on the eye that perceives it. As Martin Heidegger claims, beauty is something that *occurs*.[10] It emerges in the encounter between something that one may experience as beautiful and someone whose gaze on that something actualizes this potential for an experience of beauty. This gaze is not necessarily the gaze of the eye; the word 'gaze' here denotes the sensitive way of relating to something, which is different from the sensory or intellectual way of relating to it. Moreover, the beauty that is actualized and that

10 See Martin Heidegger, "The Origin of the Work of Art," in *Poetry, Language, Thought*, ed. and trans. A. Hofstadter (New York: Harper Perennial Modern Thought, 2013), and Dorthe Jørgensen, "Heideggers fænomenologi" (Heidegger's Phenomenology), in *Den skønne tænkning: Veje til erfaringsmetafysik. Religionsfilosofisk udmøntet* (Beautiful Thinking: Pathways to the Metaphysics of Experience. Religio-Philosophically Implemented) (Aarhus: Aarhus University Press, 2014), 275–357.

thus occurs in the sensitive gaze does not inhabit the perceived as an essential feature of it. Beauty exists only as *potential thought*, and it requires feeling, sensation, and presentiment to actualize it as experience.

As potential thought, beauty is metaphysically given. It is not a fully formed metaphysical entity after the Platonic model, but neither is it a completely subjective phenomenon dependent on taste and pleasure only. This is because the beautiful is something other and more than the nice and neat—it does more than simply please. In the eighteenth century, it was common to distinguish between the beautiful and the sublime, and today, the sublime is perceived as greater and more overwhelming, more interesting even, than the beautiful. This distinction is not a matter of course, however, but the product of a historical reduction of beauty.

It was only because the meaning of words such as 'beauty' and 'beautiful' gradually shrank that the sublime could become separated from the beautiful and challenge its position. In the past, the beautiful was sublime itself; the sublime was a dimension of the beautiful. Such was the case as far back as Horace in antiquity and as late as Nicolas Boileau-Despréaux in French classicism.[11] Even Immanuel Kant, who distinguished between the beautiful and the sublime, did not regard them as contradictory. In his *Critique of Judgment* of 1790, Kant's analysis of the sublime is an element in his development of his main concern, namely the universality of experiences of beauty, which he terms 'pure judgments of taste.'[12] For Kant, these experiences are subjective but not private. They thus provide some kind of insight.

---

11   See, for example, Horace, *The Art of Poetry: An Epistle to the Pisos*, trans. G. Colman (Gloucester: Dodo Press, 2008), and Nicolas Boileau-Despréaux, *The Art of Poetry*, trans. W. Soames (Richmond: Alma Books, 2008).

12   Immanuel Kant, *Critique of the Power of Judgment*, eds. and trans. P. Guyer and E. Matthews (New York: Cambridge University Press, 2000).

Beauty's Broadness

If we expanded our concept of beauty and reunited the beautiful and the sublime, we would be better at understanding what is happening when we not only notice the light in the park but also perceive it as loaded with a surplus of meaning. The light tells us something, but what? We would be better at understanding what is active in us when the inner cinema is open all night. A power is at work, but what is this power? Similarly, we would better understand why art and poetry can appeal in such a way that it feels like the work is speaking to us personally. The work is reaching out to us, but why and what is it offering?

If we made use of a broader concept of beauty that included everything we now attach to the sublime—being overwhelming, for instance—we could profit from past thought. In ancient and medieval beauty-metaphysical texts, there is much to inspire anyone who wishes to explore the experiences of transcendence occurring in our time. Since the introduction of the modern distinction between the beautiful and the sublime, it has become common to empty the beautiful of transcendence: the sublime supposedly bursts the frame, whereas the beautiful merely shows how well ordered the existent is. However, in previous times the metaphysics of beauty was loaded with transcendence. According to Plato, transcendence was precisely the meaning of beauty, and this idea continued into the Middle Ages, though theologically interpreted.[13]

The experience of beauty is *also* an experience of sublimity. When something really happens, when beauty really occurs, this event is sublime. This was already part of the old understanding of the beautiful as that which has value in itself and of the experience of beauty as an experience of coherence and meaningfulness, in which one sees oneself and something other as parts of something bigger, and by which one is transformed. Such an experience is unquestionably one of transcendence: it transcends the way in which we generally experience the world and is not simply a silent im-

---

13   See, for example, Plato, *Symposium*, trans. A. Nehamas and P. Woodruff, in *Plato: Complete Works*, eds. J.M. Cooper and D.S. Hutchinson (Indianapolis and Cambridge, MA: Hackett Publishing Company, 1997).

pression of everything fitting neatly together. Beauty is *not* a sweet balm. If that were the case, Plato, Aristotle, and their successors would not have interpreted beauty as a path to knowledge, which even educates the soul morally.

New Metaphysics

Obviously, we should not just repeat the ancient metaphysics of beauty. Kant's criticism of traditional metaphysics was justified: we cannot know anything about the transcendent.[14] Nevertheless, experiences of transcendence keep overwhelming us. But they are radically immanent due to our own awareness of the limit of what we can recognize with the understanding. We therefore still need metaphysics, but it must take shape as the modern philosophy of experience anticipated by not only Heidegger but also Walter Benjamin, among others.[15] We need what I call a *metaphysics of experience*.

Aesthetics, phenomenology, and the metaphysics of experience are about focusing on the *intermediate world* of which one is part before one becomes a subject that has a realization of something that the understanding treats as an object.[16] In this intermediate world, one aesthetically senses a connection between oneself and the world to which one is otherwise blind. Baumgarten was already aware of this level in our relation to the world, but his aesthetics was later replaced by the modern study of art, which is controlled by the understanding. In the twentieth century, however, hermeneutic phenomenology reintroduced an openness to the intermediate world, although now no longer referred to as aesthetic but as phenomenological.

---

14 For this criticism, see Immanuel Kant, *Critique of Pure Reason*, eds. and trans. P. Guyer and A.W. Wood (Cambridge, UK: Cambridge University Press, 1998), and Jørgensen, "Kants kritik" (Kant's Criticism), in *Den skønne tænkning*, 159–176.

15 See Jørgensen, "Benjamins metafysik" (Benjamin's Metaphysics), in *Den skønne tænkning*, 177–255.

16 Concerning 'the intermediate world,' see the chapter "The Intermediate World."

Most recently, the 'new phenomenology' and 'new aesthetics' represented by Hermann Schmitz and Gernot Böhme, respectively, also focus on the intermediate world.[17] They term it an *atmosphere*, however, in which we are lived-bodily present and aware of our presence. The *body* (*Körper*) Schmitz and Böhme regard as a delimited container separated from other things; it is determined by the understanding. The *lived body* (*Leib*), on the other hand, they consider atmospherically blurred, like noise. As lived bodies, we know a sphere that lies before the level at which we are subjects recognizing objects. It is thus as lived bodies—not as bodies or as users of our understanding—that we sense our own and something else's presence, by and with each other. Lived-bodily, we are out there among the things of the world, allowing them to "look back at us," as Benjamin said, and through which they are enlivened in our gaze upon them.[18]

Immanent Transcendence

Developments such as philosophical aesthetics, hermeneutic phenomenology, new phenomenology, and new aesthetics are only approaches to—and not full developments of—a *metaphysics of experience*. More is required if we wish to explore our experiences of transcendence philosophically in a modern way, that is, without recursion to pregiven truths but with a sense of the unconditional nature of the contingently emerging insight when beauty happens. Today we still lack a fully developed philosophy of the comprehension we obtain when we sensitively experience a coherence and meaningfulness, the significance of which we immediately feel but

---

17 For a presentation of both, see Jørgensen, "Ny æstetik, ny fænomenologi" (New Aesthetics, New Phenomenology), in *Den skønne tænkning*, 411–425.

18 Walter Benjamin, "On Some Motifs in Baudelaire," trans. H. Zohn, in *Selected Writings, Volume 4: 1938–1940*, eds. H. Eiland and M.W. Jennings (Cambridge, MA and London: The Belknap Press of Harvard University Press, 2003), 338.

have difficulties expressing verbally. It remains an unsolved task to develop a genuine metaphysics of experience.[19]

We must solve this task knowing that we might never be able to fully develop and finish the philosophy in question. While the ancient metaphysicians of beauty could base their thinking on unquestioned concepts and models of thought and were thus able to equip their experiences of transcendence with potentially comprehensible objects, in our time, everything is questionable. Not only are the objects of our experiences of transcendence volatile, but the experiences themselves seem completely objectless. Experience of this kind does not appear to provide insight into anything transcendent. It just lets us understand that transcendence is indeed possible—in immanence and without leading anywhere else. That is what I call *experiencing immanent transcendence*.[20]

Because the experience of beauty has become an experience of immanent transcendence, we must transform the traditional metaphysics of beauty into a modern metaphysics of experience, that is, a philosophy whose source and object is the experiences of modern humans. There is a need for thinking that is conscious of the modernity of these experiences but which is also aware of the continuity between what reality is for us and what reality was for others in the past, and which can therefore benefit from the philosophy of those times. Such thinking, rooted in philosophical aesthetics and hermeneutic phenomenology but also inspired by the metaphysics of beauty, can be fruitful in many places. In what follows, I briefly outline its possible significance for *the perception of art*, *ethics*, *nature*, and *the philosophy of science*.

---

19   This chapter is a translation of a text published in 2012, that is, two years before my presentation of a genuine metaphysics of experience in *Den skønne tænkning*.

20   See also Dorthe Jørgensen, "Immanent Transcendence," in *Poetic Inclinations: Ethics, History, Philosophy* (Aarhus: Aarhus University Press, 2021).

The Power of Art

Many art lovers are aware of the sixteenth-century Isenheimer Altar. Some have seen it in Colmar, perhaps even engaged professionally with it, but that does not necessarily mean that they have also *experienced* its importance. Like other modern human sciences, the study of art wishes to relate methodically to its subject matter. It turns the work of art into an object and keeps it at a distance, because the intention is to analyze the work objectively, and such an endeavor requires that one does not let oneself be influenced by the analyzed. However, the philosophical hermeneutics of the twentieth century showed that something gets lost this way, namely the possibility of experiencing what art means to us as humans. Indeed, such an experience requires that one does not keep the work at a distance but opens up to it and accepts being addressed and changed by it.

Experiencing the meaning of art is about *being present*, not just recording the formal qualities of the work or categorizing it with the understanding, but being completely present with everything in oneself, including feeling, sensation, and presentiment. It is about being lived-bodily attentive in an atmosphere that belongs neither to the work nor to oneself but is the previously mentioned intermediate world. It is about dwelling in this sphere *before* one becomes a subject that identifies what it sees and hears, that is, it is about focusing completely and totally on sensing the appeal emanating from the work.

However, the encounter that can thus take place and the experience it can lead to require not only subjective attention. They also require the suspension of everyday reality that the work performs by setting up its own world and the potential interpretations thus facilitated by the work. Poor craft and disgusting content may mean that the work has no appeal. But, ultimately, what is crucial is not the formal qualities of a work of art or its semantic content but that it *speaks to us and changes us*. The potential thought thus associated with a work of art is its beauty, and this beauty is normative. If a person has been seized by a work or art, this person begins discarding artifacts without comparable appeal. He or she considers such artifacts indifferent or at least not *good* art, or even not art at all.

The Ethics of Aesthetics

If beauty only required harmonious form to exist, that is, if it were essentially dispirited, or if beauty simply depended on private taste and preference, it would have no ethical significance. In this case, what is aesthetic would only be a source of sensuous pleasure. In recent times, it has been common to regard the aesthetic as unethical, and this view is confirmed by current aestheticization trends, not least by the propensity to categorize phenomena such as the story telling of brands selling goods or a political star's performance as aesthetic. Originally, however, the beautiful was regarded as that which is valuable in itself and associated with an experience of coherence and meaningfulness, as stated previously. The experience of beauty was an experience of transcendence and, for this reason, it was ethically important.

With the modern emptying of the transcendent, we may feel we are unable to say anything definite about *the* absolute. We are left with the mere experience *that* something can have value in itself and *that* it is possible to feel coherence and meaningfulness. Yet, ethically, this is enough. What is crucial is the very perception of something in such a way that it does not appear as a means of achieving goals set by oneself but rather as something that is self-reliant and must be treated as inviolable because it is irreplaceable.

Such experience is subjective but also common to humans. It can be communicated to other people and can, in principle, be understood by them, as it is the product of a way of thinking shared by all: *the expanded way of thinking*.[21] This way of thinking means we

---

21   I am alluding to Kant's description of *die erweiterte Denkungsart* in the *Critique of Judgment*, 173–176 (5: 293–296). Paul Guyer and Eric Matthews translate the German word *erweitert* as 'broad-minded,' and they translate Kant's term *die erweiterte Denkungsart* as 'the broad-minded way of thinking.' This is unfortunate. It causes a narrowing of the term's meaning, limiting it to something moral, and it is biased: an expression of the primarily sociological and psychological thinking of our day. John Henry Bernard and James Creed Meredith made better choices in their translations of Kant, using the expressions 'enlarged

are able to have empathy for something without identifying with it; instead, we transcend to something universal, which is a prerequisite for the ability to act morally. The experience that something can have value in itself and the experience of being part of something bigger provides a possibility of orientation that appears reliable because of the way of thinking in which it originates, and which, due to its indeterminate nature, does not prevent us from thinking for ourselves. This experience feels safe and is normative, but it is also open and undogmatic. It does not prevent but rather promotes moral behavior and ethical understanding.

Sensible or Senseless Science

For science, nature is a challenge. Science is about getting nature under control, grasping its powers and benefitting from them. Aesthetically, on the other hand, nature is a source of pleasure, not only sensuously but also intellectually, for it is *astonishing*. One cannot doubt the *beauty* of nature if one has looked out of an airplane window and seen the glacier landscape of Vatnajökull bathed in red morning light. The fact that beautiful nature is also *sublime*, however, is equally indisputable to someone who, in a snowstorm, has flown the same stretch in a helicopter. Perhaps nature demonstrates better than anything that the beautiful and the sublime are connected, and perhaps it is the impression of this duality that can surprise us the most.

However, wonder is not the engine of modern science in which the understanding's way of thinking prevails. By using the *understanding*, we distinguish analytically between things and categorize them. With *reason*, however, we produce ideas of things we cannot know anything specific about, and we navigate with reference to these ideas. It is with reason that we can reconnect what we separated with the understanding and reflect on the astonishment that nature's beauty awakens, and the thoughts aroused by

thought' and 'enlarged mind,' respectively; but it is even better to translate the term *die erweiterte Denkunstart* as 'the expanded way of thinking.'

this wonder. The point is not to reject modern science but to help reason unfold in a time dominated by understanding, for the sake of both reason and science. This requires a mobilization of the aesthetic way of thinking understood as the ability to think in the expanded way; it requires this ability to reflect creatively on the diverse.

It is neither as body nor as understanding but as lived body that we ourselves are a part of nature, which itself is part of us, if we regard it not as x number of objects and cause–effect relationships but as lived body, like us. In the intermediate world in which we and that which appears to us are physically present to one another, there is no sharp boundary between us and the things we are surrounded by. In this intermediate world, we may experience the trees watching us and hear the wind telling us alien stories. Nature is not only physically but also spiritually alive to those who experience it sensitively. Such experience most likely does not result in a clear picture of the identity of the perceived but suffices as a point of reference for a more dignified way of dealing with nature.

Improvising Reflexivity

It is a widespread assumption that cognition replicates empirical reality and that the truth of cognition depends on the relationship between copy and original. In order to make the most exact copies possible and to reproduce them accurately, the approach of modern science is methodical. However, knowledge may also be a product of *improvisation*. In this case, the result might not look like anything that exists in advance, and it is impossible to reproduce the cognition because there is no explanation of how to proceed. One has gained insight, but it is 'unscientific' according to the academic institutions' cubits. In our universities, we therefore do everything possible not to encourage students to think in the expanded way.

Real explorers in science are probably improvisers, however, and thus more related to artists than to other academics. Great physicists, biologists, and medical professionals can describe experiences similar to the experiences of musicians, painters, and writers: landmark moments in which they were one with what they were concerned about, and, in this fusion, discovered or created something on which they had not previously counted. Something of this sort may also happen to a philosopher. It is what happens to me when I really write, but then I am more of an author than an academic. The improvising reflexivity I surrender to in such moments unfolds in the previously mentioned intermediate world. It requires sensitivity and performs a searching and thus free reflexivity. It is open to impressions but also active in its receptivity: it is creative.

If the philosophy of science is to understand the creativity of science, it must revise its concept of knowledge: human cognition is actually based on a suspension of the distance between subject and object, which is otherwise regarded as the starting point of cognition. It is not only aesthetic experience but all significant cognition which presupposes that one does not relate in a distancing but an empathetic manner and thus does not make an image *of* that which one faces but lives *with* it. This emotional relation is the reason why one can later say anything at all about anything. In fact, the methods we are so eager to teach our students are *not* the path to knowledge. They are nothing but tools one uses *after* thinking to legitimize one's insight scientifically by conveying it to other academics in a comprehensible manner.

Body and Prayer

Depending on our churches, we fold our hands or kiss icons, light candles, inhale incense, let rosaries slip between our fingers, or burst into song. However, it is to open up the *lived* body for the divine that the *physical* body is mobilized. It is as something aesthetic—not just sensuous—that the formation brought about by prayer takes place in the intermediate world.[22]

Twenty Toes

She is a circus artist. She sits on the stage floor wearing a black unitard and headdress. She is face to face with the audience. Her arms and legs are in front of her, ending in bare hands and feet placed in a row with white balls in between. She is a circus artist sitting in the darkened auditorium bathed in the spotlight, looking neither human nor animal, and gazing inquisitively into the room, first slightly to one side, then slightly to the other side, until her attention is captured by what is happening in front of her. Her toes and fingers wake up slowly, first a few of them move, then others follow. Eventually they all move. They play together while she curiously observes what is happening at the end of her limbs. This is just the

---

22 See the chapter "The Aesthetics of Prayer," itself a translation of "Bønnens æstetik" in Dorthe Jørgensen, *Den skønne tænkning: Veje til erfaringsmetafysik. Religionsfilosofisk udmøntet* (Beautiful Thinking: Pathways to the Metaphysics of Experience. Religio-Philosophically Implemented) (Aarhus: Aarhus University Press, 2014). The quotation translates a passage pp. 767–768 in *Den skønne tænkning*.

beginning. Soon her entire body is awake and snakes acrobatically on the floor, while all twenty finger-toes juggle with the white balls.

Her name is Roxana Küwen and she is performing at the KUKART festival.[23] Her foot juggling belongs to a form of circus artistry called New Circus, a fusion of circus, theater, dance, music, and performance that creates short and longer stories, not just acts. Like a piece of theater, Küwen's performance has a title and, like the title of a painting by Paul Klee, it tells a story that complements the work; the title is "Twenty Toes." Accordingly, Küwen does not consider circus artistry a sport but an art form. Circus artistry makes as many demands on the body as sport does, but it is devoid of the competition element and therefore represents an opportunity to be creative and express oneself freely.[24] Accordingly, on stage, Küwen does not seem to compete with others; she pays no attention to anyone outside the relationship between her and her audience. Although Küwen's virtuosity presupposes intensive training and critical examination of her achievements, she only competes with herself. On stage, she therefore radiates calm, and her performance appears as a study in *immersion*.

Artists compete for academy positions, scholarships, and assignments, and their works are subject to evaluation, but the creative process is characterized by immersion, not competition. An artist's competition with herself takes place through an immersion in the creative process itself and what it produces, not the opinions of others or the mind of the artist. Standing at the canvas, the painter explores the composition of the picture by painting, thus developing her capability to express something that comes from elsewhere—from a world between painter and canvas to which we are otherwise blind. While dancing, the dancer studies the choreography of the ballet and, while writing, the author explores language, its shortcomings and potentialities. Study and immersion

---

23   Roxana Küwen, "Circus performer Roxana Küwen," July 25, 2017, https://www.youtube.com/watch?v=BxfHO7dg86o, accessed November 18, 2018.

24   Roxana Küwen, "Roxana Küwen: Jonglieren mit Händen und Füssen," November 30, 2016, https://www.youtube.com/watch?v=b8NKLUvZ7Dk, accessed November 18, 2018.

constitute the same art referred to as dwelling and formerly as contemplation. It is by immersing oneself in something outside oneself—that is, through *study* in this sense of the word—that one as an artist can create something that appears as created by a greater power and thus as *beautiful*, that is, as something of value in itself.

Lived-Bodily Kenosis

The word 'art' also means craft. It is the task of an artist to make room for something other than the artist herself, namely art, and it is the pastor's task to create a space in which the congregation can receive grace. The pastor solves her task by using liturgical objects and rituals, just as the artist solves hers by using artistic materials and tools. At the same time, however, their tasks also require more of them. Both pastor and artist must immerse themselves in the process, enter it and fully embrace it. They must be totally present without losing sight, take part sensitively in the process but simultaneously observe it from outside. They must move on two levels at once, being both inside and outside the process, not only sensing but also thinking. Thus, they must practice the art of *thinking aesthetically*, and this art is a craft, as one can learn it, train in it, and become better at it.[25] The artist exercises by practicing her art, and the pastor exercises at every service, assuming they immerse themselves in their work, letting it take shape as a creative process in which something larger than they themselves may appear to otherwise deaf and blind modern people.

This craft called immersion is also the way to *prayer*. Many people equate prayer and petitionary prayer, automatically assuming that praying is the same as requesting something from God. However, prayer can also take shape as praise and thanksgiving. Perhaps praise is in fact the essence of prayer, or thanksgiving is what is most fundamental to it.[26] Yet our time is dominated by an

---

25 Dorthe Jørgensen, "Hvad er æstetik?" (What is Aesthetics?), in *Æstetik og pædagogik* (Aesthetics and Pedagogy), ed. M.B. Johansen (Copenhagen: Akademisk Forlag, 2018), 35–37.

26 Merold Westphal, "Prayer as the Posture of the Decentered Self," in *The Phenomenology*

economic way of thinking, which complicates prayer understood as praise and thanksgiving, because praising and thanking do *not* rest on 'something-for-something.' Prayer fundamentally serves the incarnation of the holy in our corporeal existence by creating a space for the appearance of the holy, which, due to the dominance of the earthly economy, requires a *kenosis*. God had to gradually empty himself in order to manifest himself in the secular as non-secular through incarnation; only this way could he appear *in* the world as being *outside* the world, that is, its economy. Similarly, *we* must empty ourselves to make room for God's appearance to us; we must empty ourselves of the earthly economy to be receptive to his self-manifestation.[27]

It is when we pray that we empty ourselves of what is alien to prayer, but this kenosis is itself a prerequisite for us to pray at all. We must have left the economic way of thinking behind in order to be able to thank and praise, but the escape from the economic mindset itself requires prayer. In prayer, an emptying of the subject occurs, which is perceived as a decentering, but this occurrence is itself a prerequisite for prayer to occur. In prayer, an opening of the subject takes place, as the focus shifts from the individual to God; this is what is perceived as a decentering, but this opening itself depends on a shift of focus. Prayer opens up the understanding subject, that is, the subject modern man generally is and identifies with.[28] It opens a gate to the field of *feeling, sensation,* and *presentiment* in which prayer itself occurs.[29] Prayer lifts us out of our phys-

---

of Prayer, eds. B.E. Benson and N. Wirzba (New York: Fordham University Press, 2005), 13–31. Dieter Henrich, "Gedanken zur Dankbarkeit," in *Bewusstes Leben: Untersuchungen zum Verhältnis von Subjektivität und Metaphysik* (Stuttgart: Philipp Reclam jun., 1999), 152–193. Jørgensen, *Den skønne tænkning*, 761–762.

27 James R. Mensch, "Prayer as Kenosis," in *The Phenomenology of Prayer*, eds. B.E. Benson and N. Wirzba (New York: Fordham University Press, 2005). Jørgensen, *Den skønne tænkning*, 761.

28 The term 'the understanding subject' refers to what in German would be *das Verstandessubjekt*. It should not be confused with 'the rational subject,' that is, *das Vernuftsubjekt*, which is characterized by more comprehensive thought.

29 For my use of the phrase 'feeling, sensation, and presentiment,' see the chapters "Prot-

ical bodies and the understanding, because the sensitive field in which it takes place is the *lived body,* which is a third level. However, we must already have entered the lived body, already have surpassed body and understanding, for what is happening to qualify as *prayer*.

Aesthetic Formation

It is not only the earthly economy that prevents us from praying. Prayer is also difficult because it is a conversation between God and the soul that takes place in God's language.[30] Not only do we think in the wrong way, but we also speak the wrong language, and therefore we do not know how to pray. Yet we can try to learn. We can try to pray, even in the knowledge that we will never fully succeed, since we can only manage to suspend the earthly economy temporarily and will never be able to speak like God. Stuttering, however, we can answer the call from God. The *poetic* language is the stutter with which we approach the language of God, and this language is thus also the conversation that prayer constitutes. The poetic language lies between the language of God and our daily language, which today consists of chat and pseudoscience. The poetic language thus links the empty word with the creative Word, just as the sensitive lived body in which God and humans meet bridges the physical body and the understanding. In poetic language, which itself is sensitive and lived-bodily, not bodily or conceptual, and which is not only verbal but encompasses all sorts of poetic expression, including dance and music, the divine is afforded space in the individual, who thus approaches something greater than herself.

We cannot force God to appear, nor can we force an aesthetic experience to take place, but we can practice the art of giving room for something not mastered by us to occur. Since we can shut our-

---

estantism and Its Aesthetic Discontents," footnote 83; "The Philosophy of Imagination," footnote 311; and "The Intermediate World," footnote 323.

30   Hans Urs von Balthasar, *Das betrachtende Gebet* (Einsiedeln: Johannes Verlag, 1965). Jørgensen, *Den skønne tænkning*, 759–760.

selves within ourselves and render ourselves impenetrable to everything that we have not intended, we can also train our receptivity to the nonintentional: inspiration, thoughts not yet thought, the unexplained and mysterious, for instance. Just as the artist exercises by practicing her art and the pastor exercises by doing her work, we can exercise praying by attempting to pray. Each time we try to get beyond the economic way of thinking, we train our ability to think aesthetically and thus actually become better at thinking this way. Every attempt to express oneself poetically represents an approximation to something that we sense but cannot conceptualize; we approach something that is greater than us and thus also come closer to one another. In letting our thoughts and formulation attempts be poetic, the world grows and is enriched since something different appears to us than what we already know and possess.

In our time, it is not the body but the understanding that constitutes a problem, because it is the understanding that dominates and requires proof for anything to be true. Such is the dictate of the earthly economy. However, when the understanding is a problem, the body also becomes problematic—first, because the body is ignored for the benefit of the understanding; second, because the body, as a reaction thereto, is cultivated as the opposite of the rational. Both attitudes prevent us from perceiving the presence of anything other than what we can sense physically and explain rationally. When the understanding's demand for evidence dominates a churchgoer's consciousness, the poetry of the Bible fades out, and when the body's physical sensation of the message becomes the criterion for the message's relevance, poetry is replaced by charm and experience is reduced to impression. If one has not left the economic mindset in the porch, one cannot sense the power of the liturgy. But neither can one do this by demanding that the pastor whip around the church to be physically present and activate all of one's senses with a forty-five-minute church service. An *aesthetic formation of lived-bodily attention* must begin with oneself, even if one is a pastor. It is about using the porch for its purpose, as a screen between liturgy and economy, and imagining that something unfamiliar can happen and that the unfamiliar can be valuable. That the mystery could occur and be true.

Lived-Bodily Attentiveness

It is no art to be physically present. We are present whether we wish it or not, otherwise we would not exist. What qualifies as an art is being *lived-bodily attentive in one's physical presence.* Theology must have an eye for the whole person and therefore not ignore the body, but it faces a larger task than this. In our time, the body as well as the understanding are cultivated by both culture in general and the human sciences; the cult of the body is a consequence of the modern glorification of the understanding, just as sentimentalism mirrors scientism. Instead of contributing to this cult, theology must strengthen our lived-bodily attentiveness in our physical presence. The task of theology is not to get the body into the church. The body is already present in church—perhaps even too much, like when we are tormented by the need to urinate or feel too hot in our outdoor clothes while sitting in the pews. Instead, the task is to assist the church in making the liturgy speak to the *totality* of body and lived body, so that the service breeds experience characterized by feeling, sensation, and presentiment—that is, so that the experience qualifies as sensitive cognition rather than sense impression or intellectual cognition, and thus as something that opens and transforms the mind.

The prerequisite for theology to solve this task is that theology itself becomes aware of the *lived-bodily* dimension of the aforementioned totality. Practical theology must seek a grounding in systematic theology, which itself must develop to become relevant. It ought to be evident but is alien to many contemporaries that "God dwelt in the body of Jesus, but gave his lived body to us; in the sacrament, we ingest his spirit with the bread and wine—not body, but lived body."[31] A modern lack of imagination has made us strangers

---

31 Dorthe Jørgensen, "Etik og transcendens" (Ethics and Transcendence), in *1. Omtanke: Større end kroppen—omskæring* (1. Consideration: Larger than the Body—Circumcision), November 21, 2018, https://omtanke1.tt-eksistensen.dk, accessed November 29, 2018.

to the lived body understood as a field of attention characterized by feeling, sensation, and presentiment—the field between everything we usually divide, such as subject and object. This unimaginativeness, which originates in a combination of the Reformation and the Scientific Revolution, has made us suspicious of the intangible and unprovable and thus bad at empathizing with what we experience as unfamiliar—for instance, all that which we cannot reduce to 'body' and therefore cannot understand rationally.[32] However, art can assist theology and thus also the church. We should not even judge a body artist like Küwen by her bodily competencies, for, just like all good artists, she is rather an expert in lived-bodily attentiveness. Her ability to snake her body with props and maneuver her toes like fingers is of course impressive, but her performance conveys more than this skill and therefore moves its viewer.

Where does the power to awaken and move twenty finger-toes come from? This is one of the questions invited by Küwen's circus artistry, because she herself appears astonished on stage by the movement, which thus seems to emanate from something other than her. It is as though she did not initiate the virtuoso foot juggling. The initiating force therefore appears to be greater than her, beyond her power and will, and the result, the ball-playing snake dance, seems imbued with auratic power. It appears as unique, understood as self-reliant—in aesthetic terms, something beautiful. Good art encourages reflection because it awakens wonder. The Christian message, with its bottomless ideas of grace, forgiveness, incarnation, and trinity, should also give rise to wonder and reflection. When this does not happen, the reason may not only be the attention-demanding bodies of the churchgoers and their distracting intellectualism. It may also be a lack of imagination on the side of not only churchgoer but also pastor. If the pastor is not lived-bodily attentive in her physical presence, she does not empathize with the message and does not interpret it from within, and

---

32 Dorthe Jørgensen, *Hvorfor er vi så fantasiforskrækkede? Om reformationen og æstetikken* (Why Are We Afraid of the Imagination? On the Reformation and Aesthetics) (Frederiksberg: Eksistensen, 2017).

she thus treats the liturgy as something outward. She becomes untrustworthy.

Look at Küwen. If she is not fully attentive in her physical presence on the stage, she loses the balls. Art requires empathy. The artist must be able to empathize with something other than herself, be it the motif she is painting, the story she is telling, or the play she is performing. However, art also requires focus, concentration, and attention. One must devote one's full and continuous attention to the creative process so that one can correct potential errors with elegance (Küwen loses a ball, but picks it up with such ease that the error becomes part of her dance). Just as the artist can lose the balls, the pastor can lose the message if she is not lived-bodily attentive in her physical presence. The attentive pastor, on the other hand, adds *poetry* to the ceremonial ritual. During the service, such a pastor creates the common lived-bodily space that the word 'church' actually denotes, and, with her trustworthiness, invites the congregation to enter it. The pastor helps others to be lived-bodily attentive by performing such attentiveness herself. This way, she also helps the congregation to pray—to thank and praise rather than make requests—because prayer is not just a bodily act, not just folded hands, but a lived-bodily occurrence, an experience. When praying, we use both body and head, but we do not pray with them. We do not pray unless something moves us into the field of feeling, sensation, and presentiment constituted by the sensitive lived body. This something may be a hymn that seizes, or an icon that oscillates between visible and invisible, but it could also be the surprising trustworthiness of a pastor whose behavior incarnates the Word.

The Receptivity to Faith

Introduction

In November 2017, I walked through Venice's hazy streets with my cell phone turned off. I went to Venice by myself, had no obligations, and enjoyed being in this magical city for no other reason than just being there. Whilst there, I saw the exhibition "Intuition" in Palazzo Fortuny.[33] I spent several hours at the exhibition, immersing myself in everything that appealed to me. At one point, when I stepped out into a small courtyard behind the showroom and stood between the bare walls and green plants, I had to fight the tears. I felt the same way when I left the palace and walked into the streets, into a café, and then across the bridge to another island in the lagoon. A month later, I contributed to a newspaper article describing the exhibition I had seen in Venice—that it was the last in a series created over ten years by Axel Vervoordt and Daniela Ferretti to explore the links between philosophy, science, music, history, art, and craft; that it was about the meaning of intuition throughout history and all over the world; and that it did away with the notion of knowledge as rational and intuition as irrational. "Intuition is an emotional path to knowledge," I wrote, "of whose accuracy one is assured without having any proof of it, and from which one learns how to act without fully understanding why. 'Du must dein Leben ändern' the exhibition told me—you must change your life! Then

---

33 The exhibition was open May 13–November 26, 2017. See the catalogue *Intuition*, eds. Axel Vervoordt and Daniela Ferretti (Gent: AsaMER, 2017).

art is a source of experience rather than just impression; it is the cause of change."[34]

Digital Medialization

Keeping one's cell phone off is not easy, and reading a book can be difficult if one is used to sitting at a screen. Psychologists, neurologists, and other scientists have explanations for the addiction most people are experiencing today. There is the fear of missing out on something, feeling left out, or being unavailable. There is the risk of being stigmatized as old-fashioned and excluded from the in-crowd. There are all the influences that the brain is exposed to when the eye is bombarded with light and one's curiosity is both set and excited—the many rewards and the hunger for more that they awaken. Furthermore, for the writing person at the screen, there is the distinct feeling of being active and producing something—fingers running across the keyboard, keys singing in the ear, text growing on the screen—compared with the less noticeable feeling of being creative when, sitting reading in an armchair, one lets the characters of a novel appear in one's mind.

The example of the author at the computer shows that it is not digital technology as such that is the problem when we experience technology as exerting power and therefore criticize it. The source of the problem is our own dealing with technological possibilities. We are still not mature enough to interact with digital technology in a sensible way. Some of us remember how computers becoming common property revolutionized our lives. My 250-page MA thesis required endless (literal) cutting and pasting because I worked as though I had a computer yet I only had a typewriter. The computer's entry into my life made my job as an assistant professor, later an associate professor, and finally a professor much easier and probably also healthier, since I no longer had to work with glue and correction fluid. I instantly fell in love with the laptop version

---

[34] Dorthe Jørgensen, "Æstetik og intuition" (Aesthetics and Intuition), a part of "Trump-paradigmet" (The Trump Paradigm), eds. H. Laura et al., *Weekendavisen*, Sektion 4 (Ideer), December 29, 2017, 4.

of computers. I have traveled the world with a laptop under my arm, and have gone into symbiosis with several of them by carving holes in their keys and absorbing their chemistry through my fingers. Half human, half computer, happy writer.

The problem is not digital technology as such but the risk that we lose the ability to sit still with a book and let imagination do the writing in our minds. The risk that we are no longer able to immerse ourselves probingly in the news, because we have become accustomed to quickly scrolling on to the next piece of information. The risk that we lose the ability to watch a single movie and have a conversation about it because it is easier to binge watch a series without having to relate to other people. The risk that we will eventually not be able to go for a walk, see an exhibition, or have a conversation without being distracted by a smartphone. The word *medialization* does not refer to the media as such but their dominance: our dependence on the media and their logic when they become an independent social institution and simultaneously integrate into the work of other social institutions, so that all social interaction relies on them.[35] Similarly, the term *digital medialization* does not mean digital technology as such but the power of this technology over us as it spreads into everything and we fail to oppose this process—when all communication becomes digitally mediated and we no longer know the importance of relating directly to one another.

The Fear of Transcendence

In Venice, I saw the world with fresh eyes. This is what can happen if one lets go of the daily routine and the associated bombardment of demands and impressions. One gives oneself the opportunity not just to have impressions but also to experience the event that genuine experience represents. *Impressions* are fleeting and superficial, whereas *experiences* settle in and change the mind; they make us think. It all begins in the sensorial and historical, since we

---

35 Stig Hjarvad, *En verden af medier: Medialiseringen af politik, sprog, religion og leg* (A World of Media: The Medialization of Politics, Language, Religion, and Play) (Frederiksberg: Samfundslitteratur, 2008).

are set in the world as bodily creatures and live in certain places at certain times. The human life of the mind thus originates in impressions—we must have an impression of something in order to experience it—but experiences transcend the merely impressive. They transcend the sensorial by being sensitive themselves, which means that they are of not only a physical but also a *feeling*, *sensate*, and *presentimental* quality. Due to their sensitivity, they open a gate to something that is intangible and greater than anything of which we can have sense impressions or explain with the understanding. This is precisely why experiences settle in the mind, change it, and make us think. They arouse wonder.

Compared with impressions, experiences thus by definition distinguish themselves by being transcendent. In some cases, however, the transcending quality of the experience appears more clearly than in others. My Venice experience, with its clearly perceived 'Du musst dein Leben ändern' quality, can be taken as an example of an experience that not only transgressed the level of impressions, which all experience does, but which also clearly appeared as such a transgression—as an experience of transcendence. In such cases, where the already by nature transgressive experience manifests itself as an experience of transcendence, we have a tradition of using particular words. Such experiences were traditionally described as *experiences of beauty*, which denoted something far more comprehensive and more significant than simply having an impression of something as pretty. In this chapter, I use the phrase *experience of transcendence* as a term for all the interpretations of human transgressive experiences formulated throughout history, usually called experiences of faith and beauty or religious and aesthetic experiences.[36]

When experience in this emphatic sense of the word occurs and provides food for thought, we are badly off in our time, because the antimetaphysics of the past many years has made it difficult to relate in a thinking way. For example, Gilles Deleuze and Félix

---

36   See also the chapter "Immanent Transcendence" in Dorthe Jørgensen, *Poetic Inclinations: Ethics, History, Philosophy* (Aarhus: Aarhus University Press, 2021), and the chapter "The Metamorphosis of Beauty" in the present volume.

Guattari described transcendence with thinly veiled contempt and instead prioritized immanence, more specifically "pure immanence."[37] The words *immanence* and *transcendence* are generally identified with the worldly/sensible/physical and the otherworldly/supersensible/metaphysical, respectively. They may, however, also have a verbal meaning and denote to 'stay in' and 'go beyond,' but, in this case, they usually indicate 'staying in the immanent' and 'going beyond the immanent by transgressing into the transcendent.' Traditionally, the words 'immanence' and 'transcendence' have thus been presented as each other's opposites, which continues when postmodern philosophers insist on pure immanence, for we overcome no contradictions by prioritizing the opposite of what has so far been a priority, in this case the transcendent. On the contrary, by doing so, we involuntarily reproduce the dualistic mindset from which we otherwise wish to depart. To overcome a contradiction, one must think it through and thus, in the present case, one ends with neither transcendence nor immanence but perhaps *immanent transcendence*.[38]

Postmodern philosophers such as Deleuze and Guattari are not alone in having rejected the idea of an underlying metaphysical world of absolute referents that devalue what experience might deliver. Many modern philosophers—Immanuel Kant, Walter Benjamin, and Martin Heidegger, for instance—have done something similar. The metaphysics of experience presented in my book *Den skønne tænkning* (Beautiful Thinking) also represents philosophy that intends to take experience seriously by not operating with an underlying sphere of static entities.[39] In the metaphysics of experience, the term *experience of immanent transcendence* plays an important role in designating the historically most recent inter-

37   Gilles Deleuze and Felix Guattari, *What Is Philosophy?*, trans. H. Tomlinson and G. Burchell (London and New York: Verso 1995), 43.

38   Concerning the concept of 'immanent transcendence,' see also the references offered in footnote 36.

39   Dorthe Jørgensen, *Den skønne tænkning: Veje til erfaringsmetafysik. Religionsfilosofisk udmøntet* (Beautiful Thinking: Pathways to the Metaphysics of Experience. Religio-Philosophically Implemented) (Aarhus: Aarhus University Press, 2014).

pretation of human experience of transcendence. Unambiguous immanence is thus not the only alternative to traditional metaphysics, and the idea of pure immanence does not respect what our experiences reveal to us—a respect one would otherwise expect from a philosopher like Deleuze, who considered himself an 'empiricist.' An unambiguous immanence's closure upon itself is not the only possible way to escape traditional metaphysics dividing and opposing immanence and transcendence. The rejection of anything but immanence and the suspicion of any idea of transcendence rather expresses a *fear of transcendence*, and this ideological bigotry makes it difficult to reflect on experiences that otherwise incite thought because they are transgressive and thus arouse wonder.

The Intermediate World

In general, we imagine that where there is experience, there is also a subject having the experience and to whom the experienced has the status of an object. Experience is usually perceived as something that is initiated and controlled by a person; it is considered something that is subjectively produced, perhaps even intentionally. However, experience in the sense of experiencing transcendence is not something that we *have* but something that *happens* to us; in this sense of the word, we are rather scenes for than subjects of experience. In experience in this sense of the word, we feel, sense, and fathom the world opening up, and we gain access to otherwise inaccessible insight, which moves both us and the world. In experiences of transcendence, there is thus no subject facing an object but a subjectivity and an objectivity—a field of feeling, sensation, and presentiment, as well as a number of concrete things—which meet in and for each other as the phenomenon appearing in the experience and by which we experience a surplus of meaning, traditionally called beauty.

Experience is subjective as it takes place in subjectivity, but it is not subjective regarded as the opposite of objective. Based on the subject/object-thinking we are indebted to by the understanding, subjectivity must be found *between* subject and object, even though it actually lies *before* the constitution of subject and object. Experience occurs in what we perceive as an 'in-between,' which is why it is not subjective in the everyday sense. It is only subjective in the sense that it occurs in subjectivity—in the field of feeling, sensation, and presentiment—and operates in the aforementioned 'in-between,' referred to in *Den skønne tænkning* as the *intermediate world*.[40] Experience is personally embodied but, as a phenomenon of the intermediate world, it also holds an element of general validity and is thus not private. An experience of transcendence is not only one's own but also something that we as humans share, because it does not take place within oneself or in the object but in the intermediate world and is thus not only subjective but also *intersubjective*. In the intermediate world of feeling, sensation, and presentiment, we are always already out in, involved in, and infiltrated in both things and people. Feeling, sensing, and apprehending in the intermediate world, we relate to everything around us in such a way that brings us closer to it than the understanding does. We are not only *for* each other as mutually objectifying subjects of understanding, but, through feeling, sensation, and presentiment, we are also *with* one another in intersubjective subjectivity.

As mentioned, the experience of transcendence is not just one's own but also shared because it is not produced by oneself. However, this commonality emerges not only from the fact that the experience occurs in the intermediate world and is not intentionally produced by the individual. It also emerges from the fact that the experience is an event in which something happens to something that is bestowed upon us: *an actualization of an already given potential for insight takes place*. An experience of transcendence actualizes something metaphysically given; it is the actualization of a bestowed potential for insight. An experience of transcendence is thus by definition an experience of a surplus of meaning, but the reverse also applies. The actualizations of metaphysically given

---

40 Jørgensen, *Den skønne tænkning*, 727ff; see also "The Intermediate World" in the present volume.

potentials for insight that qualify experiences as experiences of a surplus of meaning are by definition transcending in nature in that they transgress what we consider matters of fact. They transgress but without losing connection to the present, whose inherent potentials for insight they instead actualize. It is also for this reason that experience in the described sense of this word may be personally embodied but holds an element of general validity and is therefore not private.

Anaesthetics

The intermediate world is bursting with potentials for insight and shared comprehension that do not come from us but, on the contrary, are bestowed upon us. The field of feeling, sensation, and presentiment called the intermediate world is packed with a surplus of meaning and therefore appears ambiguous. This intermediate world, which, as mentioned, lies before the understanding's constitution of subject and object but appears to us as something in-between them, is where we encounter the world poetry described in the exhibition book *Verdenspoesi* (World Poetry): "Reality is ambiguous: it has several layers. This does not concern the ancient idea that there is another world to be found somewhere else. On the contrary, this concerns the world here being multidimensional. The sensuous world is sprinkled with suprasensuous meaning. There is a surplus of meaning for those who seize the moment when the sun splits the clouds or the door is left ajar."[41] The term 'world poetry' thus denotes the dimension of a surplus of meaning available to the poetic gaze, or, as I also state in the preface to the book: "If only your eyes are open, the poetic surplus of the world is accessible."[42] Things are not just for use; they contain more and point to the beauty of that of which they are a part.

---

41   Dorthe Jørgensen, "Preface," in *Verdenspoesi: Malerier og tankebilleder* (World Poetry: Paintings and Thought-Images) (Aarhus: Women's Museum, 2011), 73. Translation modified.

42   Jørgensen, "Preface," 73.

An aestheticization of everything from politics to consumption is observable in our time, which, according to aesthetic theorists such as Wolfgang Welsch, entails an anaestheticization that, I add, can blind us to the poetic surplus of the world, just as the understanding's way of thinking does. Welsch claims that, in particular, we are witnessing a historically new duality of sensitivity and numbness; the current aestheticization, which consists of a product aesthetic and mass media-mediated bombardment of our senses and emotions, results in an anaestheticization understood as a desensitization.[43] *Aisthesis* is the subjective source of aesthetic experience and holds two poles in the form of sensation/emotion (*Empfindung*) and perception/cognition/insight (*Wahrnehmung*), respectively, but both the aestheticization and the anaestheticization make independent and cultivate the sensitive/emotional pole. Admittedly, as Welsh claims, anaesthetic numbness may be an advantage in an age of aestheticization—that is, it may be a safeguard against all the charm and emotion to which we are exposed.[44] Welsch does not realize, however, that this numbness not only (arguably) protects against sensory and emotional overstimulation but also potentially closes our minds to the poetic surplus of the world. The numbness can make us unreceptive to that which may occur as experience in the intermediate world and to which faith belongs, because the conglomerate of feeling, sensation, and presentiment (*Empfindung*) is the gateway to insight (*Wahrnehmung*), without which existence would be empty of both faith and comprehension.[45]

Faith comes not from us but by itself. It is a gift. However, if faith is to be effective in life, it must be able to take root. A receptivity to faith is required for it to manifest itself in thought and deed. This receptivity is innate to us as humans as we are born into the field of feeling, sensation, and presentiment that characterizes the

43 Wolfgang Welsch, *Ästhetisches Denken* (Stuttgart: Reclam Verlag 1993), 13f.

44 Welsch, *Ästhetisches Denken*, 20.

45 For a detailed presentation of this, see, for example, the chapter "Fornemmelse, tro og forståelse" (Sensation, Faith, and Comprehension), in *Den skønne tænkning*, 791–804.

intermediate world, a field that is not identical to the particulate feelings, sensations, and presentiments of singular individuals but which is existential. Our being situated in this field is why we do not just sense physically and think with the understanding but are sensitive beings and, compared with animals, are distinguished by this sensitivity. We cannot change our sensitive existence in the intermediate world, but we can weaken or strengthen our ability to actualize the potentials that inhabit this sensitivity. The same is true of the receptivity to faith that characterizes us as human beings due to our existence as situated in the intermediate world and the resulting sensitive human constitution. This receptivity is jeopardized when the anaestheticization makes inroads into our sensitiveness to everything that may appeal to us—that is, not only consumption goods and the media but also the higher calling heard in the world in the form of its poetic dimension, its cracks of transcendence in immanence.

The Return of the Analog

There is no distance between a teenager's body and smartphone, and, if one removes the smartphone, the teenager panics—because he is disconnected from the social community (so a parent might claim if she believes technology can promote community). However, there could also be another cause of this panic: the teenager robbed of his smartphone is forced to think for himself. Furthermore, it is not only smartphones that can foster community between people—so much else can do this—and it is not the objects themselves but how we use them that creates social communities. Moreover, a person's community-forming relationship with an object does not originate in the relation between things and humans but in the relation between people. If no socialization through interaction with adults who demonstrate caring attentiveness has taught a child how to contribute to the development of human community, the child will never really become friends with anyone on social media. It remains important that the cell phone does not have access to the dining table, that parents listen with both eyes and ears, and that children also generally experience that adults pay attention by being not only physically present but also lived-bodily attentive in their physical presence.[46]

If we do not bother to be attentive, we cannot act reasonably and do not make proper use of digital technology, for instance. Digital media thus becomes a bad excuse for not only being lived-bodily distant but often also physically absent. While some people are impressed by how naturally young people interact with digital technology and how much companionship they experience in their virtual existence in the digital world, others observe quite different phenomena that rather testify to a revival of an analog existence. Ten years ago, a Danish university lecturer could expect to meet a class of students with bright laptop screens, the content of which was unknown to the lecturer. Now many students sit with pens and notebooks, and they are not surprised that new studies show that we learn more when taking notes by hand instead of on a laptop. Moreover, these same students are among the many citizens who participate in or initiate related current phenomena such as the renaissance of salon culture, the popularity of the living word, the interest in community eating, the establishment of new cultural associations, the growing interest in the book as a medium, and the many attempts to revitalize assembly houses.

Where is the church in all this? What does the pastor think she should do in a time of not only digital medialization but also the return of the analog? What about the possible idea that the church is something special, though not sacred—that it should be used not to copy life outside the church but to qualify life in a way that only the church can? It is not only the duality of aestheticization and anaestheticization, identified by Welsch, which characterizes the current culture. It is also the described duality of digital medialization and the return of the analog. This second duality pulls in the opposite direction to that described by Welsch as early as 1993. Unlike anaestheticization, the return of the analog implies not less but more sensitivity, understood as a perceptiveness to the life actually

---

46   See also the chapter "Body and Prayer."

unfolding between people who are lived-bodily attentive in their physical presence. The digital medialization remains dominant, however, because it pays off and is an effective instrument of power in a complex modern society. The media does not prioritize the listening dialogue between concrete individuals, but the church has a choice. Does it want to copy the media in order to be fashionable, determined by an increasingly old-fashioned idea that this will result in more churchgoers? Or does the church wish to contribute to the aforementioned alternative movement for lived-bodily attentiveness in ways that only the church can—its language, tradition, and message considered? Should the church repeat postmodern society's lack of spirit or rather incarnate the Word—let the confirmed feel that nothing they have been taught matters or make them realize there is an alternative?

Protestantism and Its Aesthetic Discontents

Protestant Ambivalence

For centuries, Protestantism distanced itself from the aesthetic; ever since the introduction of philosophical aesthetics, Protestant theologians problematized this discipline. What Alexander Gottlieb Baumgarten referred to as sensitive cognition (*cognitio sensitiva*), his contemporaries mistook for sensuous experience.[47] They confused the perfect sensitive cognition with which he identified the experience of beauty with completely sensuous experience, and thus accused him of sensualist fanaticism.[48] Baumgarten's aesthetics was known primarily through Georg Friedrich Meier's dissemination of it, and Meier fortified this sensualistic misinterpretation.[49] Such a misinterpretation might partly explain the unfortunate way in which many thinkers, including Georg Wilhelm Friedrich Hegel and Søren Kierkegaard, used the words 'aesthetics,' 'aesthetic,' and 'the aesthete.' Using these words to denote something sensual

---

47   Alexander Gottlieb Baumgarten, *Reflections on Poetry: Alexander Gottlieb Baumgarten's Meditationes philosophicae de nonnullis ad poema pertinentibus*, trans. K. Aschenbrenner and W.B. Holther (Berkeley and Los Angeles: University of California Press, 1954), and *Ästhetik, Volume 1–2*, trans. D. Mirbach (Hamburg: Felix Meiner Verlag, 2007).

48   Dorthe Jørgensen, *Den skønne tænkning: Veje til erfaringsmetafysik. Religionsfilosofisk udmøntet* (Beautiful Thinking: Pathways to the Metaphysics of Experience. Religio-Philosophically Implemented) (Aarhus: Aarhus University Press, 2014), 107, footnote 191.

49   Jørgensen, *Den skønne tænkning*, 129–130; Georg Friedrich Meier, *Anfangsgründe aller schönen Wissenschaften, Teil I–III* (Hildesheim and New York: Georg Olms Verlag, 1976).

and fanatic without ethical or epistemological value hampered or even prevented the establishment of aesthetics as a philosophical discipline dedicated to the exploration of sensitive cognition. As a result, neither the Nordic nor the English-speaking countries have any tradition of philosophical aesthetics, but only of art theory and philosophy of art.[50]

Hegel's understanding of the word 'aesthetics' can be studied in his lectures on fine art, in which he mentions that it is an inadequate term for his lecture topic.[51] According to his interpretation, aesthetics is the science of sensation, whereas his lectures would present the philosophy of fine art.[52] Likewise, Kierkegaard problematized the aesthetic despite the fact that he was very conscious of the aesthetic qualities of his texts, that he showed great aesthetic sensitivity in his analyses of specific works, and that he himself lived as an aesthete. Kierkegaard's characterization of the aesthetic exudes fascination; nevertheless, he diminished the aesthetic compared with the ethical and the religious, and—although he was not entirely negative toward it—he identified the aesthetic with immediate and noncommittal pleasure.[53]

Hegel and Kierkegaard both problematized what they referred to as 'the beautiful soul' and 'the aesthete,' respectively. The beautiful soul was the eighteenth century's interpretation of the Greek idea of *kalokagathia* (beauty-and-goodness), understood as the highest ideal of man.[54] In the middle of the eighteenth centu-

---

50   See "The Relevance of Aesthetics" in Dorthe Jørgensen, *Poetic Inclinations: Ethics, History, Philosophy* (Aarhus: Aarhus University Press, 2021).

51   Georg Wilhelm Friedrich Hegel, *Aesthetics: Lectures on Fine Art, Volume 1*, trans. T.M. Knox (Oxford: Clarendon Press, 1988).

52   Hegel, *Aesthetics, Vol. 1*, 1.

53   For the so-called philosophy of stages (the aesthetic, the ethical, and the religious [a and b]), see, in particular, *Stages on Life's Way: Studies by Various Persons* and *Concluding Unscientific Postscript to Philosophical Fragments*, of which the latter is an extensive postscript to *Philosophical Fragments, or a Fragment of Philosophy*. See volumes 11, 12/1–2, and 7 in *Kierkegaard's Writings*, eds. and trans. H.V. Hong and E.H. Hong (Princeton: Princeton University Press, 1991, 1992, and 1987).

54   For the history of the beautiful soul, especially in the eighteenth century, see Robert E.

ry, Lord Shaftesbury actualized this idea when introducing his own concept of moral beauty, which spread in a personalized, interiorized, and subjectively appealing form as the beautiful soul.[55] However, in *The Phenomenology of Spirit*, Hegel criticized the fervor of the beautiful soul for being empty abstraction, and thus also for being morally ugly rather than beautiful.[56] He saw the beautiful soul as an expression of Romantic fancy, and this view was repeated in Kierkegaard's presentation in *Either/Or* of the aesthete.[57]

According to Kierkegaard, the aesthetic attitude to life is a stage on the way to the ethical and religious attitudes, although it constitutes a dimension that cannot be left behind but must be integrated. The aesthete is characterized by *not* being able to integrate the aesthetic; he is stuck in it, that is, in his spontaneous needs and immediate pleasures. The aesthetic attitude to life is most clearly described in the piece "Rotation of Crops" in *Either/Or*.[58] Here, the aesthete's demands for variety and intensity make his life fall apart and plunge him into an eternal quest. Unlike the aesthete, who thus flees from himself, the ethicist chooses himself. He takes responsibility for what he is and for his life. But this ethical attitude to life is surpassed by the religious attitude, the focal point of which is faith that suspends the ethical and cannot be rationally proved.

Norton, *The Beautiful Soul* (Ithaca: Cornell University Press, 1995). For a discussion of the original Greek idea of *kalokagathia*, also see Julius Jüthner, "Kalokagathia," in *Charisteria: Alois Rzach zum achtzigsten Geburtstag dargebracht*, eds. M. Adler et al. (Reichenberg: Verlag von Gebrüder Stiepel, 1930), and Hermann Wankel, *Kalos kai agathos* (Diss. Würzburg, Julius-Maximilians-Universität zu Würzburg, 1961).

55   Lord Shaftesbury, *Characteristics of Men, Manners, Opinions, Times*, ed. L.E. Klein (Cambridge, UK: Cambridge University Press, 1999), especially the treatise "The Moralists, a Philosophical Rhapsody, Being a Recital of Certain Conversations on Natural and Moral Subjects."

56   Georg Wilhelm Friedrich Hegel, *The Phenomenology of Spirit*, ed. and trans. T. Pinkard (Cambridge, UK: Cambridge University Press, 2018), 380–387.

57   Søren Kierkegaard, *Either/Or: Part I–II*, in *Kierkegaard's Writings, Volume 3–4*, eds. and trans. H.V. Hong and E.H. Hong (Princeton: Princeton University Press, 1988), Part I.

58   Kierkegaard, *Either/Or: Part I*, 281–300.

A Protestant Need for Aesthetics

Hegel and Kierkegaard were not alone in this ambivalent perception of the aesthetic and aesthetics. Protestantism implied an intensive subjectification of theology, as focus moved from the church and its rules to the relationship between God and the individual. The autonomy of the individual life of faith can be considered a phenomenon of modernity, just like the simultaneous autonomy of art and the reflection on the aesthetic. But the modernization process did not only result in a partial liberation of the individual person from the church institution, or in the arousal of a new fervor. In an era of modern science and demands for exact evidence for both what can be measured and what cannot, the subjectification of faith also meant that the 'truth-value' of theology became precarious. The risk of subjectivism thus associated with this subjectification was a challenge for theology, which, in the aftermath of this development, often treated aesthetics as a symbol of the problem or as the actual cause of it. Theology's relation to the aesthetic became as strained as rationalism's relation to it was *before* Baumgarten, and even in the same manner.[59]

However, ironically, it is perhaps Protestants who are in *particular* need of aesthetic imagination, and thus also of aesthetics understood as the philosophy of the experience with which this imagination is connected. The idea of incarnation is important to all Christians, but Protestantism is also characterized by the dualist way of thinking that has prevailed in modern time. Thanks to Protestantism's sharp distinction between the physical and the spiritual (when compared with Catholicism, for example), it introduced a conception of nature as profane, it subjectified and individualized the relation to God, it rejected the idea of transubstantiation, and it removed many sensuous elements from the service. It could therefore be suggested that Protestants need aesthetic imagination even

---

[59] Despite Kierkegaard's aversion to the philosophy of reason (*Vernunftphilosophie*), his philosophical and theological subordination of the aesthetic to the ethical and the religious is structurally analogous to the rationalists' understanding of the aesthetic as nothing but a precursor of the logical, but in rationalism the transition between these levels was smoother and less problematic.

more than others, so that they themselves can create a link between what in their view is more separate—the physical and the spiritual or the material and the immaterial.

The emergence of Protestantism might even be considered one of the historical prerequisites for the development of philosophical aesthetics. That is: it is a historical prerequisite for the formation of aesthetics understood as an individual philosophical discipline, the central object of which is the aesthetic experience and thus also aesthetic imagination. Until the emergence of Protestantism, theology itself dealt with aesthetic issues in the form of the philosophy of beauty, but Protestantism separated elements that previously hung together in aesthetic immediacy, and it thus paved the way for a possible exclusion of aesthetic issues from theology. As such, Protestantism furthered a theology that was hostile to aesthetics but perhaps also created a need for it, as the phenomenon called 'aesthetic experience' does not disappear just because it is banned or ignored. Whatever the case, when Baumgarten introduced philosophical aesthetics, which was indeed designed to overcome problems caused by the dualism of his day, including the contradiction between feeling and thinking, he presented a possible response to such a need.

Given the idea that Protestants might have a particular need for increased aesthetic imagination, one might expect that Protestant theologians would take a particular interest in working systematically with aesthetics. But, even nowadays, many prefer to keep theology and aesthetics apart, because, like Kierkegaard, they fear that theology will be aestheticized if it approaches the aesthetic and the philosophy of it, that is, aesthetics.[60] Kierkegaard identified the aesthetic with a sensuality and sentimentality, the autonomy of which would result in relativistic aestheticization. An aestheticization of theology would thus by definition imply a relativization of it. It would subsume the religious to the aesthetic or theology to aesthetics, make faith dependent on taste and elevate beauty high-

---

60 For notable exceptions from this unfortunate rule, see, for example, publications by Gerd Theissen such as *Transparente Erfahrung: Predigten und Meditationen* (Gütersloh: Gütersloher Verlagshaus, 2014).

er than the divine. This is why Kierkegaard distinguished systematically between the aesthetic and the ethical, and, with this distinction, also between the aesthetic/ethical and the religious.

Not Just Subjective or Objective

Be that as it may, philosophical aesthetics is actually *not* an expression of subjectivism. Baumgarten broke with the traditional objective aesthetics, as he did not regard beauty as a property of objects. But, in his aesthetics, beauty is not just a subjective construction; on the contrary, it is a phenomenon for a perceiving subject. Sensitive cognitions are thus experiences of the phenomenon that beauty forms.[61] They are sensate experiences that qualify as cognitions because they perceive not only the many marks of given objects but also some kind of unity in the diversity.[62] Sensitive cognitions let us sense the universal in the particular without losing sight of the uniqueness of the singular; that is why they bring insight. They transcend the concrete without abstracting from it, and they make us recognize not only what things are or can be used for, but what they mean to us.

Similarly, Baumgarten did not simply reproduce the traditional metaphysics; nor did he make himself guilty of antimetaphysics. On the contrary, by introducing aesthetics, he established an alternative to traditional metaphysics that differed from the latter by approaching the experience more closely. According to the new metaphysics that aesthetics thus forms, there *is* indeed something that is objectively given—but this 'something' exists only as a *possibility*, and it requires effort to turn it into subjective reality, since the sensitive cognition that is the topic of aesthetics does not identify anything present, and nor does it simply project imaginations. Sensitive cognitions are rather cognitions in which objec-

61 Sensitive cognitions are aesthetic experiences, and experiences of beauty are 'perfect' sensitive cognitions. However, the latter is the epitome of sensitive cognition; the experience of beauty is the essence of aesthetic experience.

62 I distinguish between 'sensory experience' regarded as merely sensorial (*sinnlich*) and 'sensate experience' regarded as sensitive (*empfindend*).

tively given possibilities of experiencing beauty are subjectively actualized. So that which is objectively given we know only in the subjective form in which we appropriate it, but the possibility we thus actualize is not created by us—it is something we receive.

Shortly after Baumgarten, Immanuel Kant presented his transcendental-philosophical argument for the universality of pure judgments of taste.[63] He demonstrated that experiences of beauty are individually formed but also common: they are personal but not private, for they are communicable and agreeable; they are products of the so-called 'common sense' (*sensus communis*). Through systematic attempts to move beyond the subject/object cleavage, hermeneutical phenomenologists such as Martin Heidegger later pointed out the objective 'truth-value' of subjectively experienced phenomena. Using the artwork as his example, Heidegger demonstrated that sensate experiences let us realize the very fact *that* something actually does exist.[64] Experiencing that both we and what we perceive are parts of something bigger encourages us to reflect on *why* and *how* the existent is, and such experience invites theological thought. In a similar vein, Gernot Böhme has argued, with a basis in both aesthetics and phenomenology, for an *Aisthetik* understood as a philosophy of perception (*Wahrnehmung*) that is also designed to suspend subjectivist relativism.[65] And Jean-Louis Chrétien has argued that precisely sensate and as such aesthetic-sensitive experiences are the way to God: they are revelatory.[66]

---

63   Immanuel Kant, *Critique of the Power of Judgment*, eds. and trans. P. Guyer and E. Matthews (New York: Cambridge University Press, 2000).

64   Martin Heidegger, "The Origin of the Work of Art," in *Poetry, Language, Thought*, ed. and trans. A. Hofstadter (New York: Harper Perennial Modern Thought, 2013).

65   Gernot Böhme, *Aisthetik: Vorlesungen über Ästhetik als allgemeine Wahrnehmungslehre* (München: Wilhelm Fink Verlag, 2001).

66   Jean-Louis Chrétien, *The Call and the Response*, trans. A.A. Davenport (New York: Fordham University Press, 2004).

Creative Receptivity

In spite of aesthetics' nonsubjectivist character, many theologians remain skeptical of its focus on the experience and its interest in the creative aspect of the experience, which they see as expressions of fanaticism. However, the sensate experience called 'sensitive cognition' by Baumgarten differs from logical 'intellectual cognition' not only by being productive but also by being receptive in a different manner. Sensitive cognitions not only depict but are also open; their productivity requires receptivity. Receptive to the many marks of the concrete, sensitive cognitions are also open to the 'material perfection of metaphysical truth' (as it was dubbed by Baumgarten).[67] Otherwise they would not be able to create unity in diversity, give form to something that is otherwise not accessible, and actualize the metaphysically given possibility of beauty. Only this way, that is, sensitively, are we lifted in the direction of the metaphysical, which, in the thought of Baumgarten, means in God's direction.

As it is creative, sensitive cognition is analogous to God's act of creation, but it creates subject to divine creation: cognition itself does not manufacture the truth that the metaphysically given and by cognition aesthetically seized potential for insight forms, nor does it itself produce the object of this insight. It is in the contemplation of the beautiful that we come closest to truth, which however presupposes that the contemplation itself is beautiful, that is, driven by sensitive cognition or rather by trying to perfect this cognition. Furthermore, there is an empirical subject involved in sensitive cognition and in the effort to perfect it—a subject with feelings, sensations, and presentiments, to whom the cognition happens but who does not control it, as it presupposes a metaphysically given possibility. This is one more way in which sensitive cognition is dependent on openness: one must make oneself available—for the possibility to appear.

---

67 According to Baumgarten, metaphysical truth includes both "material perfection" and "formal perfection." See Baumgarten, *Ästhetik*, §§ 559ff.

The source of the productive quality of cognition was referred to as *phantasia* by Baumgarten and as *Einbildungskraft* by Kant. The previous paragraph thus showed that fantasy or imagination brings something into the world, but that it does so in receptivity to something that fantasy or imagination itself cannot produce but must be open to.[68] In modern theology, including Chrétien's, a kindred understanding of human existence as both receptive and productive, and as productive in its receptivity, also plays an important role. Faith is interpreted as a response (that is, to a call) which is only possible if one is attentive, and this response is interpreted as an activity that by itself contributes something to the 'dialogue' between God and human. God calls us in the form of the Word, and we respond in prayer and worship that interpret the Word rather than just repeating it, so prayer and worship are cocreative. This interpretive and thus cocreative dealing with the Word can be considered a hermeneutic condition, but the awareness of it increased along with modern subjectification. We may therefore conclude that without receptivity there would be no theology; but, without simultaneous productivity, there would be no *modern* theology.

The Ethical in the Aesthetic

Imagination plays a prominent role in the theology that has approached aesthetics in recent decades. I refer in particular to the efforts made internationally to develop new disciplines such as 'theological aesthetics,' 'aesthetic theology,' and 'religious aesthetics.'[69] But genuine dialogue between theology and aesthetics is still often prevented by prejudices according to which the aesthetic is

---

68 It is often appropriate to distinguish between 'fantasy' and 'imagination,' as Kant did. However, in the present context, it is not particularly relevant to make such a distinction and it merely complicates the comparative reading of Kant and Baumgarten. For now, I therefore use the words as synonyms (for what Kant understood by imagination, not fantasy) and later I only use the word 'imagination.' For a comprehensive presentation of various historical philosophies of imagination, including Kant's philosophy and his distinction between fantasy and imagination, see the chapter "The Philosophy of Imagination."

69 See the chapter "Åbenheden i mellemverdenen" (The Openness of the Intermediate World) in *Den skønne tænkning*.

not enough in itself and faith is more fundamental than aesthetic experience.

The first of these prejudices can be found in the works of K.E. Løgstrup, which means that the problem—namely, theology's stubborn relation to aesthetics—is *not* resolved by resorting to him rather than to Kierkegaard. In *Kunst og erkendelse* (Art and Knowledge), Løgstrup says that an understanding of the aesthetic inspired by Kierkegaard "rages" in continental thought.[70] In his words, we usually "take it for granted in a Kierkegaardian sense, not only that life is split up into an aesthetic and an ethical province, but that the aesthetic is a treacherous escape from our practical life and ethical duties."[71] In continuation of this, Løgstrup differentiates between two different kinds of aesthetic experience. The term 'aesthetic experience' may denote a way of approaching life in which there is no break between vision and action. In this case, what a person experiences is a "revelation of life's wealth of possibilities and contradictions, and carried away he promptly acts out of a great spiritual surplus."[72] Far more often, however, the term 'aesthetic experience' means to relate in a pleasure-seeking way to what happens, and to which one thus fails to relate in a responsibly practical way.

According to Løgstrup, it was aesthetic experience in the latter sense of the term that Kierkegaard referred to when describing the aesthete, and his description was correct, which also means that his criticism was justified. Nevertheless, he was mistaken in using this to construct a narrow concept of aesthetics by presenting the described lack of responsibility as the essence of aesthetic

---

70 K.E. Løgstrup, *Kunst og erkendelse: Kunstfilosofiske betragtninger. Metafysik II* (Art and Knowledge: Art Philosophical Considerations. Metaphysics II), eds. S. Andersen et al. (Copenhagen: Gyldendal, 1983), 56.

71 Løgstrup, *Kunst og erkendelse*, 56.

72 Løgstrup, *Kunst og erkendelse*, 56. For example, Løgstrup also uses the expression 'aesthetic experience' in "Min tids tre fromhedsbølger: En smule subjektivt set," in which he describes the commitment of science as "an aesthetic experience and if it does not remain this way, I cannot imagine it is worth the effort." See K.E. Løgstrup, "Min tids tre fromhedsbølger: En smule subjektivt set" (The Three Waves of Piety in My Time: Somewhat Subjectively Seen), in *Solidaritet og kærlighed og andre essays* (Solidarity and Love and Other Essays), 146–157, eds. O. Jensen et al. (Copenhagen: Gyldendal, 1987), 151.

experience.⁷³ Løgstrup's objection might be right, especially if he is addressing it to Kierkegaard reception up to the end of the twentieth century, rather than Kierkegaard himself. However, Løgstrup also contributes to the pejorative use of the words 'aesthetics,' 'aesthetic,' and 'the aesthete,' for which he criticizes Kierkegaard. Løgstrup's negative charging of these words is evident in what I quoted in the previous paragraph, and it can also be observed elsewhere in *Kunst og erkendelse*. For example, concerning the error of judgment one might make when judging an object's aesthetic qualities, he says that it is caused by the fact that "in aesthetics more is always at stake than aesthetics,"⁷⁴ thus indirectly saying that something is missing in what is 'just' aesthetic. According to Løgstrup, there is always some kind of interest, that is, nonaesthetic needs and desires, involved in an aesthetic judgment, and this interest may interfere with the assessment of the aesthetic aspects of the object. Actually, what Løgstrup considers most crucial in the aesthetic is what is *not* aesthetic: "The more one manages to delude oneself into thinking that one's interest in the work of art is purely aesthetic, the more effectively its pseudobeauty serves one's nonaesthetic interests. The deeper the self-deception is, which means the more unconscious it is, the more the nonaesthetic interests are pumped up and the more the aesthetic is masked."⁷⁵

The Religious in the Aesthetic

Among the previously mentioned prejudices that still impede the dialogue between theology and aesthetics, we also find the idea nourished by some theologians—including some of those involved in the development of theological aesthetics—that the experience of faith is and must be more fundamental than any other kind of experience; therefore, it cannot spring from *aisthesis*. Or as Mirjam-

---

73 Løgstrup, *Kunst og erkendelse*, 56, footnote.

74 Løgstrup, *Kunst og erkendelse*, 83.

75 Løgstrup, *Kunst og erkendelse*, 83.

Christina Redeker puts it: "The perception [*Wahrnehmung*] of God must continue to be the criteria for any human *aisthesis* and all factual human perception."[76] A similar dogmatics is known from philosophical hermeneutics, though, in hermeneutics, it is not the experience of faith but hermeneutic understanding that is given the priority. Hans-Georg Gadamer insisted that aesthetics can only be particular, whereas hermeneutics is universal and includes aesthetics.[77] His reasoning was that the work of art—which to him was the aesthetic object, that is: he identified aesthetics with the philosophy of art—"tells us something" and thus requires understanding, which means that the work belongs to what is the topic of hermeneutics.[78] In this way, Gadamer let hermeneutics dominate aesthetics, and similarly theologians such as Redeker let aesthetics be dominated by theology when they reduce aesthetics to a theological auxiliary discipline.

In opposition to Gadamer, I demonstrated in my book *Den skønne tænkning* (Beautiful Thinking) that it is actually not the work of art but sensitive cognition that is the topic of aesthetics, and that this cognition is hermeneutic *in itself*: it brings insight.[79]

---

76   Mirjam-Christina Redeker, *Wahrnehmung und Glaube: Zum Verhältnis von Theologie und Ästhetik in gegenwärtiger Zeit* (Berlin and New York: De Gruyter, 2011), 363.

77   Hans-Georg Gadamer, "Aesthetics and Hermeneutics," trans. D.E. Linge, in *The Gadamer Reader: A Bouquet of the Later Writings*, ed. R.E. Palmer (Evanston: Northwestern University Press, 2007), 130.

78   Gadamer, "Aesthetics and Hermeneutics," 128.

79   Jørgensen, *Den skønne tænkning*, 493–503. *Den skønne tænkning* contains an English summary on pp. 947–965. The overall aim of the book was to develop, with a point of departure in philosophical aesthetics and hermeneutic phenomenology, a philosophy of experience for all kinds of experience of transcendence (aesthetic, religious, and metaphysical experiences). At the same time, its ambition was also to provide a basis for theological aesthetics with a proper philosophical grounding, that is, theological aesthetics that is well rooted in philosophical aesthetics and not just in art theory, for instance. *Den skønne tænkning* thus provides detailed interpretations of both older and newer theorists, especially Baumgarten, Kant, Heidegger, and Walter Benjamin, but also, for example, Böhme, Hermann Schmitz, Wolfgang Welsch, Martin Seel, Christoph Menke, Hans Ulrich Gumbrecht, and Richard Shusterman. Furthermore, the book contains a comprehensive religio-philosophical implementation of aesthetics discussing other theorists, including Løgstrup, Chrétien, Eugenio Trías, Hans Urs von Balthasar, Eberhard Jüngel, Klaas Huizing, Mark C. Taylor, Hannah Arendt, Hans Joas, and Dieter Henrich.

Not only hermeneutic understanding but also sensitive cognition includes, qua cognition, the element of understanding that Gadamer searched for in vain because he insisted on defining it hermeneutically rather than aesthetically. Similarly, in *Den skønne tænkning*, I explained that the theological claim for regarding the experience of faith as the measure of all other experience is based on a limited understanding of *aisthesis* and a reductive concept of *experience*. Aisthesis is regarded as devoid of faith; often it is even identified with physical sensation, and the applied concept of experience usually comprises only sensory experience, empirical experience, scientific experience, and perhaps life experience, but not experience of transcendence or a surplus of meaning.

Therefore, in *Den skønne tænkning*, I introduced a concept of *basic experience* to describe a level of experience characterized by a trinity of sensation, faith, and comprehension. Basic experience is the sensitive level of experience at which anything at all appears to us, and which by aesthetics was named 'the aesthetic.' Here we are thus *not* talking about singular experiences, but about the sensitively sentient being-there-in-the-universe-together-with-whatever-else-there-is without which there would be no consciousness. In this presence, we sensitively sense what is: ourselves in our presence and what we are together with in it. As Baumgarten noted, there is understanding, which he referred to as cognition, even at this basic level, and, in *Den skønne tænkning*, I added that this understanding is due not only to the sensitive aspect of the experience but also to the faith, in the sense of *trust*, with which we respond to the sensitively provided insight. Already at the aesthetic-sensitive level of experience, which basic experience represents, we thus find not only *sensation* but also *faith* and *comprehension*. In our sensations we sensitively comprehend ourselves, each other, and the world around us, and we spontaneously have faith in what we comprehend: we trust the insight we receive in our sensitive experience. We sense, comprehend, and have faith in what we comprehend when our experience is something that *happens* to us instead of being something we, ourselves, *accomplish*; and this is precisely what goes on at the level of basic experience, at which there is yet no subject or object but only *Dasein*.

Aesthetic Formation

Our day is not characterized by having an eye for basic experience, however, or for its elements of sensation, faith, and comprehension; on the contrary, it is dominated by intellectualism and aestheticism.[80] The allegedly rational mindset of intellectualism sees faith and comprehension, or theology and philosophy, as contrary to each other. It cultivates what it refers to as reason, but which is in fact understanding, at the expense of everything that has anything to do with faith, religion, and theology. No one expresses this ideology more explicitly than the militant atheists, but it can be observed everywhere in society. The tendency to contrast faith and comprehension is also present in Kierkegaard's works and in the reception of his thought, but here it is in reverse. We could take as an example Johannes Climacus' study in *Philosophical Fragments* of philosophy understood as the rational view of the world, and of theology defined by faith that cannot be understood rationally, or, therefore, philosophically. In this study, a distinction between reason and understanding is also missing; likewise, one misses an eye for philosophy that does not insist on comprehending everything intellectually but revolves sensitively around the intellectually incomprehensible.

    Aestheticism makes itself present in the form of a widespread tendency to reduce aisthesis to physical sensation, to identify aesthetes with fanatics, and to cultivate this sensualism and fanaticism. Even in philosophy this takes place. Michel Foucault's idea about shaping oneself and one's life as a work of art, also called "self-creation" and "aesthetics of existence," may be mentioned as

---

80 In this section, 'understanding' refers to *der Verstand* (the faculty of concepts and intellectual reasoning) rather than the aesthetic/hermeneutic *Verstehen* discussed in the previous section. Moreover, the term 'intellectualism' refers to a way of thinking dominated by understanding (in the sense of *Verstand*) and devoid of reason (*Vernunft*).

an example.[81] Whereas the Greek kalokagathia had a common ethics as its sounding board, and even the eighteenth-century beautiful soul was aware of common values, the aesthetics of existence referred to by Foucault is associated with a postmodern distrust of anything universal and of the subject regarded as the seat of moral knowledge and action. This aesthetics of existence lacks both the morals of kalokagathia and the fervor of the beautiful soul. It is the expression of an individualistic aestheticism and it thus represents what not only Hegel and Kierkegaard but also Heidegger and Gadamer criticized aesthetic man for.

However, while aestheticism can be justifiably criticized, it is wrong to link it to aesthetic man. Baumgarten referred to the aesthete as *felix aestheticus*, that is, the lucky aesthete in the sense of the successful aesthete.[82] All human beings are equipped with what is needed to cognize and think sensitively, which in short is: *feeling, sensation,* and *presentiment*.[83] The lucky aesthete is the person whose sensitive cognition is perfected and whose cognition and thinking is thus *beautiful*. This perfection requires aesthetic practice and teaching, and such aesthetic formation is important because beautiful cognition and thinking have not only cognitive but also ethical and religious significance. In the experience of beauty, something appears as valuable in itself, and we see ourselves and our surroundings as parts of something bigger. This was the message of the Greek philosophy of beauty, which was transformed by

---

81   Michel Foucault, "On the Genealogy of Ethics: An Overview of Work in Progress," in *The Foucault Reader*, ed. P. Rabinow (London: Penguin Books, 1991), 350–351.

82   Baumgarten, *Ästhetik*, §§ 27ff.

83   'Feeling, sensation, and presentiment' is the reformulation used in *Den skønne tænkning* of the conglomerate of 'lower' cognitive faculties by which Baumgarten defined sensitivity. In *Aesthetica* §§ 30–37, these faculties are described as 1) "increased sensitivity" (*acute sentiendi*); 2) "the natural disposition for imagining something" (*dispositio naturalis ad imaginandum*); 3) "the natural disposition for penetrating insight" (*dispositio naturalis ad perspicaciam*); 4) "the natural disposition for recognizing something and memory" (*dispositio naturalis ad recognoscendum et memoria*); 5) "the poetic disposition" (*dispositio poetica*); 6) "the disposition for having a taste that is not ordinary, but refined" (*dispositio ad saporem non publicum, immo delicatum*); 7) "the disposition for anticipating and expecting something" (*dispositio ad praevidendum et praesagiendum*); and 8) "the disposition for characterizing one's perceptions" (*dispositio ad significandas perceptiones suas*).

Baumgarten into a philosophy of the very *experience* formed when things appear this way to us.

But unfortunately we have become beauty-blind. We nurture our understanding and physical senses, but we overlook the sensitivity that feeling, sensation, and presentiment form, and which is where the encounter with beauty happens. We confuse the beautiful with the pretty, and we cultivate the sublime or wonderful as if they were something different, whereas, in antiquity and the Middle Ages, they were aspects of the then far richer concept of beauty. Hence, there is a need for aesthetic formation, today understood not only as the cultivation of sensitivity considered necessary by Baumgarten but as a revival of our sensitivity as such, because we have forgotten the openness it represents to what exceeds understanding and sense perception. Otherwise, if we neglect the need for aesthetic formation, we exclude revelation.[84] Kierkegaard was right in insisting that revelation is not dependent on *us*; that it is not a product of the kind of experience we ourselves act out and control. But revelation is an occurrence and thus indeed an experience, though of a kind that happens to us and the event of which we may become blind to. It is just such an insensitivity that prevails today and intensifies the need for aesthetic formation: the need to rehabilitate our sensitivity and restore our openness to what exceeds understanding and sense perception, yet is accessible in its inaccessibility, namely in interaction with our creative receptivity.

---

84 Not only in Chrétien's *The Call and the Response* but also in his *Hand to Hand*, for example, one can find support for this view. Jean-Louis Chrétien, *Hand to Hand: Listening to the Work of Art*, trans. S.E. Lewis (New York: Fordham University Press, 2003).

The Metamorphosis of Beauty

Beauty has been an anathema for two centuries, but it is anachronistic to sustain this suspicion of it. Romantico-modern art and aesthetics are actually not based on a simple rejection of beauty, but on a dethronement of one perception of beauty by another. In other words, beauty is not identical to 'traditional beauty' but also includes 'modern beauty.' It therefore makes better sense to: 1) examine the metamorphosis of beauty in the history of aesthetic ideas, 2) draw attention to the relevance of beauty in our time, and 3) explore what a current form of beauty may involve.

The Experience of Divinity

In the *Republic*, Plato presented a theory of art and its role in the state guided by a wish to educate man, and modern aesthetic theory has shown more interest in this educational ambition than in his metaphysics of beauty.[85] It is the metaphysics of beauty in Pla-

---

[85] Plato, *Republic*, trans. G.M.A. Grube, rev. C.D.C. Reeve, in *Plato: Complete Works*, eds. J.M. Cooper and D.S. Hutchinson (Indianapolis and Cambridge, MA: Hackett Publishing Company, 1997). I distinguish between 'the metaphysics of beauty,' 'art theory,' 'philosophy of art,' and 'philosophical aesthetics.' The metaphysics of beauty, which is about the nature and appearance of beauty (the laws of the cosmos; the beauty of God or nature), and art theory, which is about the formal aspects of works of art (the immanent laws of art, including the laws of the beauty of art), were introduced in antiquity. The philosophy of art and philosophical aesthetics, on the other hand, are modern inventions; the former deals with the question of what art essentially is (the question of the nature of the work of art) and the latter deals with aesthetic experience understood as a kind of true cognition. I introduced these distinctions in Dorthe Jørgensen, *Skønhedens metamorfose: De æstetiske idéers historie* (The Metamorphosis of Beauty: History of Aesthetic Ideas) (Odense: Odense University Press, 2001).

to's *Symposium*, however, that has played the greatest part in the history of aesthetic ideas.[86] This metaphysics was inspired by Homeric poetry and Pythagorean cosmology, and the Greek poets and cosmologists did not think ethically, but religiously. Homeric poetry thus contained the idea that poetry originates in 'divine madness' (*theia mania*) and the Pythagoreans honored the idea that the beauty of the cosmos is due to its 'divine order' (*pankalia*). To summarize, we may conclude that this period's perception of beauty was the expression of an *experience of divinity*, and, through Plato's metaphysics of beauty, such experience was transferred and reinterpreted in a tradition ranging from Plotinus through Byzantinism, Gothic, and Renaissance Neoplatonism to Romanticism and modernism.

With his metaphysics of beauty, Plato presented a philosophy of the beauty of pure forms that dealt with both the beautiful and the ability of humans to recognize the beautiful, and in which poetry and art as well as human recognitions of beauty referred to the divine. This philosophy of beauty holds the key to a dimension of Western philosophy in which thinking not only revolves around the human being and its morality but also around forces greater than this being and around the manifestation of these divine forces in the form of beauty. However, in his *Poetics*, Aristotle cut the link between beauty and divinity formulated by Plato, thereby releasing art for secular purposes.[87] Hitherto, art and poetry were regarded as essentially different—poetry was considered divinely inspired, whereas art was considered the result of human knowledge-based skill. Aristotle, however, regarded not only art but also poetry as a product of *techne*, and he interpreted the poet's potential elation of his audience not religiously but psychologically and medically.

The Aristotelian tendency to secularize and empower art continued in Hellenistic-Roman times, but here the interest in the

---

86 Plato, *Symposium*, trans. A. Nehamas and P. Woodruff, in *Plato: Complete Works*, eds. J.M. Cooper and D.S. Hutchinson (Indianapolis and Cambridge, MA: Hackett Publishing Company, 1997).

87 Aristotle, *Poetics*, trans. I. Bywater, in *The Complete Works of Aristotle: The Revised Oxford Translation, Volume 2*, ed. J. Barnes (Princeton: Princeton University Press, 1984).

edifying potential of art was abandoned in favor of its ability to appeal to the emotions. In late antiquity, attention was thus directed to the ecstasy evoked by art and the experience of transcendence that may be associated with such ecstasy. This development culminated in Plotinus' philosophy about the metaphysical experience of the light emanating from the One, and with his metaphysics of beauty, the experience of divinity was again central to aesthetics. Late antiquity's interest in the experience of ecstasy continued into the Middle Ages, where it was interpreted in a Christian manner; the experience of divinity consisted no longer in a poetic, cosmological, or metaphysical experience of divinity but in the religious experience of God's presence. In the early Middle Ages, religious experience was interpreted as experiencing the beauty of God's creation, which also testified to its truth and goodness, whereas later it was interpreted as experiencing the glory of God himself. Although the influence of ancient Greek ideas partly held medieval man's gaze on the surrounding world and its beauty, Christianity invited him to turn his gaze inward toward the feeling accompanying the experience of the beauty of God's creation or the Creator. The experience of beauty became more subjective, resulting in theoretical considerations that, due to their emotional anchoring, already seemed to anticipate modern aesthetics.

Early in the Middle Ages, the church fathers compared God to the artist in order to illustrate His creative skills. This tradition of comparing God and the artist continued in the Renaissance, but in reverse: now the creative artist was compared to God in order to give an impression of the artist's genius. With this development, the Homeric idea of divine madness returned, but in a Neoplatonic and modern worldly form as an aesthetic experience: it was now the beauty of the sensuous (the concrete form, not least the human body) that was subject to experience. At the same time, the Pythagorean idea of *pankalia*, which referred to the beauty of the universe, was actualized, but without the medieval fear of the possible danger of beauty. Many Renaissance thinkers and artists admired Neoplatonic philosophy, mysticism, and magic, but they also surrendered without much reservation to enjoying the sensuous manifestations of beauty.

The eighteenth-century German philosopher Alexander Gottlieb Baumgarten was the first to introduce a genuine theory of aesthetic experience, which he did by founding philosophical aesthetics as the theory of sensitive cognition (*cognitio sensitiva*).[88] 'Sensitive cognition' was Baumgarten's designation of aesthetic experience (essentially the experience of beauty), which he considered different from both sense perception and intellectual cognition, as a kind of cognition that originated in feeling, sensation, and presentiment.[89] For Baumgarten, aesthetic experiences were true and valid. Since he regarded philosophical aesthetics as the theory of sensitive cognition and thus of aesthetic experience, he considered it the task of philosophical aesthetics to supplement logic. However, Baumgarten's and later eighteenth-century aesthetics were preceded by the aesthetics of taste of the seventeenth century, which was a doctrine of the good life rather than beauty's truth value; this aesthetics of taste became the source of an undercurrent of ethics (and politics) in modern aesthetics. This is evident from, for example, Immanuel Kant's interpretation of beauty as a symbol of morality, Friedrich Schiller's theory of aesthetic education, and various relics of kalokagathia in modern aesthetics.[90] Due to this

---

88 Alexander Gottlieb Baumgarten, *Ästhetik, Volume 1–2*, trans. D. Mirbach (Hamburg: Felix Meiner Verlag, 2007).

89 'Feeling, sensation, and presentiment' is the reformulation used in *Den skønne tænkning* of the conglomerate of 'lower' cognitive faculties with which Baumgarten defined sensitivity. See Dorthe Jørgensen, *Den skønne tænkning: Veje til erfaringsmetafysik. Religionsfilosofisk udmøntet* (Beautiful Thinking: Pathways to the Metaphysics of Experience. Religio-Philosophically Implemented) (Aarhus: Aarhus University Press, 2014). See also the chapter "Protestantism and Its Aesthetic Discontents," footnote 83, in the present volume.

90 See Immanuel Kant, *Critique of the Power of Judgment*, eds. and trans. P. Guyer and E. Matthews (New York: Cambridge University Press, 2000), § 59, and Friedrich Schiller, *On the Aesthetic Education of Man in a Series of Letters*, eds. and trans. E.M. Wilkinson and L.A. Willoughby (Oxford: Clarendon Press, 1967). Schiller's idea of human liberation through aesthetic education was inspired by the linking of the good and the beautiful in the Greek educational ideal, which in antiquity was expressed in the idea of *kalokagathia* (*kalos kai agathos*, literally 'beautiful and good'), and a great part of modern aesthetics replays the theory of Schiller.

undercurrent of ethics (and politics), philosophical aesthetics was never really developed as the epistemology it was originally conceived to be.

The Hegemony of the Form

The Homeric idea of divine madness is one of the very first European testimonies of aesthetic reflection. However, the Pythagoreans had already begun focusing on the form of the experienced rather than the source of experience, that is, the divine order of the cosmos rather than the inspiration in which poetry originated. This shift from source to form later manifested itself in the art theory developed in relation to ancient art. The classical art of the Greeks was supposed to mirror the harmony of the cosmos in the symmetry of temples and sculptures, for instance, and, due to the anthropometric scale used, in addition to the challenge of the idea of inspiration thus implied, anthropos and ethos also challenged cosmos and logos. With classical art's anthropometrical translation of cosmology, the Pythagorean experience of divinity was thus transformed into an *aesthetics of form* that defined itself by symmetry and to which a normativity with ethical implications was attached. This aesthetics of form and the associated ideology have influenced the majority of Western art and aesthetics.

Both classical art and the corresponding theory of art managed to find support in the metaphysics of beauty, but it was the Aristotelian theory of art that propagated the aesthetics of form throughout history. Likewise, Aristotle did not dissolve the ancient Greek distinction between art and poetry because he considered art divinely inspired like poetry but because he considered poetry, like art, a result of *techne*. He expanded the field of the aesthetics of form from visual art to poetry, which resulted in a purification of poetry from its original reference to divine madness. He confronted not only temples and sculptures but also Greek tragedy with the characteristic demands of art theory and subjected catharsis to a psycho-physical interpretation that limited its connection to divinity.

Later, the classic Hellenic concept of beauty was replaced by the Hellenistic-Roman understanding of beauty. In this connection, the doctrine of symmetry had to give way to that of eurythmics (the idea that the proportions of an object need not *be*, but merely *appear* symmetrical), and the catharsis doctrine of art's ability to purify the soul was reinterpreted through stylistic considerations of the sublime's ability to appeal to the emotions. During this process, the Greek perception of beauty was challenged, but only within its own form-aesthetic framework, and the change was thus a variation on the same theme rather than a genuinely new idea. With the transition from the Hellenic to the Hellenistic-Roman perception of beauty, beauty therefore underwent a metamorphosis, since the beautiful now became synonymous with the sublime, but the truly great change first occurred with Plotinus' philosophy of the light emanating from the One. Plotinus' processing of Plato's metaphysics of beauty and the Greek aesthetics of form led to an addition of a Near Eastern component that resulted in a new *aesthetics of light*.[91]

The Middle Ages inherited both the Greek aesthetics of form and the new aesthetics of light, linking them to the Old Testament's *aesthetics of the symbol*. The Christian aesthetics resulting from this syncretism may be considered one great attempt to reconcile the Greek harmony of form with the Jewish dynamics of the symbol: an alloy of the beauty of peace and the beauty of life. However, this attempt was performed differently in the domains of the Greek Orthodox Church and the Roman Catholic Church. In the Byzantine Empire, Dionysius the Areopagite's interpretation of the aesthetics of light contributed to the mediation, which resulted in a metaphysical aesthetics focusing on the true in the beautiful. In the Roman Catholic arena, on the other hand, Augustine's interpretation of the moral doctrine of the New Testament formed the basis of the association, which resulted in an ethical-ascetic aesthetics focusing on the good in the beautiful.

---

91   Plotinus, "Ennead I.6: On Beauty," trans. A.H. Armstrong, in *Ennead, Volume I: Porphyry on the Life of Plotinus. Ennead I*, trans. A.H. Armstrong (Cambridge, MA: Harvard University Press, 1969).

The medieval Christian reconciliation attempt thus relied on the Greeks reflecting not only on the form-experience of a Pythagorean origin but also the Plotinian experience of light, and it relied on the Jews not only formulating the Old Testament's image ban but also nurturing a Near Eastern pleasure in the material and its potential symbolism. However, since the aesthetics of light constituted a feature of Greek philosophy related to Near Eastern thought, it was particularly well suited to mediate between the Hellenist experience of the form's aesthetic beauty and the Near Eastern experience of the material's symbolic significance. Furthermore, the aesthetics of the symbol in Christian aesthetics included a pan-perspectivism, which did not exist to the same extent in antiquity, and the aesthetics of light, the aesthetics of the symbol, the synthesis of Greek and Jewish thought, and pan-perspectivism are all evident from Byzantine icons.[92] These icons attempted not to portray Christ in a naturalistic way but to refer to the divine light, and they therefore folded several worlds together into the same image.

The medieval pan-perspectivism, which was characteristic of both Roman Catholic and Greek Orthodox art, was rejected, however, as the Greek aesthetics of form was actualized in a purer form by the Italian Renaissance of the fourteenth to the sixteenth century. The investment in the form performed in the Renaissance resulted in the construction of the central perspective, and medieval pan-perspectivism had to give way to the 'gathering' of the image carried out by the central perspective, a gathering strengthened to the utmost in the High Renaissance. The aesthetics of form characterized by central perspectivism was exemplary in the production of the Florentine school, and the beauty ideal associated with this aesthetics dominated almost exclusively for centuries. In this period, the hegemony of form was challenged only on a small

---

92 Pan-perspectivism is the opposite of central perspectivism. Central perspectivistic images are characterized by having one focus, while pan-perspectivistic images have many focuses and are characterized by flat frontality instead of spatial depth. Medieval visual art was distinctly pan-perspectivistic and so is modern art. See Werner Hofmann, *Die Moderne im Rückspiegel: Hauptwege der Kunstgeschichte* (München: C.H. Beck Verlag, 1998).

scale, that is, through the light aesthetic interpretation of form introduced by the Venetians, the fragmentation of form performed by mannerism, and the dynamism of the baroque. Moreover, in the eighteenth century, the aesthetics of form characterized by central perspectivism was revived as the philosophy of liberation inspired by humanism made use of the neoclassicism of that time in relation to its ambition of enlightenment and its educational project. Georg Wilhelm Friedrich Hegel also maintained the aesthetics of form, not least in its classical Greek interpretation, and his philosophical strengthening of the Greek profile of aesthetics became crucial for the art-historical thought of the nineteenth century.

Peace and Life

The German Romantics of Hegel's time, Friedrich Schlegel in particular, problematized the hegemony of form described in the previous section. Moreover, at the end of the nineteenth and the beginning of the twentieth century, art finally abandoned the aesthetics of form characterized by central perspectivism. The light was liberated through modern colorism, and cubism resumed pan-perspectivism in a modern form. Through a new *mysticism of form* and *magic of things*, the twentieth-century modernist use of elements from the medieval aesthetic universe thus entailed innovative interpretations of both the aesthetics of light and the aesthetics of the symbol.[93] However, modernism's abandonment of the aesthetics of form stemming from the Renaissance also implied a recursion to the Near Eastern element of the European history of aesthetic ideas. This Near Easternization of modern art differed

---

93 Wassily Kandinsky is the most prominent representative of the modernist *mysticism of form*; see his *Concerning the Spiritual in Art*, trans. M.T.H. Sadler (New York: Dover Publications, 1977). This mysticism of form was not merely an extension of the form-aesthetic tradition but was rather the result of an alloy of the aesthetics of form and the aesthetics of light, in which color values played an important role, and which was characterized by pan-perspectivism. The *magic of things*, on the other hand, was recognizable in the art of Marcel Duchamp and the surrealists, for instance. In addition to wishing to dissolve the art institution by uniting art and life, it attempted to collect, express, and reflect on the experiences of a suprasensuous surplus that may happen to modern humans.

from the neoclassical heroification of classical Greek aesthetic thought, and was akin to the Romantic criticism of classicism.

But what does it mean to suggest that a romantico-modern Near Easternization took place? The suggestion is based not only on the observation that the European history of aesthetic ideas contains both a Greek-Roman and a Jewish-Eastern component. It also assumes that these two components are interrelated in a historically changeable way. In ancient times, the Jews had only one God, whereas the Greeks cultivated many humanlike gods, and this difference had implications for the art and aesthetic thought created in Greece and the Near East, respectively. Greek art and aesthetic thought gave priority to form and visibility, which was in keeping with the mythological myriad of humanlike Greek gods. Similarly, with the help of philosophy, the Greeks sought to obtain insight into the existent and to recognize it intellectually. The God of the Jews, on the other hand, was invisible (in principle), and the Old Testament's ban on images forbade any attempt to depict him visually, especially in sculptural form. Unlike the Greeks, the Jews therefore did not give priority to form and visibility but favored intensity and fervor, and they were action-oriented rather than philosophically tuned. They did not act for the existent but for the coming, in an attempt to follow the commandments of their religion.

The Greek culture was one of images and philosophy, just as Greek art and aesthetic thought were governed by vision and intellect and marked by an ethical interest in 'the human.' The Jewish culture, on the other hand, was one of sound and religion, and Jewish art and aesthetic thought were governed by hearing and feeling and characterized by eschatology and messianism. For the Greeks, however, sight was attached to not only the outer eye but also a kind of inner eye, and it was directed to form in both a material and an intellectual sense. There was thus no contradiction between the sense of sight and the intellect; on the contrary, in mystical vision and the associated metaphysics of light, eye and intellect fused in exemplary ways. Similarly, for the Jews, there was no contradiction between hearing and feeling, and the Jewish hearing was open to immaterial as well as material sound since it was connected to not only an outer but also an inner ear.

With the Hellenization of the Mediterranean during the centuries leading up to the birth of Christ, and with the Christianization of the Greco-Roman people, the Greek and Jewish legacies—that is, image and sound, or philosophy and religion—had to unite. Medieval Christian art inherited this task, which was difficult to solve because the Greeks enjoyed the love of duration and thus elevated the static and stable, whereas the Jews enjoyed the love of becoming and thus praised dynamism and development. Accordingly, Greek philosophical thought, which gave priority to visuality and *stasis*, was expressed aesthetically in sculpture characterized by intellectuality, whereas Jewish religious thought, which gave priority to audibility and *dynamis*, manifested itself in music and prophetic narrative characterized by emotionality. Simultaneously, both Greek and Jewish art were loaded with paradoxes. Jewish art was fervent but also more sensuous than Greek art, although the latter was more naturalistic despite its idealism. Similarly, Greek philosophy was more abstract than Jewish religion, but the Jewish God was transcendent, whereas the gods of the Greeks resembled and moved among humans.

Since the eighteenth century, it has been common to concentrate on the differences between the Greek and Jewish legacies, including the difference between philosophy and religion, but one may also take the paradoxes seriously and consider why it has been difficult to reconcile Greek and Jewish art. Perhaps the differences were exaggerated when reconciliation became a task at the beginning of the Middle Ages. While the difference between Greek and Jewish art and culture was underscored between the eighteenth and the twentieth centuries, new knowledge of exchanges between Greece and the Near East that took place long before the Hellenistic-Roman period was gained in the second half of the twentieth century.[94] The interrelations across the Mediterranean were intense as

---

94 See, for example, Cyrus H. Gordon, *The Common Background of Greek and Hebrew Civilizations* (New York and London: W.W. Norton and Company, 1965), and Walter Burkert, *The Orientalizing Revolution: Near Eastern Influence on Greek Culture in the Early Archaic Age*

early as the Bronze Age (especially in the fourteenth and thirteenth centuries BC) and not least in the Homeric era (around 750–650 BC). The latter period was so marked by syncretism between the different cultures of the Mediterranean area that it is now referred to as not only the Archaic but also the Orientalizing period.[95] Therefore, it should not come as a surprise that, in their own time, the Romantics could celebrate ancient Greek art and simultaneously initiate a Near Easternization of art. For it was Archaic poetry and Archaic temple ruins that caught their attention and, unlike classical art, Archaic art was not genuinely 'Greek' but already itself a product of a culture of Near Easternization.

Form and Fragmentation

While medieval art attempted to balance Greek and Jewish art in a Christian way, Renaissance art attempted to actualize a more genuinely Greek source. During the Renaissance, the musicality of the Gothic patchworklike art was thus replaced by the monumental architectonics of the Greeks, which meant that calmness, duration, and solidity prevailed over movement, becoming, and finality. However, this Grecophilia was problematized by baroque art's attempt to unite architectonics and musicality, and, since Romanticism, art has swung between a Greek will to form and Near Eastern dynamics. Admittedly, it is a common assumption that modern art, best known for its fragmented nature, is devoid of any will to form, but the experience of modernity is not identical to the experience of fragmentation, and romantico-modern art is not identical with prioritizing fragmentation over form. Romantico-modern art rather expresses and reflects a stronger awareness of a conflictual relation between the experiences we have and our established ways to

---

(London and Cambridge, MA: Harvard University Press, 1992).

95   Burkert, *The Orientalizing Revolution*.

express and interpret human experience, resulting not only in fragmentation but also in a tension between form and fragmentation.[96]

The romantico-modern awareness of the aforementioned conflict originates in modern humans' experiences of modernity but is actually a variation of an older European theme, namely a longing for unity that has accompanied European culture ever since it began to develop from two different sources: the Greek-Roman and Jewish-Eastern traditions. Medieval thinkers believed that the legacies of the Greeks and the Jews were difficult to unify but trusted that Christianity could reconcile them. However, the modern secularization of society eroded the belief in the Christian power of the incarnation mystery, which meant that the wound once again opened and the contrast between visuality and musicality, image and banned image, or *stasis* and *dynamis* manifested itself once more in the romantico-modern, but was now interpreted as a conflict between form and fragmentation. As early as mannerism and the baroque, the outlines of this development, and thus also of early modernity, were perceivable, but it was in the art of the nineteenth and twentieth centuries that the tension between the will to form and the experience of fragmentation became the center around which everything revolved.

For a long time, only modern art's interest in fragmentation and not its will to form caught scholarly attention. This imbalance is caused by the fact that the relationship between tradition and modernity has mainly been treated as one between contradictions. However, modernism did not regard it as its task to reject tradition and renounce the form as such. It was instead characterized by the attempt to create a balance between the inherited and the self-experienced and thus also between the will to form and the experience of fragmentation. Since the Renaissance, however, tradition

---

[96] For more on the experience of modernity, romantico-modern art, and the relation between form and fragmentation, see Dorthe Jørgensen, *Aber die Wärme des Bluts: Et studium i den romantisk-moderne dialektik imellem vilje til Form og erfaring af faktisk fragmentering. I anledning af G.W.F. Hegels fortrængning af modernitetserfaringen* (Aber die Wärme des Bluts: A Study in the Romantico-Modern Dialectic between the Will to Form and the Experience of Actual Fragmentation. On the Occasion of G.W.F. Hegel's Displacement of the Experience of Modernity) (Aarhus: Modtryk, 1996).

had been identical with the legacy of the Greeks and European culture had inherited the task of reconciling the Greek and Jewish legacies. We may therefore regard it as a historically conditioned task for modern artists to resume the aesthetics of nascent life, human finality, and the fleeting movement. In other words: the inherited demand to balance the Greek and Jewish components of European art and aesthetic thought combined with secularism's hollowing out of confidence in the Christian model required modern artists to resume the Jewish-Eastern legacy but in a modern version, that is, as an expression of modernity.

Consequently, two different currents occur in romantico-modern aesthetic phenomena. On the one hand, these phenomena contain traces of a Hellenic aesthetics awakened from its hibernation by the Renaissance and dominated by a will to form. On the other hand, they also contain traces of a Jewish-Eastern aesthetics actualized by Romanticism and characterized by dynamics and discontinuity. This duality has a historical genealogy: in the Renaissance, the surviving Grecophilia undermined the Christian construction that was dominant in the Middle Ages, and Greek aesthetics began to replace Christian religiosity, but in Romanticism, the neo-Greek construction created by the Renaissance was undermined by the equally inherited Jewish-Eastern component. The legacy of Jewish-Eastern aesthetics thus challenged the legacy of Greek aesthetics, but this challenge was concealed by the conflict between the classical and the modern that erupted in the eighteenth century.

The Near Easternization of art initiated by Romanticism became a reality with modernism, which actualized the Near Eastern tradition to such an extent that it referred even further back than the Middle Ages. This became obvious with modernism's dynamization of art. Modernism brought time into art, which, since the emergence of the central perspective, had primarily been spatially oriented. For example, cubism reintroduced pan-perspectivism, which resulted in a fragmentation of the form, and Orphism attempted a colorist reproduction of the effect of light on the eye rather than merely depicting light mimetically. However, an actual Near Easternization was initiated by expressionism and the avant-garde. Expressionism broke both formally and spiritually with the Renaissance's aesthetics of form characterized by central perspectivism, and the avant-garde problematized the modern art institution as such. With this development, it became obvious that modern beauty is not simply the opposite of traditional beauty. Modern beauty revealed itself as a particular version of beauty that is secular and immanent, and which is not reserved for an aesthetic encounter with art but is available for anyone at anytime and anywhere. With reference to Walter Benjamin, we may term the modern interpretation of beauty a 'profane aura' that transcends immanence without leaving it, and which thus represents a particular way of experiencing divinity, namely as *immanent transcendence*.[97]

Like European culture as a whole, the romantico-modern is characterized by a pendulum movement between the Greek-Roman and the Jewish-Eastern, that is, between harmony and movement, or a will to form and the experience of fragmentation. However, the pendulum swings faster in the romantico-modern era than it did previously. The will to form is no longer slowly replaced by fragmentation and vice versa; there is instead coincidence between the provision and dissolution of form. It is due to this romantico-modern simultaneity of form and fragmentation

---

97   In "Little History of Photography" and "The Work of Art in the Age of Its Technological Reproducibility," Benjamin describes a historical loss of 'cultic aura' (traditional beauty) but also the emergence of a new type of aura. Inspired by Benjamin's notion of 'profane illumination' in "Surrealism," I have in several books referred to the new aura (modern beauty) as 'profane aura.' I originally described the concept of the aura in Dorthe Jørgensen, *Nær og fjern: Spor af en erfaringsontologi hos Walter Benjamin* (Near and Far: Traces of an Ontology of Experience in Walter Benjamin) (Aarhus: Modtryk, 1990). An updated interpretation is available in the chapters "Skønhedsfilosofi" (The Philosophy of Beauty) and "Iagttagelse og mimesis" (Observation and Mimesis) in Jørgensen, *Den skønne tænkning*, 211–238. See also the chapter "Immanent Transcendence" in Dorthe Jørgensen, *Poetic Inclinations: Ethics, History, Philosophy* (Aarhus: Aarhus University, 2021), and the chapter "Sensuousness and Transcendence" in the present volume. For the aforementioned texts by Benjamin, see Walter Benjamin, "Little History of Photography," trans. E. Jephcott and K. Shorter, in *Selected Writings, Volume 2: 1927–1934*, eds. M.W. Jennings, H. Eiland, and G. Smith (Cambridge, MA and London: The Belknap of Harvard University Press, 2001); "The Work of Art in the Age of Its Technological Reproducibility: Second Version," trans. E. Jephcott and H. Zohn, in *Selected Writings, Volume 3: 1935–1938*, eds. H. Eiland and M.W. Jennings (Cambridge, MA and London: The Belknap Press of Harvard University Press, 2002); and "Surrealism: The Last Snapshot of the European Intelligentsia," trans. E. Jephcott, in *Selected Writings, Volume 2*.

that modern humans interpret their potential experiences of divinity as secular experiences of immanent transcendence. This kind of experience and the relation to divinity to which it testifies are both a product of the European history of ideas and the secularization reserved for the modern. The experience of modernity is rooted in an account between Greek and Jewish thought, which is peculiar to Europe but which owes its characteristics—its quality as secular and immanent—to the historical conditions of modern life.

Beauty's Variability

The amount of fragmentation in the modern experience of beauty sheds light on the contemporary darkening of beauty as a theme. The modern fascination with the fragmented includes a reference to what was previously considered beautiful; it refers negatively to the traditional perception of beauty renounced by Romanticism and modernism. The perception of beauty represented by the classicism of the sixteenth and seventeenth centuries and the neoclassicism of the eighteenth and nineteenth centuries insisted on the harmonious proportionality expressed by the ancient symmetry doctrine. The classical, the classicist, and the neoclassicist perceptions of beauty differed in other aspects—for instance, whether there should be unity in both form and content—but, within their form-aesthetic tradition, the demand for symmetry was never abandoned. It was, at most, only interpreted differently. Romanticism's acceptance of the fragmentation of form, on the other hand, represented a dismissal of the aforementioned demand and the related wish for organic unity, and romantico-modern products are thus 'ugly' compared with what was traditionally considered 'beautiful.' Expressed differently, romantico-modern art and aesthetics invite a distinction between 'traditional beauty' and 'modern beauty.'

If we examine the history of aesthetic ideas more closely, we discover various understandings of beauty, as shown in the previous sections, and we recognize that the history of beauty is one great metamorphosis. Even in antiquity, the Middle Ages, and the

Renaissance, the form-aesthetic tradition's idea of beauty understood as harmonious proportionality and organic unity did not go unchallenged. These periods also saw a light-aesthetic idea of beauty, which demanded clarity rather than symmetry. Moreover, it appeared that the experience of beauty originates in an experience of transcendence and that, in the course of history, this experience was subject to various interpretations. With reference to the Homeric notion of poetry's origin in divine madness, the experience of transcendence was originally interpreted as an experience of divinity. Later it was associated with the art-theoretically supported idea of the beauty of the harmoniously and organically formed, but it is also present in our time, now interpreted as the experience of immanent transcendence happening to modern humans. Finally, it appeared that the experience of transcendence nourished various aesthetic ideas resulting in the two traditions mentioned previously: the aesthetics of form and the aesthetics of light.

Due to its fragmentation of the classicistic form, romantico-modern art primarily defined itself in opposition to the form-aesthetic tradition, especially the neoclassicism of the eighteenth century. Compared with what was traditionally considered 'beautiful,' romantico-modern art was thus 'ugly.' However, if we take both art theory and the metaphysics of beauty into account, different understandings of what constitutes beauty become recognizable. We recognize that the beauty of a work of art originates not only in its form but also in its reflection of the experience of transcendence. A work of art containing such reflection does not necessarily adhere to the rules of proper form prescribed by tradition but seeks the source of any experience of a transcending quality. Works of art that are beautiful in this sense of the word we find in previous epochs, as well as in the romantico-modern era. However, the sublime has long been cultivated as the designation of any element of transcendence in contemporary art and literature. The Romantics have been praised for reintroducing the sublime, because they, unlike their neoclassical predecessors, allegedly discovered the connection between divinity and sublimity, thus abandoning the tradition of the beautiful in favor of a new sublime form of art and literature. However, this interpretation is based on the unfounded belief that beauty is identical to traditional beauty and thus obsolete, and that the sublime, on the other hand, is the opposite.

In a modern world rich in asymmetry and the absence of organic unity—that is, in a world full of fragmentation—beauty becomes an anathema when its definition remains traditional. This also explains the current tendency to reserve divinity or transcendence for the sublime rather than the beautiful. The sublime is associated with a paradoxical pleasure in the horror associated with the encounter with something overwhelming and impossible to illustrate, which is assumed to be characteristic of modern humans' experiences of transcendence and that which finds expression in the broken and disharmonious form of romantico-modern art. However, as shown in the previous sections of this chapter, it appears that, whenever the interpretation of the experience of transcendence changed in the course of history, beauty took on a new form: it underwent a metamorphosis. The different historical epochs nourished different ideas of what is beautiful, but this historical variability of beauty remains unrecognizable if one insists on an undifferentiated concept of beauty, that is, if one simply identifies beauty with what was traditionally considered beautiful. In this case, Hellenistic-Roman and Romantic beauty appear not as specific forms of beauty but merely as expressions of the sublime's dethronement of beauty. However, Horace regarded the sublime as synonymous with the beautiful, and even for Longinus the sublime was not the opposite but a variation of the beautiful.[98] Similarly, there is no reason to reserve our experiences of divinity or transcendence for the sublime. Not only Romantics overwhelmed by sublime storms but also Pythagoreans contemplating the beauty of the starry sky were in touch with unimaginably great powers. In fact, the sublime was unimportant as an individual category until the eighteenth century, and, when it finally achieved such importance, it did not represent a rejection of beauty but a variation of

---

98   Horace, *The Art of Poetry: An Epistle to the Pisos*, trans. G. Colman (Gloucester: Dodo Press, 2008). Longinus, "On the Sublime," trans. W.H. Fyfe, in *Aristotle, Poetics. Longinus, On the Sublime. Demetrius, On Style* (Cambridge, MA: Harvard University Press, 1995).

it. The sublime became the term for the beauty of the beautiful, its source and expression.

Experience, Metaphysics, and Immanent Transcendence

Modern Scientism

Western philosophers have long striven to think scientifically, based on an ideal they have found in the modern experimental sciences. This effort to turn philosophy into science has meant that the former has moved away from the original wisdom-seeking *philosophia*. The traditional notion of truth as correspondence dominates as usual; moreover, the mental copying of something empirical with which cognition is so often identified is now expected to follow the methodological ideal of the experimental sciences.[99] According to this ideal, we only have cognition if the content is knowledge that is true in the sense that it is consistent with the empirical data. This correspondence is only ensured if it is possible to explain the process of cognition so precisely that others can emulate it and come to the same result. Consequently, the acquisition of true knowledge requires the use of a method that is clearly defined and can be adopted by others. Experience is thus not only identified with *empirical* experience; it is also regarded as something conducted by a *subject* to whom that which is learned has the status of an *object*. Both empirical experience and scientific knowledge rooted in this

---

99 Most of the philosophical positions referred to in this chapter are of a German origin. In English the German word *Erkenntnis* may be translated in many ways, not only as 'cognition' but also as 'recognition,' 'comprehension,' 'acknowledgment,' 'understanding,' and 'knowledge.' However, in order not to confuse what in German is called *Erkenntnis*, *Verstehen*, and *Wissen*, respectively, I primarily use the word 'cognition' when referring to *Erkenntnis*. In a few specific cases I do, however, deviate from this rule.

experience are thus considered to be something that we, ourselves, control.

Although the methodical approach of the sciences prides itself on transparency, much is taken for granted when we make use of it. For example, there is no discussion concerning what is real and what can be realized. The reality is limited to what can be observed empirically, and cognition is supposed to require a methodical processing of the material obtained in this manner. To the extent that cognition is accredited with any possibility of transcendence, its ability to transcend only consists in being able to reach out for data making up a reality that is given in advance, and which does not evoke *wondering*. Within the framework of this approach, no room exists for the kind of experience and cognition that modern thinkers and artists such as James Joyce and Walter Benjamin were concerned about.[100] The sudden appearances of otherwise inaccessible reality—the experiences of a dimension of the world of which we are not otherwise aware, referred to by Joyce as 'epiphanies' and by Benjamin as 'higher experiences'—are excluded. There is no opportunity to reflect on the unexpected experiences of a 'more'—*a transcendence in the immanence*—that deviate from our usual experiences and cognitions of the world in which we live.

Sensitive Cognition

It is a long time since the Enlightenment philosopher Alexander Gottlieb Baumgarten problematized a notion of cognition that acknowledges no other experience than empirical experience. Thanks to this questioning, he not only introduced philosophical aesthetics but also prepared the aforementioned experience of immanent transcendence. Baumgarten's rationalist contemporaries only had eyes for sense and intellect seen as faculties of *sense perception* and

---

100   See James Joyce, *A Portrait of the Artist as a Young Man*, ed. J. Johnson (New York: Oxford University Press Inc., 2008), and Walter Benjamin, *Berlin Childhood around 1900*, trans. H. Eiland, in *Selected Writings, Volume 3: 1935–1938*, eds. H. Eiland and M.W. Jennings (Cambridge, MA and London: The Belknap Press of Harvard University Press, 2002).

intellectual cognition, a limitation still prevalent today.[101] In analogy to other rationalists of his time, he distinguished between a lower and a higher part of the cognitive faculty; but he broke with the established notion that the lower part is nothing but a provider of material for the higher part and does not, by itself, result in cognition.[102] According to Baumgarten, the lower part of the cognitive faculty does in fact generate a certain kind of cognition, which he referred to as sensitive, and by which he did *not* mean sensuous. As early as in *Reflections on Poetry* he stressed in § 116 that the *aistheta* (sensations) observed by the lower part of the cognitive faculty are not identical to mere sense impressions.[103] The aistheta comprise all sensitive ideas, including imaginations, and they are perceived differently depending on whether they are *obscure* or *clear*. Furthermore, clear ideas can be *distinct* and lead to 'intellectual cognition,' or they can be *confused* and lead to 'sensitive cognition.' It was the latter (the confused clear ideas, which Baumgarten also referred to as *extensively* clear ideas) he was concerned about, not only in *Reflections on Poetry* but in *Aesthetica,* too.[104] He dealt with these ideas not only because of the sensitive cognition they allow for but also because of the *beautiful thinking* associated with this kind of cognition.

Because the sensitive cognition is a product of the lower part of the cognitive faculty it is not intellectual, but sensitive; so it is not logical or conceptual, but aesthetic and intuitive. However,

---

101   Besides seeing sensation as merely sensuous and cognition as purely intellectual, we nowadays even confuse reason and understanding, limiting the former to the latter. See the chapters "Philosophy at a Crossroads" and "Toward an Aesthetics of Well-Being" in Dorthe Jørgensen, *Poetic Inclinations: Ethics, History, Philosophy* (Aarhus: Aarhus University, 2021).

102   The word 'faculty' applies to both the cognitive faculty as such with its two parts (a lower and a higher, respectively) and the various particular faculties (for example, sense, imagination, and reason) constituting the dispositions of those parts.

103   Alexander Gottlieb Baumgarten, *Reflections on Poetry: Alexander Gottlieb Baumgarten's Meditationes philosophicae de nonnullis ad poema pertinentibus*, trans. K. Aschenbrenner and W.B. Holther (Berkeley and Los Angeles: University of California Press, 1954).

104   Alexander Gottlieb Baumgarten, *Ästhetik, Volume 1–2*, trans. D. Mirbach (Hamburg: Felix Meiner Verlag, 2007).

sensitive cognitions do have epistemic value, and they even represent an individual aesthetic-intuitive kind of cognition that is not subordinate but analogous to the logical-conceptual cognition. As a consequence of this acknowledgment, Baumgarten eventually abandoned the conventional distinction between two parts of the cognitive faculty. He began distinguishing, instead, between two independent cognitive faculties: a lower and a higher, respectively, the former being the origin of sensitive cognition.

According to Baumgarten, philosophical aesthetics is the philosophy of sensitive cognition, and for this reason aesthetics is a kind of epistemology. Philosophical aesthetics explores the epistemologically rather unexplored phenomenon that sensitive cognition was at the time of the emergence of aesthetics, and which it still is. Before the formation of philosophical aesthetics, the epistemologists took nothing but rational knowledge seriously, and the kind of cognition leading to such knowledge had only logical and metaphysical truth to relate to. Only conceptual thinking, which formulates explanations and provides proofs by subsuming particular phenomena under general concepts, and which therefore is characterized by abstraction, was regarded as true. Valid thinking thus only comprised thinking that results in general concepts and logically constructed explanations of relations. But philosophical aesthetics made it possible for epistemologists to explore *aesthetic* experiences as well, and thanks to philosophical aesthetics there was now also an *aesthetic* truth to relate to. Baumgarten's aesthetics created the basis for examining a beautiful thinking, which thanks to its eye for the uniqueness of the particular retains the complexity of observation and, thus, is characterized by liveliness. Henceforth, thinking leading to truth could also consist of thinking resulting in knowledge marked by palpability and meaningfulness.

As stated in *Aesthetica* § 14, it is the perfection of sensitive cognition that is the goal of aesthetics, and perfection is identical to beauty. Logic is not just about intellectual cognition, but aims at the *correct* intellectual cognition. Similarly, philosophical aesthetics is not just about sensitive cognition, but strives for *perfect* (that is, beautiful) sensitive cognition.[105] Furthermore, Baumgarten regarded perfection/beauty as a matter of *unity in diversity*. Intellectual cognitions explain specific phenomena and causal relations by subsuming them under general concepts. Therefore, rational knowledge is characterized by abstraction, and it is marked by unity only. Sensitive cognitions, on the other hand, are specific and characterized by both unity and diversity. They are distinguished by not moving from the particular to the general, but rather alternating between the poles. Therefore, in sensitive cognitions, the many individual marks of the specific are not lost in abstraction, and not only complexity is experienced, but meaning as well. In sensitive cognitions, we not only sense a multitude of marks. We also perceive a whole that is characterized both by liveliness thanks to this wealth, and by meaningfulness thanks to inner consistency.

According to Baumgarten, the optimum solution is to allow the beautiful thinking associated with sensitivity to supplement the logical thinking of the intellect. The *aestheticological* (both aesthetic-intuitive and logical-conceptual) knowledge that this may result in is the highest it is humanly possible to reach cognitively.[106] If we really want to obtain significant insight, we need both aesthetic openness and logical rigor. Both intellect and sensitivity are of an individual epistemic value and give true knowledge, but they each do so in their own way, and they should complement each other.

---

105   Baumgarten's contemporaries misinterpreted this, believing that his aesthetics was about the *completely* sensitive cognition, even regarded as completely *sensuous*—a conception that is still prevalent. However, as Baumgarten stressed in a foreword to the third edition of his *Metaphysics*, his aesthetics was actually about the *perfect sensitive* cognition. It was about improving our sensitive cognitions, and thus cultivating our ability to think beautifully. Alexander Gottlieb Baumgarten, *Die Vorreden zur Metaphysik*, ed. and trans. U. Niggli (Frankfurt am Main: Vittorio Klostermann, 1998), 53–55.

106   This idea of 'aestheticological knowledge' is based on Baumgarten's concept of 'aestheticological truth' (*veritas aestheticologica*); see Baumgarten, *Ästhetik*, § 427.

Creativity

Baumgarten was aware of the creative aspect of the aesthetic experience, which means that it contributes to what is being experienced. This is evidenced, among other things, by his presentation of what he called *felix aestheticus*, the lucky aesthete, that is, the successful aesthete.[107] *Felix aestheticus* is Baumgarten's term for a person whose sensitive cognitions are of the perfected kind and who thus meets the goal of aesthetics. Such an aesthete is equipped with "innate natural aesthetics" in the form of a natural disposition in all of his soul for beautiful thinking.[108] This natural disposition requires that the person is in possession of an "innate graceful and tasteful spirit," understood as a talent for letting the different dispositions of his lower cognitive faculty be encouraged, work together in appropriate distribution, and thus contribute to tastefulness in his cognition.[109] And such a graceful spirit requires a certain measure of higher dispositions for cognition (that is, intellect and reason),[110] as well as the following dispositions of the lower cognitive faculty: 1) "increased sensitivity" (*acute sentiendi*); 2) "the natural disposition for imagining something" (*dispositio naturalis ad imaginandum*); 3) "the natural disposition for penetrating insight" (*dispositio naturalis ad perspicaciam*); 4) "the disposition for recognizing something and memory" (*dispositio naturalis ad recognoscendum et memoria*); 5) "the poetic disposition" (*dispositio poetica*); 6) "the disposition for having a taste that is not ordinary, but refined" (*dispositio ad saporem non publicum, immo delicatum*); 7) "the disposition for anticipating and expecting something" (*dispositio ad praevidendum et praesagiendum*); and 8) "the disposition for characterizing one's perceptions" (*dispositio ad significandas perceptiones suas*).[111]

---

107   Baumgarten, *Ästhetik*, §§ 27ff.

108   Baumgarten, *Ästhetik*, § 28.

109   Baumgarten, *Ästhetik*, § 29.

110   Baumgarten, *Ästhetik*, § 38.

111   Baumgarten, *Ästhetik*, §§ 30–37. The innate natural aesthetics also includes an innate

Concerning the creative aspect of the aesthetic experience, it is worth noticing dispositions number two and five, which are related to the faculties referred to in Baumgarten's *Metaphysics* as "the imagination" (*phantasia*) and "the faculty of invention" (*facultas fingendi*, also called the "poetic" faculty).[112] Imagination is the basis of the *capacitas infinita* of the human being, that is, our inclination and ability to imagine something that does not already exist. Without imagination the poetic faculty would not function, and imagination is, in fact, a prerequisite for all the dispositions of the lower cognitive faculty, including memory.[113] However, according to Baumgarten imagination as such is not creative, but merely reproductive. It is the ability to restore a bygone state, and therefore it is bound to the perceptions and the related representations recalled and made palpable by its mental images (*phantasmata*). But in analogy to reason, the poetic faculty is genuinely creative, and this faculty is thus particularly characteristic of the lucky aesthete, who is essentially a *poeticus*. This aesthete is the creative person who poetically calls forth new worlds, thus making new insights possible. Therefore, unlike the traditional notion of what it means to cognize and think, the cognition and thinking of the lucky aesthete constitute not a passive gazing that simply copies something mentally, be it ideas or anything else, and in which truth is thus a matter of correspondence between the observed and its imprint in the mind. In addition to being contemplative, the aesthete's sensitive cognition and beautiful thinking are formational, and are therefore by their very nature creative acts. They are not only dependent on the usual cognitive potential of the human being. They

---

aesthetic temperament. Furthermore, being a lucky aesthete requires not only natural aesthetics but also aesthetic exercise, aesthetic education, etc.

112   Alexander Gottlieb Baumgarten, *Metaphysics: A Critical Translation with Kant's Elucidations, Selected Notes, and Related Materials*, eds. and trans. C.D. Fugate and J. Hymers (London: Bloomsbury Academic, 2014), §§ 557ff. and 589ff.

113   Although the faculty of sense does not presuppose imagination, sensation and imagination are deeply interrelated. The faculty of sense produces representations of the present (ideas of what is being sensed); imagination produces representations of the past (ideas of what has been sensed).

also rely on the *poiesis* acting among the dispositions of the lower cognitive faculty, namely in the form of imagination and the poetic faculty.

Although the lucky aesthete does not follow the principles of intellectual cognition when he cognizes and thinks, he is not merely fantasizing. He wishes to effectualize not only aesthetic "plenitude" (*ubertas*) but also aesthetic "magnitude, truth, clarity, certitude, and liveliness" (*magnitudo, veritas, claritas, certitudo et vita*).[114] Thus, besides the logical clarity and distinctness characterizing intellectual cognition and the associated logical thinking, a specific *aesthetic* clarity and distinctness is possible in sensitive cognition and beautiful thinking. Moreover, there is both a light emanating from the things, and a light that we ourselves make the things shine with.[115] Our sensitive cognitions take place in the space established by this duality of objectively given and subjectively added light, and they take shape as unfinished and fundamentally infinite processes unfolding in a field in which it is difficult to keep subject and object strictly separated from each other. Consequently, despite Baumgarten's rationalist point of departure he actually negated the rationalist separation and opposition of subject and object, thereby opening the paradigm of the dualist philosophy of mind from within.[116] His understanding of the aesthetic experience as an unfinished and fundamentally infinite process that unfolds in the space of light between subject and object and commutes in a constant alternation between the particular and the universal implied that he actually regarded the aesthetic experience as an *event*, and that he also considered this event to be *creative*.[117] The aesthet-

---

114 Baumgarten, *Ästhetik*, § 22.

115 For Baumgarten's reflections on 'aesthetic light' (*lux aesthetica*), see *Ästhetik*, §§ 614–630.

116 Although Baumgarten wanted to expand rationalist epistemology, he cannot be said to have wished to leave the dualist philosophy of mind behind. However, thanks to his way of understanding sensitive cognition, his aesthetics did indeed hold the potential for such a maneuver.

117 Steffen W. Gross has also noticed Baumgarten's anticipation of the contemporary un-

ic experience brings something forth—aesthetic knowledge—that would not exist if no aesthetic experience was taking place.

Phenomenology is Aesthetics

The latter point shows that Baumgarten's conception of sensitive cognition contained traits of hermeneutic phenomenology, but philosophical aesthetics often had a bad reputation among hermeneutic phenomenologists. Through Hans-Georg Gadamer's criticism of the so-called aesthetic consciousness (the aesthetics of Immanuel Kant and Friedrich Schiller, primarily), this aversion can be traced back to Martin Heidegger's critique of aesthetics *as such*.[118] According to Heidegger, aesthetics is an expression of metaphysics, just like logic and ethics, and he criticized *modern* aesthetics for subjectivism, too. In this context, the word 'metaphysics' means 'objectifying scientific theory.' Because Heidegger did not distinguish between art theory and philosophical aesthetics, he thought that aesthetics arose as early as antiquity, when Plato and Aristotle expected to be able to explain art theoretically. The way of thinking introduced by them included a distinction between matter and form, as well as an understanding of the exterior as an expression of something interior, which has since paved the way for the subjectivism of our days.[119] According to Heidegger, this subjectivism was what determined Baumgarten's focus on sensitive cognition. The result was an understanding of art that—besides turning the

---

derstanding of the aesthetic experience as an event. See *Felix Aestheticus: Die Ästhetik als Lehre vom Menschen. Zum 250. Jahrestag des Erscheinens von Alexander Gottlieb Baumgartens "Aesthetica"* (Würzburg: Verlag Königshausen and Neumann, 2001), 132.

118 As for Gadamer's criticism of the aesthetic consciousness, see Hans-Georg Gadamer, *Truth and Method*, trans. J. Weinsheimer and D.G. Marshall (London and New York: Bloomsbury Academic, 2013), 81–91. Heidegger's aversion to aesthetics is evident in several of his texts, for example, Martin Heidegger, *Nietzsche, Volume 1: The Will to Power as Art; Volume 2: The Eternal Recurrence of the Same*, ed. and trans. D.F. Krell (San Francisco: HarperSanFrancisco, 1991), *Vol. 1*, 77–91 (in particular).

119 In *Nietzsche*, Heidegger finds the origin of the conceptual pair matter–form (*hyle–morphe, materia–forma*) in Plato's idealistic conception of beings, which also contains the seed for the distinction between interior and exterior (Heidegger, *Nietzsche, Vol. 1*, 80).

work of art into an object of scientific study—thought of it as an expression of an artist's subjective feelings and notions that caters to the subjective feelings and notions of a viewer. This understanding meant that now there was only an eye for the emotional side of the work of art, while its roots and origin faded away completely.[120] In order to avoid this, Heidegger, by contrast, related to the artwork in a phenomenological way. He wanted to describe the work of art as it appears to us, and he therefore abstained from the usual focus on the artist or the viewer. He wished to let the work of art appear as what it truly is, thus making way for the possibility that truth could happen again in the field that had been called 'aesthetic' since Baumgarten.

Nevertheless, Heidegger's texts also show that emotions actually played an important role in his thinking—including for cognition and even for the experience of truth. "What we call a 'feeling' is neither a transitory epiphenomenon of our thinking and willing comportment, nor simply an impulse that provokes such comportment, nor merely a present condition we have to find some way of coping with."[121] On the contrary, feelings can be better promoters of insight than the rational way of thinking, because the latter makes us think of the existent as something present-at-hand. "Finding ourselves attuned not only unveils beings as a whole in various ways, but this unveiling—far from being merely incidental—is also the fundamental occurrence of our Da-sein."[122] This emotionally given disclosure is identical to the *aletheia* (unconcealedness) introduced by Heidegger as his alternative to the traditional concept of truth as correspondence. In attunement, we are next to

---

120   After the time of Baumgarten and Kant, both scientism and subjectivism showed themselves in the psychological aesthetics of the late nineteenth century, since this took the shape of a modern science about emotionality regarded as the actual feelings of empirical individuals. Perhaps Heidegger's aversion to aesthetics was due, primarily, to the mixture of scientism and subjectivism that he observed in his contemporaries, but it was the philosophical aesthetics of the eighteenth century his criticism was aimed at.

121   Martin Heidegger, "What Is Metaphysics?," trans. W. Kaufmann, in *Pathmarks*, ed. W. McNeill (Cambridge, UK: Cambridge University Press, 1998), 87.

122   Heidegger, "What Is Metaphysics?," 87.

what is both the most distant and the closest, that is, Being. However, Heidegger's reflections on the fundamental importance of emotionality do not only refer to the way of thinking with which he tried to do away with traditional metaphysics. They also arouse associations with Baumgarten's philosophical aesthetics. As stated previously, the sensitive cognition so crucial to aesthetics is an insight of emotional origin, and sensitive cognitions are not only analogous to the cognitions provided by the intellect. They even surpass them, at least potentially.

This is not to say that there is no significant difference between Baumgarten's and Heidegger's ways of thinking; Baumgarten belonged to the dualist philosophy of mind, whereas Heidegger was an existential philosopher. Nevertheless, they shared an interest in a felt kind of 'cognition,' as well as the view that the logical-conceptual way of thinking is of a limited scope. Furthermore, they both considered the notion of a subject who only recognizes conceptually to be an abstraction, and they were both of the opinion that the language of philosophy must be processed—for the sake of thinking.

According to Heidegger, even truth understood as correspondence is based on aletheia, because no cognition can correspond to anything without something having shown itself.[123] The more 'poetic' experience that aletheia is considered to be is therefore a precondition for conceptual knowledge. In *Being and Time* Heidegger thematizes this as a matter of attunement and of the understanding opened by attunement regarded as a precondition for all knowledge, including theoretical-scientific knowledge.[124] This also points back to Baumgarten's aesthetics, that is, sensitivity understood as something fundamental and sensitive cognition seen as an independent kind of knowledge that is distinguished by an individual strength compared to intellectual cognition. Further-

---

123 Martin Heidegger, "The Origin of the Work of Art," in *Poetry, Language, Thought*, ed. and trans. A. Hofstadter (New York: Harper Perennial Modern Thought, 2013), 50.

124 Martin Heidegger, *Being and Time*, trans. J. Stambaugh, rev. D.J. Schmidt (Albany: State University of New York Press, 2010), 134.

more, it points back to the aestheticological truth regarded as the furthest and highest humans can reach cognitively, and the aesthetic, that is, sensitive, aspect of the associated aestheticological cognition seen as the source of this cognition's strength. Therefore, in my book *Den skønne tænkning* (Beautiful Thinking) I conclude that Baumgarten's philosophical aesthetics anticipated the hermeneutic phenomenology of our time, and that the latter is aesthetic by nature.[125] Hermeneutic phenomenology actualizes the potential in the form of which philosophical aesthetics wintered during the dominance of the study of art in the nineteenth and twentieth centuries. However, to the detriment of aesthetics, thinkers such as Heidegger have practiced this actualization without any awareness of their own debt to aesthetics. Indeed, they have even shown contempt for aesthetics.

The Nature of All Things

The book *Den skønne tænkning* is subtitled "Veje til erfaringsmetafysik" (Pathways to the Metaphysics of Experience). Our different experiences of transcendence, including aesthetic and religious experiences, and not least experiences of immanent transcendence, are the subject matter of what I call *metaphysics of experience*. This philosophy is formulated in opposition to the current trend of having an eye for two options only, meaning *either* we commit to metaphysics (which today is perceived as problematic) *or* we reject all kinds of metaphysics (from which follows that there really is only one way forward, namely to leave metaphysics behind). This trend is based on a widespread belief that metaphysics represents a historically invalidated doctrine of two worlds, one of which is immanent whereas the other is transcendent—or perhaps that metaphysics is identical to the theoretical-scientific way of thinking dis-

---

[125] See in particular "Baumgartens æstetik" (Baumgarten's Aesthetics) and "Heidegger's fænomenologi" (Heidegger's Phenomenology), that is, pp. 83–158 and 275–357 in Dorthe Jørgensen, *Den skønne tænkning: Veje til erfaringsmetafysik. Religionsfilosofisk udmøntet* (Beautiful Thinking: Pathways to the Metaphysics of Experience. Religio-Philosophically Implemented) (Aarhus: Aarhus University Press, 2014).

cussed by Heidegger that reduces Being to a being. However, the word 'metaphysics' can also be used to denominate something else, and this is precisely the case in what I call 'metaphysics of experience.' According to this third use of the word, philosophical thinking is metaphysical by nature, and the metaphysics thus referred to is characterized by something as significant as: 1) being open to experiences that are different from sensory/empirical experiences; 2) being willing to reflect systematically on one's experiences of this other kind; and 3) doing the latter in a meaning-seeking way, which requires interpretation and, hence, openness to something that goes beyond the experience itself (something that is more universal—a wider context or an idea).

It follows from this third understanding of metaphysics that philosophical thinking was metaphysical from its very beginning. Even the so-called natural philosophers (Thales, Anaximander, Anaximenes) thought metaphysically, that is, they looked for more in the world than what can be observed empirically, and it was this 'more' they were concerned about. Furthermore, the natural philosophers endeavored to consider the thus experienced supersensible systematically, and in the light of something more comprehensive than the experience itself—in the light of their idea of the 'nature of all things' (*physis*)—they tried to formulate meaningful interpretations of it. Often the natural philosophers have been portrayed as representatives of a kind of early science, and it was therefore postulated that their philosophy broke with the contemporary realm of religious thought.[126] However, as long ago as a century comparative studies of philosophy and religion sowed doubt about this understanding.[127] The philosophy of the natural philosophers was probably not as different from the religiosity of their day as was previously presumed. Indeed, something new happened when they began to argue systematically for their conception of the nature of

---

126 For example, Patricia O'Grady, *Thales of Miletus: The Beginnings of Western Science and Philosophy* (Aldershot and Burlington: Ashgate, 2002).

127 For example, Francis MacDonald Cornford, *From Religion to Philosophy: A Study in the Origins of Western Speculation* (Princeton: Princeton University Press, 1991, orig. 1912).

reality, but the religious understanding of this reality as something divine was inherited in the theories they formulated.

Aristotle is the supplier of our knowledge concerning Thales. According to him, Thales raised the question about the nature of the one source from which everything else comes, and in asking this question he tried to determine the nature of all things, which he identified as "water" (*hydor*).[128] Because of this interest in nature, philosophers such as Thales have been regarded as exponents of a new and more secular mindset in antiquity. However, in their mental environment the water just mentioned was not merely an empirical natural phenomenon, but a materialization of 'supersensible nature.'[129] They saw nature as a living and holy-sacred organism, and in their view *physis* was a divine "soul-substance" pervading all things.[130] This is also the reason why Thales could say that "all things are full of gods," thereby aiming at the nature of all things understood as something divine and subject to admiration.[131] In accordance with this, the natural philosophers' expectation of finding a 'higher' nature in empirical nature rested, as mentioned, on an assumption of a religious origin, namely the idea that everything comes from a single source. This source is the power that is present in everything and thanks to which anything exists, or the supersensible that has inspired everything with divine nature. On the whole, the thinking of the natural philosophers was probably not as different from the religiosity of their time as was often assumed. On the contrary, it originated from an experience of a divinity inherent in nature, and it was shaped as a homage to this sacred nature.

---

128   Aristotle, *Metaphysics*, trans. W.D. Ross, in *The Complete Works of Aristotle: The Revised Oxford Translation, Volume 2*, ed. J. Barnes (Princeton: Princeton University Press, 1984), I.3, 983b20.

129   Cornford, *From Religion to Philosophy*, 127 ff., 136.

130   Cornford, *From Religion to Philosophy*, 128.

131   Aristotle, *On the Soul*, trans. J.A. Smith, in *The Complete Works of Aristotle: The Revised Oxford Translation, Volume 1*, ed. J. Barnes (Princeton: Princeton University Press, 1984), I.5, 411a9–10.

Nevertheless, although religion and philosophy had a common experiential ground early in antiquity, they were media for different interpretations of what was experienced. The understanding of reality remained the same because the conception formulated by the philosophers was expressed in their understanding of nature, the content of which was of a religious origin; but the way of dealing with the supersensible reality changed with the emergence of philosophy. Magic, mythology, and religion had an intuitive and action-oriented approach to reality: they cultivated the supersensible in its symbolic manifestations and expressed themselves in a poetic language. Philosophy, on the other hand, had an intellectual and speculative approach to the supersensible: the philosophers tried to define the nature of the one source and dealt with it in an abstract conceptual language. However, the values of religious thought affected the thinking of the philosophers, and philosophy was thus cut in two directions: a 'scientific' direction represented by Anaximander, and a 'mysterious' direction represented by Pythagoras. The first direction was an expression of humans' need for 'explanation' acquired through their mastery of nature, while the latter testified to the human need for 'understanding' gained through a union with nature. Both of these directions were rooted in the realm of religious thought, however. Anaximander's scientific philosophy was associated with Homer and the Apollonian religiosity, while Pythagoras' mystical philosophy was linked to the Orphic and Dionysian religiosity.

New Metaphysics

According to Heidegger, philosophers such as Thales did not reduce Being to a being, and this is the reason for his interest in them. They did not yet think in a theoretical-scientific way. If the philosophy of our time is to approach the question concerning the meaning of Being, it must, according to Heidegger, learn from these thinkers. Modern philosophy must drop its tendency to metaphysics, that is, the tendency to reflect in a theoretical-scientific way. However, if we do *not* follow Heidegger's pejorative use of the word 'metaphysics,' but refer to the third definition of that word's meaning as formulated previously, metaphysics is something *other* than scientific theorizing. Pursuant to this other understanding of metaphysics, metaphysics is thinking that is sensitively open to different dimensions of the world, including a supersensible one, and to the interrelationships and connections between these dimensions. From this perspective, Heidegger's own thinking was metaphysical—meant as a mark of distinction. It was experiential-philosophical by its very nature, and being a philosophy of experience it operated with an expanded concept of experience. Furthermore, the experiential-philosophical rather than idealistic character of Heidegger's hermeneutic phenomenology means that it actually represents a *new* and *different* kind of metaphysics. This is consistent with the fact that it was not metaphysics as such, but traditional metaphysics only, that is, scientific theorizing, that Heidegger addressed in his criticism of metaphysics.

We find metaphysics of a new and different kind in an even stronger form in Benjamin, whose thinking was especially concerned with experience. It was about experience in the expanded sense of the word, and this was the case all the way from the text "'Experience,'" written in 1913, to "On the Concept of History" from 1940.[132] Benjamin's expanded concept of experience is manifest, for instance, in "On the Program of the Coming Philosophy," in which he introduced his notion of *higher experience* and also expressed a desire to develop a *new metaphysics* understood as a philosophy about this experience.[133] According to Benjamin's program, all epistemology is confronted with two realities: an empirical and a meta-

---

132 Walter Benjamin, "'Experience,'" trans. L. Spencer and S. Jost, in *Selected Writings, Volume 1: 1913–1926*, eds. M. Bullock and M.W. Jennings (Cambridge, MA and London: The Belknap Press of Harvard University Press, 2002), and "On the Concept of History," trans. H. Zohn, in *Selected Writings, Volume 4: 1938–1940*, eds. H. Eiland and M.W. Jennings (Cambridge, MA and London: The Belknap Press of Harvard University Press, 2003). My presentation of Benjamin's thought is based on my book *Den skønne tænkning*. See in particular "Benjamins metafysik" (Benjamin's Metaphysics), *Den skønne tænkning*, 177–255.

133 Walter Benjamin, "On the Program of the Coming Philosophy," trans. M. Ritter, in *Selected Writings, Volume 1: 1913–1926*, eds. M. Bullock and M.W. Jennings (Cambridge, MA and London: The Belknap Press of Harvard University Press, 2002).

physical reality, respectively. This is because humans not only have empirical experiences but also witness a kind of metaphysical experience, that is, higher experience. Empirical experiences are about the spatiotemporal world, whereas higher experience is about what transcends this world. Moreover, these empirical and metaphysical realities constitute two analytical fields, each of which contains its own critical question about the truth of empirical experience and the eternal validity of higher experiences. The natural sciences are based on empirical experience, precisely as they should be, but philosophy is mistaken, thought Benjamin, when it rejects any possibility of higher experience, as has usually been the case since Kant. To remedy this deficiency, Benjamin wanted to develop an epistemology shaped as a philosophy about the epistemic value of higher experience.

Benjamin acknowledged Kant's recognition that what matters in philosophy are the questions being asked and how they are asked, but he turned this insight against Kant himself. He thought that Kant's critique of knowledge was weakened by the question formulated in his *Critique of Pure Reason*, or rather by his way of asking.[134] Instead of asking *how* true cognition is possible in metaphysics, Kant raised the question of *whether* it is possible at all. Just as mathematics and the natural sciences tell us, according to Kant, that true cognition is possible within these fields of knowledge, our higher experiences tell us, according to Benjamin, that true cognition is possible in metaphysics. Therefore, in philosophy the most relevant and fruitful question is not *whether* such cognition is possible, but *how* this can be the case, that is, how do we formulate a philosophical understanding of this cognition. For Kant, however, it was not possible to practice metaphysics with such a starting point, because he ruled out the possibility of metaphysical *experience* in advance. As per Benjamin, the reason for this was an inadequate concept of experience, which limited experience to empirical experience. Furthermore, Benjamin criticized Kant for giving this

---

[134] Immanuel Kant, *Critique of Pure Reason*, eds. and trans. P. Guyer and A.W. Wood (Cambridge, UK: Cambridge University Press, 1998).

kind of experience a metaphysical status in mathematics and the natural sciences that it does not deserve.

Since the question of how true cognition is possible in metaphysics is also a matter of formulating the philosophy of this cognition, Benjamin did not only want to *ask* the question. As mentioned previously, he also wished to develop a form of metaphysics—though not in the sense of a philosophy about transcendent objects; rather, it would be about metaphysical experiences. Despite his criticism of Kant, Benjamin supposed that Kant's critical method could serve this purpose. Kant investigated the conditions of the possibility of knowledge before he commented on its scope and depth. A similar study of the conditions of the possibility of higher experience should, according to Benjamin, enable a systematic determination of this experience, whereas attempts to define the higher experience without considering its fundamental conditions would result in nothing but empty speculation. However, although Kant's critical method was applicable, Benjamin criticized his philosophy as such for containing remnants of the dualist philosophy of mind; elements revealed by the fact that Kant did not always escape presenting reality as an object for a subject of cognition, even though he himself rejected such a notion of reality. These remnants were also the reason why he tied experience and cognition to the empirical consciousness of the human being, which pursuant to Benjamin resulted in a psychological mythology of cognition causing subjectivism and relativism in Kant's criticism, and which Benjamin therefore also problematized.

As a result, Benjamin wished to purify Kant's system of rudimentary metaphysics, that is, to remove the remnants of the dualist philosophy of mind and the psychological mythology of cognition. However, behind Kant's rudimentary metaphysics Benjamin also noticed a tendency toward genuine metaphysics, and he wanted to save this impulse and unfold it in the form of a new and different kind of metaphysics. Consequently, Benjamin did not plan to tear down Kant's system, but rather to rebuild it. The speculative features of the system should be subject to criticism, but this criticism should serve the purpose of saving the system's inherent tendency toward new metaphysics, and this rescue should be carried out by anchoring the higher experience thematized by Benjamin in the reconstructed system. Such a 'rescuing critique' of Kant's philosophy would potentially liberate his epistemology from speculation while addressing the lack of genuine metaphysics with a systematically reasoned new metaphysics.

Immanent Transcendence

Benjamin's notion of higher experience is certainly about experiencing transcendence, and so are similar concepts of experience found in his texts, for example of the 'aura' and the 'profane illumination.'[135] Furthermore, Benjamin treated religion and theology with an open mind: several of his texts, not least "On Language as Such and on the Language of Man," are religiously and theologically inspired.[136] However, experiences of transcendence may be irreligious, and Benjamin's concepts of experience, for instance higher experience, were not specifically religious. Religious experiences have an object in the sense of a god called by name, whereas other experiences of transcendence may be without any object. If someone has a religious experience, she has the feeling that she knows somehow what she is experiencing, namely the presence of what she believes to be her god, but an experience of transcendence does not necessarily have anything specific as its object. For this reason, experiences of transcendence may simply be referred to as *experiences of a surplus of meaning*, that is, intensified meaning. Further-

---

[135] As for the aura, see Walter Benjamin, "Little History of Photography," trans. E. Jephcott and K. Shorter, in *Selected Writings, Volume 2: 1927–1934*, eds. M.W. Jennings, H. Eiland, and G. Smith (Cambridge, MA and London: The Belknap of Harvard University Press, 2001), as well as "The Work of Art in the Age of Its Technological Reproducibility: Second Version," trans. E. Jephcott and H. Zohn, in *Selected Writings, Volume 3: 1935–1938*, eds. H. Eiland and M.W. Jennings (Cambridge, MA and London: The Belknap Press of Harvard University Press, 2002). Concerning Benjamin's notion of profane illumination, see "Surrealism: The Last Snapshot of the European Intelligentsia," trans. E. Jephcott, in *Selected Writings, Volume 2*.

[136] Walter Benjamin, "On Language as Such and on the Language of Man," trans. E. Jephcott, in *Selected Writings, Volume 1: 1913–1926*, eds. M. Bullock and M.W. Jennings (Cambridge, MA and London: The Belknap Press of Harvard University Press, 2002).

more, these experiences may be interpreted in such a way, by the person having them, that they qualify as *experiences of immanent transcendence* understood as something different from religious or aesthetic experiences, for instance.

The term 'immanent transcendence' does, indeed, appear as a religious term, while aesthetics, on the other hand, is concerned with worldly phenomena. However, this contrast only applies if we equip the words 'transcendence' and 'immanence' with religious connotations and if we detach the aesthetic from the religious, but we might just as well refrain from doing so. It is customary to identify transcendence with *the* transcendent, and to think of the transcendent as something *divine*. Furthermore, it is common to perceive the word 'immanence' as if it necessarily indicates that something divine is manifested in the worldly. Following this line of thought, immanence is inevitably associated with incarnation or pantheism, for instance. However, the word 'immanence' may also be applied without implying the presence of something divine. It may be used as a neutral term for the sphere of everything in our immediate vicinity, of which we ourselves are part. We are in the immanence. The world we live in is the immanence, understood not just as materiality, but as everything, including everything intangible in culture, that represents the world around us. This is consistent with the literal meaning of the Latin term *in manere*, which the word 'immanence' comes from and which means 'to remain in.'

Similarly, the word 'transcendence' may be employed without being a synonym for *the* transcendent, whether the latter is understood as divine or not. Instead, the concept of transcendence may be a concept of experience, that is, transcendence regarded as identical to *experience* of transcendence. Instead of being the concept of a 'something,' transcendence thus denotes movement. This movement does not lead into the transcendent understood as a world beyond the immanence. It is rather a 'movement on the spot'—a movement in the immanence, a disturbance of its opacity. This movement has no subject in the sense of a controlling agent. Behind the movement that the experience of transcendence constitutes, there is neither a particular transcendent god whose will penetrates the immanence, nor a human ego exceeding the immanence. Experience is, however, a fact and it happens in the immanence—in the sphere of that which is in our immediate vicinity. Experience is essentially *for us* as it happens, that is, it happens in the immanence that subjectivity constitutes.

When we think of the words 'transcendence' and 'immanence' as an expression of two conflicting versions of the divine (that is, the divine understood as absolutely distant and inaccessible to human beings, and the divine understood as present everywhere and immediately accessible to everyone), the concept of immanent transcendence probably appears meaningless. However, it is indeed very meaningful if we do something else, that is, if we let it refer to a specific experience, and if this experience is an event that may happen to anyone: it happens whenever it feels as if the world suddenly opens up and lets intensified meaning come forward. In other words, the notion of immanent transcendence makes good sense to a phenomenological account of what may happen to us as human beings.

What today is called aesthetic experience is one of several possible interpretations of experiencing transcendence. In antiquity and the Middle Ages, the event formed by this experience of transcendence was interpreted, not least, as an experience of *beauty*. The epistemic value of the experience was expected to rely on the fact that it gave an insight into things it was possible to say something specific about, that is, the beautiful regarded as something objective (a transcendent idea; the quality of an object). However, in the philosophical aesthetics and hermeneutic phenomenology of our time it is the experience *itself* that is considered to be beautiful. Furthermore, even if it is an experience of transcendence, when the experience is interpreted in the particularly modern way formulated by Benjamin, for instance, it does not have anything transcendent as its object. Nevertheless, the experience is still of a transcending character: it is larger than empirical experience. But instead of leaving what is usually considered to be the realm of experience, the experience transcends to another dimension of this very realm. In the case of such an experience of *immanent tran-*

scendence, the transcending character of the experience is identical to the fact that it opens up the world without leaving it, and to the fact, too, that this opening up lets everything appear in a light that is different from what we are used to seeing. The experience of immanent transcendence is not an experience of anything transcendent, and it does not open up to something that can be explained by the intellect or understood by reason. It simply opens up—thereby transforming everything there is.

Expanded Thinking

It is not only in experiences of immanent transcendence—Benjamin's higher experience, for example—that transcendence happens without anyone abandoning the immanence. In some cases this is also applicable to aesthetic experiences: not to the interpretations of such experiences formulated by traditional metaphysics, but to modern interpretations such as Baumgarten's notion of sensitive cognition and Kant's of aesthetic judgment. To explain this commonality between philosophical aesthetics and the metaphysics of experience, it is relevant to turn to Kant's reflections on 'the expanded way of thinking.' In the *Critique of Judgment* he differentiates between three ways of thinking, one of which is appertained to the aesthetic power of judgment and characterized by being expanded, that is, marked by empathy.[137] It adheres to the principle of being able to identify oneself with others and to take many views into consideration, without submitting to any one of these. By thinking in an expanded way it is possible to elevate oneself above individual interests and reconsider the common weal. According to Kant, this expanded way of thinking is a prerequisite for bringing reason's consistent way of thinking to fruition: without aesthetic judgment it would not be possible to act morally. Kant only draws this moral consequence, but the expanded way of thinking

---

137   Immanuel Kant, *Critique of the Power of Judgment*, eds. and trans. P. Guyer and E. Matthews (New York: Cambridge University Press, 2000), 173–176 (5: 293–296). Paul Guyer and Eric Matthews translate the German word *erweitert* as 'broad-minded,' but for reasons stated in the chapter "The Significance of Sensitivity," footnote 21, I prefer 'expanded.'

may be considered to be a prerequisite for cognition of a truly well-informed character as well, and, thus, for philosophical thinking. As Ernst Cassirer has put it, philosophical thinking aims at the cognition of unity in diversity.[138] This does *not* mean that philosophical thinking will obliterate all the empirical differences to replace them with a single, common denominator. Philosophical thinking does *not* aspire to simplification, but, on the contrary, to finding something that unites. When philosophical thinking is truly philosophical it aims at a harmony between items that are different from one another—and not similar to one another.

However, as modern human beings controlled by intellectualism we usually think in an unphilosophical way.[139] We are liable to view unity and variety as contrasts: often we end up thinking 'either/or' instead of 'both/and.' Due to the expanded way of thinking, aesthetic judgment may help us to reflect in a less rigid, that is, a less theoretical, but more philosophical way. Then, in our thoughts, we may be in several places at the same time, thinking what is not, otherwise, to be reflected upon, for instance that immanence and transcendence are essentially interrelated. Thinking in this aesthetic way, we come closer to an understanding of the human beings we are than we do when we cling to the widespread dualist way of thinking. As pointed out by hermeneutic phenomenology, the simultaneity of immanence and transcendence is in a sense far more the rule than an exception, because we are both intellectual and corporeal creatures, at one and the same time. In our thoughts we are constantly transcending many things—ourselves, the given, the here and now. According to widespread prejudices, thinking thereby leaves the material, the immanence, the actual behind. But this is a misunderstanding. We only do so in the case of the conceptual cognition produced by the intellect. Or to be more precise, we only do so in this cognition's traditional rationalist way of understand-

---

138 Ernst Cassirer, *An Essay on Man: An Introduction to a Philosophy of Human Culture* (New Haven and London: Yale University Press, 1974), 222–223.

139 The term 'intellectualism' here refers to a way of thinking dominated by understanding (in the sense of *Verstand*) and devoid of reason (*Vernunft*).

ing itself, contrasting itself with immanent materiality (the body and its physical senses, for instance).

This rationalist way of thinking is still dominant, and pursuant to it, transcendence and immanence are necessarily mutually antagonistic. However, it was this way of thinking that philosophical aesthetics was introduced to criticize. Furthermore, we do in fact overcome the rationalist way of thinking whenever we think in the expanded way appertained to judgment. We overcome its binarism when we do not rely on sense perception or intellectual cognition only, but also include feeling and presentiment, for instance. Philosophical aesthetics sees the human being as a transcending as well as an embodied creature, because it is essentially situated as well as self-transcending. Transcendence is happening all the time, since we cannot help thinking, and we feel a strong need to reflect on our impressions and experiences, in particular. However, this transcendence does not make us abandon immanence, or it only does so when we practice and understand our thinking in a rationalist way. This is not to say that thinking in general and experience of immanent transcendence as such are identical. Instead, the experience of immanent transcendence tells us something crucial about humans as embodied *and* transcending creatures. Furthermore, this experience does not only tell us what sensitive cognition or aesthetic experience also tells us, namely that humans are both. The experience of immanent transcendence also tells us how human beings living nowadays might interpret the simultaneity experienced and the surplus of meaning it allows for. Being able to transcend in our thoughts is universal to humans as such. Experience of immanent transcendence is what this ability of transcendence turns into when it feels like there is no 'frame' available for the person trying to get a hold on what is happening to her during the transcendence.

Sensuousness and Transcendence

Duck's Eggs or Aestheticism

"Duck eggs. Shaved ice mixed with syrup and put in a silver bowl. Wisteria blossom. Plum blossoms covered with snow. A pretty child eating strawberries."[140] This list of *elegant things* is found in Peter Greenaway's film *The Pillow Book*, which was inspired by *The Pillow Book of Sei Shonagon* from the tenth and eleventh centuries.[141] The Japanese lady-in-waiting Sei Shonagon writes that her book was begun when she decided to fill a stack of notebooks with everything from poems, tales, reflections, and diary notes to lists of things.[142] When Greenaway, who is himself known to be manically obsessed with numbers and with collecting, first read this book in 1972, its lists were among the things that appealed to him.[143] Sei Shonagon says that during her notations she was especially interested in things she found magnificent and charming, whereas Greenaway has, in movies such as *The Cook, the Thief, His Wife, and Her Lover*,

---

140   Peter Greenaway, *The Pillow Book*, DVD (1996; Stockholm: Atlantic Film AB, 2006), 6:25–7:15.

141   Sei Shonagon, *The Pillow Book of Sei Shonagon*, trans. I. Morris (London, Melbourne, and Kuala Lumpur: Oxford University Press, 1967). Greenaway's film is not a screen version of this book, but quotes freely from it.

142   Shonagon, *The Pillow Book of Sei Shonagon*, 267–268.

143   Peter Greenaway, *The Pillow Book*, movie script (Paris: Éditions Dis Voir, 1996), 5.

cultivated not least the macabre and morbid.[144] *The Pillow Book* is not entirely devoid of either death or unseemly intercourse with corpses, but Greenaway must have been beguiled by Sei Shonagon's preference for the pleasanter sides of life. At least, in this film one is confronted not only with the aforementioned list of elegant things but also, for instance, a list of *things that make the heart beat faster*: "To pass a place where a baby is playing. To sleep in a room where fine incense is burning. To notice that one's elegant Chinese mirror has become a little cloudy. A lover on his second night-time visit."[145] And a list of *splendid things*: "Chinese brocade. A sword with a decorated scabbard. The grain of wood in a Buddhist statue. An Imperial procession led by the Empress. A large garden covered in snow. Indigo-colored silk. Anything colored indigo is splendid. Indigo-colored flowers. Indigo thread. And especially indigo paper."[146]

Elegance, grandness, and charm are things suitable for an aesthete's attention. This is true whether one was a lady-in-waiting in the Land of the Rising Sun centuries ago or is a present-day British multiartist. Greenaway is regarded as a particularly visual filmmaker, who paints rather than edits his films, and, not least, who uses the screen to create baroque visual tableaus. He is also regarded as an artist who is more concerned with form than with content, and is therefore easily categorized as postmodern. On the face of it, Greenaway and his art must therefore be an obvious subject for the criticism of the aestheticism of the modern era, formulated by Hans-Georg Gadamer in *Truth and Method*.[147] This criticism deals with what Gadamer calls *aesthetic differentiation*, and considers the result of an abstract way of thinking appertained to the aesthetic consciousness. With the term 'aesthetic consciousness,' he refers to an attitude that came into being at the end of the eighteenth

144 Shonagon, *The Pillow Book*, 267–268. Peter Greenaway, *The Cook, the Thief, His Wife, and Her Lover*, DVD (1989; London: Fabulous Films, 2016).

145 Greenaway, *The Pillow Book*, DVD, 7:21–8:24.

146 Greenaway, *The Pillow Book*, DVD, 11:38–12:40.

147 Hans-Georg Gadamer, *Truth and Method*, trans. J. Weinsheimer and D.G. Marshall (London and New York: Bloomsbury Academic, 2013).

century. It is characterized by disregarding the origins of things in order to focus solely on their purely aesthetic qualities—typically the formal, rhetorical, or performative aspects of the things in question. Thus, the aesthetic is made autonomous, and it becomes visible in its difference from, say, the ethical, religious, or political. According to Gadamer, this is historically a step forward, but one that has come at a price. When something is thus made into an *aesthetic object*, it can no longer be seen as part of the practical world where it could mean something to people. As an aesthetic object it can only be part of the aesthetic world of the aesthetic consciousness, giving rise to mere impressions marked by sensuous pleasure, but offering no opportunity for experience.[148]

In *Truth and Method* Gadamer primarily addresses the consequences of the aesthetic consciousness for the understanding of *art*, namely that the abstraction leads away from the work's original context of life: the religious or secular function that originally gave the work significance and motivated the spectator to evaluate it broadly, rather than purely aesthetically.[149] Art thus becomes autonomous, and the work of art becomes visible as a 'pure work of art,' but it is also deprived of its place and the world it derives from, and loses contact with what really distinguishes art, namely that it can give rise to experience of cognitively crucial value. Altogether, the aesthetic consciousness results in a wholesale levelling of all values other than the purely aesthetic impression of the aesthetic, because it indiscriminately regards *everything* aesthetically, dissolving content and context. The gaze of the aesthetic consciousness is thus marked by simultaneity—an equalization of everything, no matter where and when it is from—which results in historicist and eclectic relativism. However, according to Gadamer we do have other options than regarding works of art as aesthetic objects. They may instead be regarded as play, symbol, and festival. Understood

---

148 The word 'impression,' alternatively 'mere impression,' is used as a translation of the Danish word *oplevelse* in order to distinguish in English, too, between what in Danish (and German) are called *oplevelse* (*Erlebnis*) and *erfaring* (*Erfahrung*), respectively.

149 Gadamer, *Truth and Method*, 81–91.

as *play*, the work of art sets up a world one can be drawn into and changed by if one is willing to join the play, that is, experience instead of witness.[150] This has to do with the fact that the work, understood as *symbol*, shows more than it contains in a literal sense. It coproduces meaning that only exists by virtue of the work itself, and gives rise to experience that is not just of the moment. In this experience the work is dwelled on, and ordinary time must give way to a differently charged time. This latter fact is the reason the work of art is also *festival*, suspending chronometric time and opening up to community between people in the true sense.

If *The Pillow Book* is to be criticized for aesthetic consciousness, this presupposes that the gaze expressed in the film levels out all values, or that the film in its entirety does not draw its audience into its dominion, but only titillates their senses and reduces their view of the world. These two things are interrelated and can only be separated analytically. If the work does not draw us into itself, we will not be able to notice anything in the gaze expressed by the film that furthers true cognition.[151] We will only have access to the sensuously pleasurable quality of that gaze. Conversely, we cannot be drawn into the work unless it, in addition to its character of play, also has the symbolic and festive character of a gaze that appreciates meaning. As for Greenaway himself, he is clearly fascinated by sensuous forms and colors, and he culls from the tradition as he pleases. He pulls things out of their usual context and makes

---

150   Here 'witnessing' is synonymous with having an impression—understood as less than experiencing.

151   The philosophical terms 'Erkenntnis,' 'Verstand,' and 'Vernuft' are difficult to translate adequately into English. Referring to heterogeneous philosophical positions, here not only Alexander Gottlieb Baumgarten's rationalistic and Immanuel Kant's critical philosophies but also various phenomenological and hermeneutic philosophies such as Gadamer's, compounds the problem. For example, 'Verstehen' (understanding) does not mean the same to both Kant and Gadamer. Therefore, both 'Erkenntnis' (cognition, comprehension, etc.) and 'Wahrheit' (truth) also mean something different to them. Furthermore, Kant's term 'Verstand' is traditionally translated as 'understanding,' though 'Verstehen' (understanding) means something other than 'Verstand,' not least in Gadamer's interpretation. For the sake of consistency in the presentation of my own thought, I primarily call the phenomenon in question 'cognition' (or 'knowledge'), not 'understanding,' because in Baumgarten it is termed 'Erkenntnis' (*cognitio*), and because to hermeneutic philosophers understanding is, indeed, a kind of cognition—only not intellectual but sensitive cognition.

free with their original meaning. In interviews, however, he gives expression to strong opinions rather than to aestheticism, and in *The Pillow Book* he does not simply empty things of meaning without infusing them with new meaning. Greenaway's gaze is *creative*. He signs his own name to the things he borrows, and thus breathes new life into them. Such is the gaze that finds artistic expression in *The Pillow Book*. Therefore, this film does not confront its audience with a levelling of the value of the things it dwells on, but on the contrary demonstrates a sense for beauty. It is a gaze that captivates—it opens up a world and presents more than is physically given—and hence it also gives the spectators of the film the possibility of experiencing beauty themselves.

The Appearance of the Beautiful

In *Truth and Method*, Gadamer aims precisely at experience of beauty, not aesthetic impression. Like the ancient Greeks, he regards the beautiful as everything that has value in itself, and which thus differs from the useful by having its purpose in itself—in the very fact of it existing. The beautiful comprises everything "that is not part of the necessities of life but is concerned with the 'how,' the eu zen [the good life]."[152] In spite of this connection between the beautiful and the good, only the beautiful distinguishes itself by the fact that it "of itself presents itself, ... makes itself immediately evident (einleuchtend)."[153] As per Gadamer, this entails that the beautiful has the most important ontological function in existence, namely that of mediating between idea and phenomenon. As concepts and therefore transcendent, the true and the good do not show up in the immanent sphere as themselves, but in the shape of what we call beautiful things, including beautiful thoughts and actions. The beautiful, however, though a concept and therefore transcendent, shows up as itself when it appears in the immanent sphere as the beauty of the things we find to be beautiful. Accord-

---

152   Gadamer, *Truth and Method*, 493.

153   Gadamer, *Truth and Method*, 497.

ing to Gadamer, the philosophy of beauty, that is, the metaphysics of beauty, therefore illuminates what he as a hermeneutic philosopher appreciates as true cognition and terms 'understanding.' Studying the appearance of the beautiful contributes to the understanding of the evidence of the understandable, because both the experience of beauty and the cognition of truth are *events*, and because both these events are characterized by *immediacy*. Whereas the aesthetic consciousness says something about what prevents true cognition, namely the dominance of mere impression, the metaphysics of beauty instead reveals what distinguishes cognition that qualifies as true. It is able to do so because the experience of beauty is already a kind of true cognition.[154]

Following this line of thought, we are far from what is usually understood by 'truth' and 'cognition' today. Since the scientific revolution in the sixteenth and seventeenth centuries and the Enlightenment's subsequent reformation of philosophical thought, cognition has been defined as an experiential identification of empirical—not least causal—matters, and truth has been conceived as a question of correspondence between thought and experience. Cognition is thus regarded as a mental act, performed by a mind that in order to execute its act of cognition consciously reaches out for something that consequently takes on the character of an object. Cognition is here something a subject 'does' and necessarily must 'do' in order to attain knowledge of something other, whose status is that of an object, which consequently means that this other does not do anything itself, that is, from a cognitive point of view. However, according to Gadamer's thinking, which was articulated in terms inspired by Martin Heidegger, cognition is not an act, but an event, and thus cognizing happens to the subject, rather than being controlled by it. In this kind of cognition the subject is therefore not really a subject, but mere Dasein, and it is rather the 'object' of cognition that does something: it shows itself to Dasein. The resultant event is both the cognition, and the truth about what

---

[154] Regarding the concept of beauty, see also my book, *Skønhed—En engel gik forbi* (Beauty—An Angel Passed By) (Aarhus: Aarhus University Press, 2006).

shows itself, as well as about what cognition is, and about what it means to be present—in the midst of being, among beings. As Gadamer notes, such an understanding of truth and cognition does not make its first appearance in his and Heidegger's philosophies; it was already a factor in the metaphysics of beauty in antiquity and the Middle Ages, though they termed it 'beauty'—but indeed beauty understood as an event characterized by immediacy.[155]

In this metaphysics of beauty and Gadamer's hermeneutic use of it, we are not only far from the concepts of truth and cognition that are prevalent today. We are also a long way from the interpretation of aesthetics that has held sway for centuries. Since the days of Søren Kierkegaard, aesthetics—by him considered the aesthetic that is worshipped by the aesthete—has been accused of subjectivism and relativism. An aesthete is allegedly characterized by finding sensuous pleasure in particular phenomena, and by being different from the ethicist or the religious person due to an inability to recognize or commit him- or herself to anything universal. It is this negative use of the word 'aesthetic' that echoes in Gadamer's criticism of the aesthetic consciousness—a kind of consciousness he believes he can trace back to Immanuel Kant's *Critique of Judgment* and not least to Friedrich Schiller's use of this work.[156] As Gadamer notes, Kant's concept of knowledge is reductive, and this reductionism has consequences for the latter's aesthetics.[157] However, in *Truth and Method*, Gadamer ignores the very ambition of Kant's analysis of aesthetic judgment: not to make the judgment of taste autonomous, but to argue for its universal validity. For the same reason, he fails to notice the true result of Kant's analysis, namely that the judgment of taste is not only emptied of all knowledge (in the sense of logical cognition), but simultaneously endowed with

---

155   Gadamer, *Truth and Method*, 493–506.

156   Immanuel Kant, *Critique of the Power of Judgment*, eds. and trans. P. Guyer and E. Matthews (New York: Cambridge University Press, 2000), and Friedrich Schiller, *On the Aesthetic Education of Man in a Series of Letters*, eds. and trans. E.M. Wilkinson and L.A. Willoughby (Oxford: Clarendon Press, 1967).

157   See, in particular, the chapter "Transcending the Aesthetic Dimension" in "Part One" of Gadamer's *Truth and Method*.

insight (led by reason rather than by understanding). As per Kant, the beautiful is the symbol of the morally good, and even though the judgment of taste delivers no knowledge, it does give us insight, into ourselves and into our possibility of developing as the freely acting and thinking creatures equipped with reason we are by nature, according to Kant.

While we are far from the prevalent concepts of truth and cognition, as well as the concept of aesthetics according to which the aesthetic is noncommittal sensuality, we are, on the other hand, right at the center of *philosophical aesthetics*. When Alexander Gottlieb Baumgarten founded aesthetics in the eighteenth century, it was, indeed, neither as a philosophy about intellectual cognition nor as a theory about sense perception and lack of morals.[158] On the contrary, he introduced aesthetics as philosophy about what he called *sensitive cognition* and regarded as synonymous with the experience of beauty.[159] Translated into current terminology, Baumgarten founded aesthetics as a philosophy about aesthetic experience understood as a kind of true cognition that has the beautiful as its object and is itself beautiful, too. In other words, philosophical aesthetics is philosophy about what appears by itself, in both an objective and a subjective sense—both as a property of the object and as a quality of the cognition. Philosophical aesthetics, more precisely, is the philosophy of beauty understood as something third, that is, as a *phenomenon*. According to hermeneutic phenomenology, a phenomenon is exactly *"what shows itself in itself, what is manifest."*[160] Already for this reason—but also for oth-

---

[158] Regarding the philosophical aesthetics introduced by Baumgarten, see the part on Baumgarten in my book *Den skønne tænkning: Veje til erfaringsmetafysik. Religionsfilosofisk udmøntet* (Beautiful Thinking: Pathways to the Metaphysics of Experience. Religio-Philosophically Implemented) (Aarhus: Aarhus University Press, 2014).

[159] Sensitive cognition is equal to aesthetic experience, whereas perfect sensitive cognition is equal to experiencing beauty. However, the perfection of sensitive experience is the purpose of aesthetics, and the experience of beauty is thus the epitome of aesthetic experience. See Alexander Gottlieb Baumgarten, *Ästhetik, Volume 1–2*, trans. D. Mirbach (Hamburg: Felix Meiner Verlag, 2007), § 14.

[160] Martin Heidegger, *Being and Time*, trans. J. Stambaugh, rev. D.J. Schmidt (Albany: State University of New York Press, 2010), 27.

ers that must remain unaddressed here, however[161]—aesthetics can be said to have approached phenomenology from the beginning. Focusing on the experience of beauty, it deals with what shows itself by itself, only more explicitly and in a more direct way than the metaphysics of beauty did previously. Conversely, hermeneutic phenomenology can likewise be said to have been aesthetic from the beginning. Hermeneutic phenomenologists such as Heidegger and Gadamer did indeed reject the concept of aesthetics, and the aesthetics introduced by Baumgarten, but by focusing on phenomena they themselves dealt with something that shows itself by itself, and in itself—and thus appears in the same way as the beautiful.

The Symbol and Peripheral Vision

This will become more explicit if we return to *The Pillow Book*. The film begins with the young Japanese woman Nagiko's memory of two rituals her father and her aunt performed on her birthday when she was a child: he calligraphed on her face and the aunt read aloud from Sei Shonagon's pillow book. Nagiko's father, who always completed his work by writing his signature on the back of her neck, said while calligraphing: "When God made the first clay model of a human being, He painted in the eyes, the lips, and the sex. Then He painted in each person's name lest the person should ever forget it. If God approved of His creation, He brought the painted clay model into life by signing His own name."[162] As an adult, Nagiko yearns to experience again the meeting between body and brush to which her father introduced her, just as she, a little less consciously, also yearns to actualize herself as an author. Image and literature are in general so intimately conjoined in Japan that their histories coincide, Greenaway says in an interview from 1997.[163] It is this

---

161   See *Den skønne tænkning* for a more detailed discussion of the relation between philosophical aesthetics and hermeneutic phenomenology.

162   Greenaway, *The Pillow Book*, DVD, 2:20–3:55.

163   Christopher Hawthorne, "Flesh and Ink," *Salon Magazine* June 6, 1997, https://www.salon.com/1997/06/06/greenaway970606/, accessed July 21, 2020.

connection he adopts in *The Pillow Book*, and here transforms to a correspondingly close relation between flesh and word. Every time you see flesh, you see text, Greenaway says in the same interview, and flesh and text are so intimately conjoined that the pleasures in them intersect. The transcendent is present in the immanent; the carnal, corporeal, or sensual is charged with meaning. Representing the naked body as text in *The Pillow Book*, Greenaway adds something to it that it does not contain when seen only as the object of physical desire. The body is the material incarnation of the immaterial word, and it is therefore not just pretty, but beautiful. Greenaway saturates the body with meaning that does not refer to anything anywhere else, but to something more within the body itself: the word it incarnates. It is precisely not as flesh, but as symbol, that the body is beautiful.

This understanding of the body as symbol and of the symbol as something that transcends in an inward direction, to meaning in the symbol itself, is difficult to understand today. Nowadays the symbolic is often misunderstood as something that refers us to some other place. It is understood as representation, and representation is regarded as building on a traditional metaphysical opposition of immanence and transcendence. Thus the symbol is regarded as something that points away from the immanent of which it itself is part, toward the transcendent that it symbolizes, thereby bridging a gulf, the actual existence of which it simultaneously confirms. According to Gadamer's way of thinking, which as demonstrated is close to the metaphysics of beauty, this is not how symbols actually function, however. A symbol does not point beyond itself but into itself—to an extra layer of meaning found there. It does not symbolize something distant that the symbol reaches out to but can never entirely reach because the symbol and the symbolized are different—they are immanent and transcendent, respectively. On the contrary, the symbolized is totally present, thanks to the symbol, which does not refer to anything in a distant transcendence, but points to what in the symbol itself is constituted by the symbolized. The meaning that the symbol contains in the form of the symbolized is thus given with the symbol and found nowhere else than in the symbol, which in its immanent presence is itself thus saturated with transcendence. So when we experience the meaning of a symbol, we are quite literally experiencing *immanent transcendence*.[164] This kind of experience we all know, but many perhaps only from their childhood, because modern man's world is emptied of content that generates meaning—it is profane and pragmatic. In reality, the world is presumably still studded with possibilities of experiencing cohesion and meaningfulness, but modern man is blind.

If we are blind, the world is a sum of objects that can be used and consumed, but do not give occasion for contemplation of a 'dwelling' character, that is, lingering. This narrow perception of the world is coupled with a primitive conception of metaphysics, according to which it represents a way of thinking that opposes something distant with something close. Such a notion of metaphysics causes problems for our understanding of not only the symbol but also the body. It hinders us in comprehending the holistic relationship between body and mind that philosophical phenomenologists try to articulate in order to go beyond modern epistemology and its burden of dualism. Among these phenomenologists we find Maurice Merleau-Ponty, whose phenomenology of the body has inspired Juhani Pallasmaa to think of human experience as multisensory. In *The Eyes of the Skin*, Pallasmaa distinguishes between the *focused vision* that confronts us with the world, and a *peripheral vision* that envelops us in the flesh of the world.[165] The focused vision is visual, whereas the peripheral is multisensory, and, not least, tactile. "All the senses, including vision, are extensions of the tactile sense," Pallasmaa writes, and he is therefore of the opinion that "all sensory experiences are modes of touching."[166] Because the periph-

---

164 I usually ascribe a different meaning to the term 'immanent transcendence,' that is, I usually use it to designate a specific modern form of experiencing transcendence. See, for example, the chapter "Experience, Metaphysics, and Immanent Transcendence" in the present volume, and the chapter "Immanent Transcendence" in Dorthe Jørgensen, *Poetic Inclinations: Ethics, History, Philosophy* (Aarhus: Aarhus University Press, 2021).

165 Juhani Pallasmaa, *The Eyes of the Skin: Architecture and the Senses* (Chichester: John Wiley and Sons, 2005).

166 Pallasmaa, *The Eyes of the Skin*, 10.

eral vision is primary for human experience, experience, according to him, builds more on tactility than on visibility. It is with 'the eyes of the skin' that we experience the world; with the eyes we have in our heads we only view the world from without. Yet it is the sense of vision and the focused vision that dominate, for example in modern architecture and town planning, which for that reason make us feel left out. If instead we built with respect for the peripheral vision, our buildings and cities would enfold us in their space, as nature and historical places do. We would have a spatial and bodily experience, because "peripheral vision integrates us with space, while focused vision pushes us out of the space, making us mere spectators."[167]

Pallasmaa criticizes the *ocularcentric paradigm* that, in his opinion, has dominated in the West ever since antiquity—its isolation of the eye, suppression of the other senses, and reduction of experience to visual impression. Such a critique of imbalance has an immediate appeal, which is also true of Pallasmaa's desire for a multisensory architecture that furthers the feeling of belonging to and being integrated into our environment. Privately, many people try to create spaces that accommodate needs of this kind; spaces that enclose without being too tight—that embrace, and through which one may breathe peacefully. Yet Pallasmaa's treatment of the relation between body and mind is not entirely unproblematic. In *The Eyes of the Skin*, he does not only criticize the hegemony of the eye. Nor does he only think that its growth "seems to be parallel with the development of Western ego-consciousness and the gradually increasing separation of the self and the world."[168] He also associates this with "the consequent spectator theory of knowledge in Western thinking."[169] However, in *Praise of Theory* Gadamer states that the originally visionary quality of *theoria* did not at all consist in 'seeing' in an external ascertaining way, but in an immanently

---

167 Pallasmaa, *The Eyes of the Skin*, 13.

168 Pallasmaa, *The Eyes of the Skin*, 25.

169 Pallasmaa, *The Eyes of the Skin*, 19.

lingering way.[170] "Theoria is not so much the individual momentary act as a way of comporting oneself, a position and condition. It is 'being present' in the lovely double sense that means that the person is not only present but completely present."[171] The spectator theory of knowledge mentioned previously is, then, in reality a theory of *lingering*—or at least was so originally—and therefore has more to do with the peripheral view than with the focused. For the same reason we may not have to seek out the body at all, in order to let go of modern epistemology's worshipping of the mind. The body may not be the solution.

Flesh or Felt Body

Unlike the epistemologists of the modern era, Merleau-Ponty—whose body-phenomenology Pallasmaa is inspired by—regards body, mind, and the world as inextricably conjoined. In the *Phenomenology of Perception*, he therefore replaces the Cartesian cogito with a bodily cogito, understood as a *prereflective cogito*.[172] According to Merleau-Ponty, the world is not a sum of objects of a conscious mind, but appears phenomenally to the body, and the body is not merely the physical body, but lived corporeality and as such incarnated subjectivity. This body, referred to by Merleau-Ponty as *le corps propre*, has already perceived and created meaning before any reflection sets in, and body and mind cannot therefore be separated.[173] All knowledge has its roots in an immediate bodily kind of experience, in which the body is in direct contact with the world, and all thinking presupposes bodily preconsciousness in the

---

170   Hans-Georg Gadamer, *Praise of Theory: Speeches and Essays*, trans. C. Dawson (New Haven and London: Yale University Press, 1998).

171   Gadamer, *Praise of Theory*, 31.

172   Maurice Merleau-Ponty, *Phenomenology of Perception*, trans. D.A. Landes (London and New York: Routledge, 2012).

173   Donald A. Landes translates *le corps propre* as 'my own body' (or 'one's own body'), which "should not be heard as the body 'I possess,' but rather the body that I live as my own" (*Phenomenology of Perception*, 512, endnote 6).

form of bodily sensation and signification. The lived corporeality Merleau-Ponty refers to is a state in which we do not *have* a body, but *are* body. It predates the experience of the body as mere physical object, and it is always situated, which means that by definition we have to do with *being-in-the-world*. In later works, such as *The Visible and the Invisible*, Merleau-Ponty, however, finds that his earlier ideas were not enough to escape epistemology's prioritizing of the mind, and he therefore introduces the concept of 'flesh' (*la chair*).[174] This concept he coins to designate a chiasmus between body and world: the common tissue that is situated before or under subject and object, and from which these two entities develop into independent poles in our cognition. Thus, it is in the flesh that the immediate experience takes place on which all knowledge builds, and this experience is therefore precisely a fleshly experience.

The French word for flesh, *chair*, can also be translated as the *lived body*—an extremely important term for phenomenologists such as Hermann Schmitz and Gernot Böhme, who both systematically distinguish between *Körper* and *Leib*, by Schmitz in English called "material body" and "felt body."[175] "When I speak of the felt body I do not have in mind the human or animal body that can be viewed or touched," Schmitz says in *Der unerschöpfliche Gegenstand* (The Inexhaustible Object), "but instead what one senses of oneself in its proximity without access to a 'sense organ' such as eye or hand."[176] The felt body is a state that one senses emotionally, and it has spatial extension, a little like noise. The felt body is "the essence of such corporeal impulses as, for example, fear, pain, lust,

---

174   See the chapter "The Intertwining—The Chiasm" in Maurice Merleau-Ponty, *The Visible and the Invisible: Followed by Working Notes*, trans. A. Lingis (Evanston: Northwestern University Press, 1968).

175   The English terms 'felt body' and 'lived body' are synonymous translations of the German word 'Leib.' For an introduction in English to Schmitz's phenomenology, see Hermann Schmitz et al., "Emotions outside the Box—the New Phenomenology of Feeling and Corporeality," *Phenomenology and the Cognitive Sciences* Vol. 10, No. 2 (2011): 241–259. For Böhme, see Gernot Böhme, "The Concept of Body as the Nature We Ourselves Are," *The Journal of Speculative Philosophy* Vol. 24, No. 3 (2010): 224–238.

176   Hermann Schmitz, *Der unerschöpfliche Gegenstand: Grundzüge der Philosophie* (Bonn: Bouvier Verlag Schmitz, 1990), 115.

hunger, thirst, disgust, vigor, tiredness, emotional affection."[177] The material body, on the contrary, is a physical thing that one may view and hold in one's arms, and it is spatially limited like a receptacle. Böhme writes similarly in *Ethik leiblicher Existenz* (The Ethics of Felt Bodily Existence) that "the body is the nature that we ourselves are."[178] In his interpretation, the term 'material body' represents an experience of our nature as something alien, whereas the term 'felt body' represents an experience of nature understood as an experience of self. As material bodies, we are things among other things, whereas being felt bodies we are a given, for ourselves as ourselves. Both Schmitz and Böhme think that modern man has forgotten his felt corporeality and constantly regards and treats himself as material body. According to Schmitz, early phenomenology—that is, Edmund Husserl's—was too much a dualist philosophy of mind to solve this problem, so he has introduced a so-called *new phenomenology*, which focuses on the felt body rather than on the conscious mind. Correspondingly, Böhme argues for a *new aesthetics*, which takes interest in our felt bodily presence and the emotional effect things have on us. Such an aesthetics is necessary, in his opinion, because the philosophy of art reduces art and other phenomena to aesthetic objects, that is, objects of the conscious mind, and because not even Schmitz's new phenomenology has reformulated aesthetics in sufficient depth.

Merleau-Ponty's term *chair* is usually translated 'flesh' (German *Fleisch*), the word used so far in this chapter. This translation, however, creates an obstacle on our way to understanding the experience Merleau-Ponty had in mind as something other and more than physical sensation. The word 'flesh' has connotations of blood and muscle tissue, dead bodies, refrigerated counters with chopped meat, and the 'meat markets' of night life, but Merleau-Ponty was thinking of the experience of significance that brings about mean-

---

177   Hermann Schmitz, *Kurze Einführung in die Neue Phänomenologie* (Freiburg and München: Verlag Karl Alber, 2009), 34–35.

178   Gernot Böhme, *Ethik leiblicher Existenz: Über unseren moralischen Umgang mit der eigenen Natur* (Frankfurt am Main: Suhrkamp Verlag, 2008), 156.

ing, albeit experience produced by the senses. It is therefore an obvious idea instead to translate *chair* as 'felt body,' which at the same time synchronizes his, Schmitz's and Böhme's philosophies. In favor of such a synchronization it can be mentioned that all three have problematized the dualist way of thinking in modern epistemology by seeking out a level of experience that predates the experience of things as objects. Even though the flesh in which the immediate experience takes place is precisely *not* to be understood as the physical body, according to Merleau-Ponty, it is, however, difficult to read his texts without imagining something rather physical. He wants to put behind him the way of thinking found in the dualist philosophy of mind and its oppositions, for example that between body and mind, but his terminology (*corps*, *chair*) and examples (for instance, a blind man's impression of his stick as a part of his arm, or the sensation of the body as both exterior and interior that anyone can have by folding one hand around the other) suggest that in his texts he really just shifts the existing focus on mind to a focus on the body. In other words, his terminology and examples give the impression that he turns the usual relation between body and mind upside down, rather than really putting the dualist way of thinking behind him; that he does not in fact bring some third possibility into focus, but prioritizes the body rather than the mind, which invariably reduces the body to the physical body, for it is the latter that is in contrast to the mind.

As mentioned previously, Merleau-Ponty realized that he remained fettered by the way of thinking found in the dualist philosophy of mind as long as he kept speaking about the body 'only'; therefore, he introduced the concept of flesh. The question is, however, whether by choosing this terminology he perhaps aggravated the problem in question, instead of solving it. 'Flesh' is supposed to denote something that is neither purely physical nor purely of the mind, but the word does not give the impression of some third position; it rather gives the impression of more body, even more *physical* body. As long as the word 'body' (or 'flesh' or the like) is used—precisely as if the word 'mind' were used—it may be difficult not to reproduce the traditional way of thinking, only now in reverse. This could at least explain why it is apparently so difficult for recipients of Merleau-Ponty's phenomenology, for example Pallasmaa, to avoid a reduction of experience to sensory experience, even though the ambition is to arrive at something that *cannot* be categorized as either (just) sensorial or concept-engendered. In spite of their distinction between *Körper* and *Leib*, not even the German phenomenologists found a terminology that was entirely unproblematic. Just like *Körper* and *Fleisch*, the term *Leib* automatically calls to mind images of physical phenomena, except it sounds more old-fashioned. However, even apart from its philosophical use, the word *Leib* distinguishes itself by sometimes denoting something other than a physical phenomenon, for instance, something as closely connected to 'the intermediate world' as religious phenomena or astral bodies.[179] This is utilized by the German phenomenologists, as is seen when Schmitz tries to exemplify what he understands by felt bodily experience and mentions feelings such as fear, disgust, or vigor, and not the impression of a stick as part of the arm.

The Sense of Beauty

Merleau-Ponty begins in the body because it is the opposite of the epistemologically profiled mind, but he searches the limit of the physical body, the transition between body and flesh, since that is where the body meets the world and all knowledge begins. Contrariwise, Schmitz begins in the mind, as it is the starting point of modern thought, but he seeks out the shadowy side of the conscious ego, where it is still just coming into being, and still coheres with everything, for it is in this emotional corporeality that all knowledge begins. In a sense, Merleau-Ponty's and Schmitz's phenomenological philosophies take their points of departure at opposite ends of the paradigm of the dualist philosophy of mind, but in a common attempt to go beyond that very paradigm—beyond both body and mind, understood as independent entities, to explore the

---

179 Concerning the notion of 'the intermediate world,' see the chapter "The Intermediate World."

human being-in-the-world, whether the 'locus' of it be described as the flesh or the felt body. It is the very experience associated with being in the world—sensing alertly and with an open mind—that is interesting to phenomenological thinking. It is this presence—of a both sensuous and cognitive character, or rather of a feeling, sensate, and presentimental character—that philosophical phenomenology was created to interpret, by absorbing itself in and exploring the phenomena that appear to it. Or this is at least the case when philosophical phenomenology takes on a hermeneutic guise, which is (in part) what happens in Schmitz and Merleau-Ponty, in both cases helped on by Heidegger, who founded hermeneutic phenomenology and thus created what was also the point of departure for Gadamer's philosophical hermeneutics.

The aesthetic consciousness criticized by Gadamer actually more or less does to things what the conscious mind (here termed the reflective movement) does to the body, according to Merleau-Ponty in the *Phenomenology of Perception*. "The experience of one's own body ... is opposed to the reflective movement that disentangles the object from the subject and the subject from the object, and that only gives us thought about the body or the body as an idea, and not the experience of the body or the body in reality."[180] As mentioned previously, the aesthetic consciousness isolates things as singular objects and thus strips them of meaning. It tears them out of the context to which they originally belonged, and ignores their original function, to instead focus exclusively on so-called aesthetic qualities. Conversely, this also means that if the body is regarded aesthetically (in the sense of the word used here) it will be regarded in the very way Merleau-Ponty tried to escape. Instead of being perceived as something we *are*, and through which we are connected to everything else that is, the body is perceived as something we *have*, and which we can shape and change beyond all recognition. This relation to the body is not science fiction; it is widespread today, where the so-called aesthetic attitude makes us remove superfluous body fat with scalpels and fill facial crevices

---

180   Merleau-Ponty, *Phenomenology of Perception*, 205.

with Botox. We deal with our bodies in a beauty-industrial way that affirms Gadamer's judgment when he claimed that an aesthetic gaze of this character is levelling. The beauty industry apposes all bodies without taking the provenance and history of the individual into account. It measures them by the same standard and reshapes them into copies of the same prototype, whose only characteristic is that the model is wholly defined as Western.

In *The Pillow Book*, however, something else happens when Greenaway has the child Nagiko feel the calligraphy on her face or the adult Nagiko and her lovers cover each other's skin with characters. Here, the gaze on the body is rather aesthetic, understood as directed by a sense of beauty, than it is aesthetic in Gadamer's negative sense of the word, and the beauty involved is not the beauty-industrial prototype, but transcendence in immanence. As mentioned previously, the beautiful is everything that has value in itself. It is the absolute and unconditional in which the true and the good come together and find a way to appear—not as themselves, but as beauty. In other words, the one who has an aesthetic eye for the beauty of this world does not just see and praise something nice and neat, but senses something of both cognitive and moral value. It is therefore meaningless to regard the beautiful as the tame opposite of the sublime, as has long been common. This opposition of the beautiful and the sublime, in which the beautiful is reduced to something harmonious and the sublime has a monopoly on all that is exciting, on disharmony and transgression, on transcendence in immanence, is not a matter of course. It presupposes that beauty is reduced to a question of harmonious proportionality.[181] Only when beauty has deteriorated into a shadow of itself is it necessary to describe the transcendent as sublime rather than beautiful. In the metaphysics of beauty, in which the ancient understanding of the beautiful was intact, the word 'beauty' was absolutely sufficient—

---

181 Similarly, the thoughts phrased by Kant in his *Critique of Judgment* about the beautiful and the sublime are built on a distinction between understanding and reason that is only possible in a time when intellectual cognition is no longer followed up on by more comprehensive thinking; science is no longer both philosophical and empirical, but only empirical. Moreover, not even the latter is obvious, since it is a product of a historical development: the farewell of the modern era to the more holistic thought of the past.

even as the designation of something so absolute and unconditional as the divine, and even in spite of the double character of the divine, at once close and distant.

However, it is not for us as subjects, but as subjectivity that is connected with the world, and therefore, in a way, is asubjective, that the beautiful is given, and with it so much else. It is precisely when we are *emotionally present* that the transcendence occurring in immanence may happen. As human beings we are present by definition, according to Heidegger, but we may be present in several ways. In the speech "Memorial Address," it is described as a question of thinking in a calculative or a meditative way.[182] In contradistinction to "meditative thinking," which is suitably *gelassen* (released), "calculative thinking," because of its intentional character, prevents Dasein from being aware of what shows itself.[183] Meditative thinking, in contrast, allows Dasein to be what it is, that is, allows it to show the openness so characteristic of Dasein to what shows itself. From *Being and Time* we additionally learn that Dasein is fundamentally defined by attunement (*Befindlichkeit*) and understanding (*Verstehen*), and that they are equiprimordial.[184] Being present, we sense the world and are already by sensing it familiar with the world. The observed is interpreted and is thus meaningful not only when we process it intellectually but already in our immediate experience of it. Noise is never only noise, but for example the sound of a car; light is never merely light, but for example sunlight. In *Truth and Method,* Gadamer consequentially describes the human as the interpretive being, whose way of being in the world is so fundamentally characterized by understanding that we will never reach a point before understanding, though we may forget that understanding precedes everything else. This leads to Gadamer's idea of the *universality of hermeneutics*: that hermeneutics is about what is most fundamental to the human Dasein, and which forms the ba-

---

182   Martin Heidegger, "Memorial Address," in *Discourse on Thinking: A Translation of Gelassenheit*, trans. J.M. Anderson and E.H. Freund (New York: Harper and Row, 1966).

183   Heidegger, "Memorial Address," 46.

184   Heidegger, *Being and Time*, §§ 29, 31.

sis of everything, philosophical thought included, so that philosophy is conversely hermeneutic by nature.

Aesthetic Transcendence

Already Baumgarten's philosophical aesthetics pointed to a basic simultaneity of attunement and understanding. In his aesthetics, human cognition has its roots in a sensitivity that is fundamental to cognition—and which we cannot discard, though we may forget it, as we often do. We cannot reach a point before this sensitivity, which by itself, however, already constitutes a kind of cognition. Therefore, philosophical aesthetics, as it was founded by Baumgarten, invites us to challenge Gadamer's idea of the universality of hermeneutics with a hypothesis of the *universality of aesthetics*.[185] Such a challenge may be necessary, because Gadamer's attempt at integrating aesthetics in hermeneutics seems to let attunement (sensitivity) fade out in favor of only understanding (cognition). Thus a point is lost, which—albeit unacknowledged by phenomenology— is common to aesthetics and phenomenology, namely that attunement and understanding are equiprimordial: that we know, as soon as we sense emotionally. This, however, does *not* mean that aesthetics and phenomenology are *identical*. Philosophical aesthetics was conceived by Baumgarten within the framework of a dualist philosophy of mind and introduced as a philosophy about the subjective faculties that are the source of sensitive cognition. So far aesthetics represents the kind of epistemological thinking that phenomenology has tried to distance itself from. However, thanks to the focus of aesthetics on sensitivity rather than intellectuality, early philosophical aesthetics spoke about human cognition in a way that was partly at variance with the framework of its own dualist philosophy of mind. Aesthetics sowed a seed that phenomenology later had the

---

185 My book *Den skønne tænkning* provides a comprehensive, systematic argument for the universality of aesthetics and the related reinterpretation of hermeneutics.

opportunity to bring to fruition, although still without being able to realize and acknowledge its debt to aesthetics.[186]

The paradigm-disrupting aspect of philosophical aesthetics does not only consist in the shaking of the subject—defined by rationalism as an agent of intellectual (not sensitive) cognition—that occurred when Baumgarten studied sensitivity from the point of view of his philosophical aesthetics. The subject, understood as the conscious instigator and controller of cognition, also became endangered because what Baumgarten now studied comprised *imagination*, among other things. Imagination produces notions of things that are not directly given in an empirical sense, and it is therefore by nature of a transcending character. It thus by definition goes beyond what the subject of logical cognition can control: it exceeds what is accessible to understanding, as it proceeds to a dimension that is only comprehensible to reason. In other words, imagination has access to what in Kant is called *ideas*, and which he does not see as something transcendent somewhere else, but as a 'more'—a transcendence—in the immanent sphere. This imagination, according to Kant, is given particularly free rein in the work of the aesthetic power of judgment, where understanding does not restrain imagination's production of thoughts (representations) with its concepts. This, however, is also to say that the subject does not control the thinking practiced by aesthetic judgment, which Kant called *expanded*.[187] With its expanded way of thinking, the aesthetic power of judgment unites different things in thought, without reducing difference to sameness. It transcends to something universal, but without losing what is unique about the particular. The aesthetic power of judgment is capable of this expanded way of thinking thanks to imagination's contribution of free reflexivity to the working of the power of judgment, which also, conversely,

---

186   For a more thorough exposition of the thoughts presented here I must again refer to my book *Den skønne tænkning*.

187   Kant, *Critique of Judgment*, 173–176 (5: 293–296). Paul Guyer and Eric Matthews translate the German word *erweitert* as 'broad-minded,' but for reasons stated in the chapter "The Significance of Sensitivity," footnote 21, I prefer 'expanded.'

means that this expanded thinking suspends the subject as it was defined by rationalism and adopted by Kant.[188]

Understood as the way of thinking of the aesthetic power of judgment, expanded thinking is aesthetic thinking. Baumgarten's interest in sensitivity and the related sensitive cognition already initiated the exploration of this thinking, and so, in a way, began the substitution of the subject with Dasein, which was later carried out by hermeneutic phenomenology. Thus, there is on one hand an abyss of difference between the original subject of aesthetic philosophy and Dasein as understood by phenomenology. On the other hand, there is also a bridge of similarity: Dasein and the subject of sensitive cognition have in common the transcendence associated with imagination, for imagination is central among the 'lower' cognitive faculties dealt with in early philosophical aesthetics, and Dasein, according to Heidegger, distinguishes itself by being ecstatic, that is, self-transcending.[189] Regarded as Dasein, man is indeed transcending by nature, not only understood in the sense that we can ignore our bodies or have an eternal soul, but in the sense that a force is active in us that expands our awareness—in both time and space. It is not that we transcend in the epistemological sense; that we ourselves consciously reach for something, be it incomprehensible or not. But it is about being *open to transcendence*, to sensing what happens in the immanence, sensing occurrences of an evidential character.[190] Being present, we are constantly expanded, constantly brought beyond ourselves, to something other than ourselves, by which we are present—both in the present space

---

188 For the thought connected with the expanded way of thinking, see the chapter "Dannelse til humanitet" (Formation for Humanity) in *Den skønne tænkning*, 361–375.

189 Concerning the centrality of imagination to the 'lower' cognitive faculties, see the chapter "Experience, Metaphysics, and Immanent Transcendence"; and concerning the imagination as such, see "The Philosophy of Imagination." For Heidegger's notion of Dasein as self-transcending, see *Being and Time*, and for his notion of imagination, see Martin Heidegger, *Kant and the Problem of Metaphysics*, trans. R. Taft (Bloomington: Indiana University Press, 1997).

190 My use of 'evidential' alludes to Gadamer's use of 'einleuchtend,' translated by Joel Weinsheimer and Donald G. Marshall as 'evident' (see the section "The Appearance of the Beautiful").

and in memory. As said previously, this Dasein is of the felt body (in distinction to the material body or the mind) and its characteristic openness to transcendence is an aesthetic or properly *aisthetic* openness to that in the sensible world which transcends the merely sensuous.[191]

In *The Pillow Book* imagination also plays an important part. Imagination is what Nagiko misses in the man she is unwillingly married to for a while. The husband is an inane boor, who refuses her wish to feel the brush against her skin. He does not understand the spirituality associated with this physical act; he does not have the imagination to follow her in his mind. If the body is to be seen as a symbol, and if the symbol is to be understood as something that transcends into itself to otherwise inaccessible meaning, what is needed is precisely imagination. Thus, it is lack of imagination that is the real scourge in a time like ours, where bodies are reduced to physical flesh, symbols are misunderstood as allegories for something distant and inaccessible, and metaphysics is ridiculed as an outmoded idea belonging to another world. Where imagination is absent, the sensuous world is not, like in *The Pillow Book*, an occasion for aesthetic pleasure that is more than merely sensuous, that is, a way to experiencing what Theodor W. Adorno called the aesthetic "more."[192] Aesthetics is, therefore, not—as Gadamer demanded—to be integrated into hermeneutics, but hermeneutics must be founded on aesthetics, because we already know when we sense; understanding already takes place in the attunement. If understanding is separated from its source in the aesthetic experience and made independent, the result will be everything that Gadamer himself criticized and wanted to depart from. Understanding shrinks to intellectual explanation, what Heidegger called calculative thinking. Aesthetic experience is reduced to aesthetic

---

191 The word 'aisthetic' derives from the ancient Greek word *aisthesis*, which, as opposed to what is often said about it today, in antiquity did not only mean sense perception but also—and this is important—experience in a wider sense of this word.

192 Theodor W. Adorno, *Aesthetic Theory*, eds. G. Adorno and R. Tiedemann, trans. R. Hullot-Kentor (London: Athlone Press, 1997). See, for instance, the section "'More' as Semblance" in the chapter "Art Beauty: Apparition, Spiritualization, Intuitability."

impression, and sensitive cognition is confused with sense perception. Philosophical aesthetics disintegrates into the study of art, works of art become objectified as aesthetic objects, and the many possibilities of aesthetic transcendence in our existence end in an empty worship of mere bodily pleasure.

The Experience of Divinity

Thinking back, Nagiko associates her childhood birthdays with a Japanese form of congratulation—which she also refers to as her father's 'blessing.' In *The Pillow Book*, Greenaway mixes European and Asian elements in a willful filmic interpretation of the aesthetically mediated experience of transcendence. Experiences of transcendence can be understood as *experiences of divinity*, and the sense of beauty artistically expressed by the film thus appears as a *disposition for experiencing divinity*. In fact, the aesthetically mediated experience of transcendence is neither the same as nor something entirely different from the experience of divinity. In so far as we talk about experience, and not just impressions, aesthetic experience is by definition experience of transcendence. This has been said already by the metaphysics of beauty; the same message is found in philosophical aesthetics, and even, as was demonstrated, in hermeneutic phenomenology as well, whether the aesthetic experience is treated as an experience of beauty or as an experience of the sublime. Religious experiences are of course also experiences of transcendence, but the object of religious experience is something transcendent, regarded as God by the religious person. Conversely, the object of aesthetic experience is something immanent that is regarded as secular by the experiencer, and which has in modernity been limited to the formal side of a universe of objects generally classified as art. As mentioned, both religious and aesthetic experiences are experiences of transcendence, however, and if we want to reflect on this fact, we must have a terminology for the relation. One possibility is to simply speak in abstract terms about transcendence, in order not to repel people who reject religion. Another is to use the term 'experience of divinity,' but devoid of any religious meaning.[193]

Dasein does not only transcend; it is not just ecstatic, not only in a state of already being elsewhere, along with something else. Dasein also interprets permanently, already understands, by virtue of its emotional sensitivity, and its interpretations are historically situated. We sense and understand in the place where we find ourselves, and with the load of knowledge and experience we have in that context. The same thing can, therefore, be interpreted differently, depending on who interprets and where and when the interpretation takes place, but what is interpreted is—at least partly—still the same. It is exactly such a duality of rupture and continuity that characterizes what in *Skønhedens metamorfose* (The Metamorphosis of Beauty) and later works was called 'experience of divinity,' and which is a reference to experience of transcendence. In these works the term 'experience of divinity' is not used synonymously with 'religious experience,' but serves to denote what is *common* to, for example, religious and aesthetic experiences. Conversely, this also entails that both religious and aesthetic experiences are *interpretations* of experience of divinity; they are different interpretations of the same common element of transcendence. The term 'experience of divinity' thus denotes the very experience of a surplus of meaning characterized by cohesion and meaningfulness according to which there is something with intrinsic value, and accordingly also something that is absolute. It was this surplus of meaning that the metaphysics of beauty was al-

---

[193] I introduced the concept of 'experience of divinity' used here in 1999, in the article "Profan metafysik: Om det guddommelige i metafysikken" (Profane Metaphysics: On the Divine in Metaphysics) in *Kritisk forum for praktisk teologi* (Critical Forum for Practical Theology) Vol. 78 (1999): 80–94. This concept became more widely known when in 2001 I published the book *Skønhedens metamorfose: De æstetiske idéers historie* (The Metamorphosis of Beauty: History of Aesthetic Ideas) (Odense: Odense University Press, 2001). Since then I have elaborated it in *Historien som værk: Værkets historie* (History as a Work: The Work's History) (Aarhus: Aarhus University Press, 2006), *Skønhed—En engel gik forbi*, and *Aglaias dans: På vej mod en æstetisk tænkning* (Aglaia's Dance: Toward an Aesthetic Thinking) (Aarhus: Aarhus University Press, 2008), and it is commented on in *Den skønne tænkning*. See also the chapter "Immanent Transcendence" in *Poetic Inclinations*, and the chapter "The Metamorphosis of Beauty" in the present volume.

ready aware of and termed 'the beautiful.' It is the same surplus of meaning various theologians have contemplated, but spoken about as 'God' and 'the beauty of God,' changing experience of beauty into religious experience. It was also this surplus of meaning that modern philosophers began to treat as something aesthetic, moving the focus from God and his creation to the man-made work of art and its secular beauty.

The term 'experience of divinity' is inspired by the early testimony about interpreting the experience of transcendence that is constituted by the Homeric tale about the genesis of poetry: that poetry comes into being when a poet is seized by *divine madness*, and thrown into *inspired ecstasy*. Thus, 'experience of divinity' basically refers to the event Homer thought the birth of poetic language was—rather than aiming at anything religious in a theological sense. This justifies the use of 'experience of divinity' as a term for the experience of transcendence as such—and not specifically religious experience (which is itself, however, an *interpretative manifestation* of the experience of divinity). The interpretative history of the experience of divinity is long, and in *Skønhedens metamorfose* and kindred works of mine the latest addition has been termed 'experience of immanent transcendence.' However, in the previous pages the term 'immanent transcendence' was also used in a wider sense. It was used to denote the occurrence, *pure and simple*, of transcendence in immanence. Conversely, in *Skønhedens metamorfose* and kindred works, the same term was used in a narrower sense, referring to a specifically contemporary interpretation of the experience of divinity.[194] In that case, the designation 'experience of immanent transcendence' presupposes not only transcendence in immanence but also an *absence of ability to interpret the event that the experience of transcendence essentially is*. In the case of experience of immanent transcendence in this narrow sense, the one who is thrown into the experience is hesitant as to what is happening. The person is unable to interpret it with reference to the

---

194 As mentioned earlier, this understanding of 'immanent transcendence' is also applied elsewhere in the present volume and in *Poetic Inclinations*.

traditional religions and philosophies—he or she has no clue to the meaning of what occurred. This, too, is an experience of a surplus of meaning, but here the occurrence remains indefinite and therefore it is all the more disturbing to the daily order of things.[195]

In *The Pillow Book*, it is not only the words about divine creation uttered by Nagiko's father, when he calligraphed on her face, that call the religious to mind. For example, Greenaway alludes to the sacrifice of Christ when he has Nagiko's lover, Jerome, offer her something that in the film is actually termed a sacrifice, and which he eventually dies of, while she actualizes herself as an author. However, the gaze that finds artistic expression in *The Pillow Book* is, as stated previously, of a creative nature; this characterizes the idiom of the film, with its experiments with the fragmented images of TV and computer games. Furthermore, the creative aspect of the gaze expressed in this film is also evident in its content, where Greenaway steers clear of all dogmatism. He presents his own artistic

---

195   To address the phenomenology of experience comprising experience of divinity as such and the interpretations of it that consist of its various manifestations, for example religious and aesthetic experience, I proposed in the article "Guddommelighedserfaring i en moderne verden" (Experiencing Divinity in a Modern World) that a discipline called *aesthetics of religion* be developed. See Dorthe Jørgensen, "Guddommelighedserfaring i en moderne verden," in *Interesse for Gud: Ni essay* (Interest in God: Nine Essays), eds. H. Brandt-Pedersen and N. Grønkjær (Frederiksberg: Anis, 2002). In 2004, a German translation by C. Diehn titled "Erfahrung von Göttlichkeit in einer modernen Welt" was published in *Gelebte Religionen: Untersuchungen zur sozialen Gestaltungskraft religiöser Vorstellungen und Praktiken in Geschichte und Gegenwart. Festschrift für Hartmut Zinser zum 60. Geburtstag*, eds. H. Piegeler et al. (Würzburg: Königshausen and Neumann, 2004).

The term 'aesthetics of religion' has been used in Germany since 1988 for a discipline of *religious studies* of a nontheological and thus actually also a nonphilosophical character. However, in my aforementioned article, I introduced it as a term for a *philosophical* discipline. My message was that a philosophical concept of aesthetics of religion can be of service to the development of—and is necessary to—the theoretical foundation that both theology and religious studies need when working with aesthetic phenomena, not least to enable them to approach a thematization of not only religious or aesthetic experience, for instance, but also the experience of divinity.

However, the already established meaning in religious studies of the term 'aesthetics of religion,' and its connotation of cultural analysis rather than systematic thought, is difficult to escape. This is one of several reasons why, in a number of recent works, like *Den skønne tænkning* and the article "Teologisk æstetik i Norden?," I argue for *theological aesthetics*. See Dorthe Jørgensen, "Teologisk æstetik i Norden? Den 'æstetiske vending' til diskussion" (Theological Aesthetics in the Nordic Region? Questioning the 'Aesthetic Turn'), in *Kontinuitet og radikalisme* (Continuity and Radicalism), eds. K. Garne and R. Vangshardt (Copenhagen: Vartov, 2013).

interpretation of late modern man's experience of aesthetically mediated transcendence, and the result suggests how people without firm points of reference might handle the openness to transcendence to which Dasein is doomed. As Dasein, we have always already interpreted what we sense, but as late modern people, for whom tradition has been eroded, we no longer understand what we understand. It could be so easy: something has intrinsic value and so it *is*—we all experience this. Instead, however, it is infinitely difficult. Today few dare use the words 'God' or 'beauty.' We therefore need works such as Greenaway's—works that take up the phenomenon, the experience of transcendence that still occurs, and give it artistic expression without forcing on anyone anything that can stand in the way of the phenomenon itself.

The Philosophy of Imagination

Introduction

"Reading is a waste of time for those who dislike spending time with images," wrote Gaston Bachelard.[196] To allow the images in a text to emerge—that is the aim of reading. It is a waste of time, then, to rush through a text in order to get to something other than simply reading it. One must devote oneself to what is written and to enjoying it; one must become absorbed in reading the text at hand and allow its images to nourish the mind. One must spend time with these images and allow the imagination to be stimulated, which also allows for the possibility that the reader and author will meet. We meet in the realm of imagination, for the images are its product, and not only in the reader's vision of it, but also in the author's. "A word is a bud attempting to become a twig. How can one not dream while writing? It is the pen which dreams. The blank page gives the right to dream."[197]

With Bachelard, we are a long way into the history of imagination and deep into its philosophy. His reflections on 'reverie,' as he also called it, are from the twentieth century, and they presuppose a history that has roots deep in antiquity, in both Greek and Jewish thought. We must be familiar with the paths leading back into this

---

[196] Gaston Bachelard, *Earth and Reveries of Will: An Essay on the Imagination of Matter*, trans. K. Haltman (Dallas: The Dallas Institute Publications, 2002), 212.

[197] Gaston Bachelard, *The Poetics of Reverie: Childhood, Language, and the Cosmos*, trans. D. Russell (Boston: Beacon Press, 1971), 17.

history for several reasons: in order to understand the thoughts formulated by Bachelard, in order to assess other interpretations of the imagination, and in order to be in a position to express ourselves with precision and relevance regarding the matter. The aim is to make a philosophical contribution to our contemporary understanding of the imagination, and to do so with an eye to what was written about it by earlier thinkers. However, in this chapter it is not possible to treat all the interpretations of imagination that have been formulated in the course of history; therefore we will focus on a selection of the most important ones.

Plato and Aristotle represent two great traditions in the history of the ancient interpretations of imagination: one based on a theory of inspiration, and the other based on epistemological considerations. These two traditions were fused in the philosophy of Immanuel Kant, whose 'Copernican revolution' with regard to thought became an unavoidable presupposition for later philosophy. His philosophy has left its mark on hermeneutic phenomenology in particular, which has not only taken account of his 'revolution,' but also attempted to get beyond the subjectivism it implied. The result has been a desubjectification of the imagination, the roots of which can be traced back to Kant's time. In what follows, theories of imagination by Plato, Aristotle, and Kant will be presented along with interpretations of their thinking from the hermeneutic phenomenological tradition. Other important positions from the medieval and modern periods will also be addressed, including those of Giambattista Vico and Alexander Gottlieb Baumgarten. Furthermore, a sketch of the current research scene will be provided, and the chapter will conclude with an alternative to the current trends: an interpretation of imagination grounded in a philosophy of experience.

The Roots of Imagination
Even in the Bible it is possible to see the contours of later understandings of imagination, particularly in the notions that it is a creative power or a cognitive faculty. Using the Hebrew word *bara*, the

biblical creation story in Genesis 1:1 tells of God's creation of the universe, which was brought forth out of nothing, through a power that only He possesses. Though *bara* does not necessarily mean to create something out of nothing, the Bible only uses it of God. Genesis 2:7, on the other hand, speaks of the creation of man from dust, which is described with the word *yatsar* (to form or fashion). This indicates the ability to create by giving shape to matter, an ability that is common to both God and humans. Based on that, *yetser* (form or frame) became the term for imagination understood as the ability to participate in the divine power of creation, and seen as something that can be both 'good' and 'evil.'[198] The 'good imagination' (*yetser hatov*) is the source of the I–thou dialogue between human being and Creator. The 'evil imagination' (*yetser hara*), on the other hand, is an expression of the desire to transcend the boundaries designated by God, a desire that Adam and Eve were infected with when they attempted to appropriate His insight and power of creation.[199] The prohibition in the Law of Moses against making an image of God was aimed at the latter form of imagination, here understood as the desire to depict something we ought not depict because we could never represent it correctly.

In the beginning, the Greeks also associated the imagination and its images (*phantasia* and *phantasmata*) with the divine. Homer's idea that poetry originates from *theia mania* (divine madness) infused by the muse into the poet, together with the *enthusiasmos* (enthusiasm) that thus seizes him and makes him break into song, can be viewed as a mythological expression for imagination.[200] Plato inherited this Homeric 'theory of inspiration' but combined it with his own 'mimetic theory';[201] in addition, he made a distinc-

---

198 J. Robert Barth, "Imagination," in *New Dictionary of the History of Ideas, Volume 3*, ed. M.C. Horowitz (New York: Charles Scribner's Sons, 2005), 1102.

199 Barth, "Imagination," 1102–1103.

200 Homer, *The Odyssey*, ed. L.R. Loomis, trans. S. Butler (Cabin John: Wildside Press, 2007), 90 (Od. 8.62–65 and 8.73–74).

201 For example, Plato, *Phaedrus*, trans. A. Nehamas and P. Woodruff, in *Plato: Complete Works*, eds. J.M. Cooper and D.S. Hutchinson (Indianapolis and Cambridge, MA: Hackett

tion between *eikasia* and *phantasia*, as well as between 'good' and 'bad' *eikasia/phantasia*.[202] Another mythological expression of the connection between imagination and divinity is the Greek myth about how Prometheus stole fire from heaven and passed it on to mankind. Plato treats this myth in *Protagoras*, where Prometheus' theft is viewed as much more than an appropriation of fire in the usual sense, that is, as an appropriation of the gods' source of energy.[203] Fire is a condition for "wisdom in the practical arts": the ability to produce and engage in actions that bring about change.[204] Even though Prometheus gave humankind this ability, his gift did not bring human beings to the same level as the gods. Human actions and products remained imperfect copies of the actions and products of the gods.

Since the ancient Greeks, then, there has been a tradition of two different philosophical conceptions of imagination. It has been either associated with creativity and irrationality, or understood as a capacity of the soul to connect sense and intellect, thus serving to bring about rational knowledge.[205] While both conceptions of the imagination can be traced back to Plato, the former is nevertheless often spoken of as 'Platonic' and the latter as 'Aristotelian.' The 'Platonic' conception characterized Christian mysticism, for example, while the 'Aristotelian' conception was a hallmark of scholasticism.

In both traditions, the imagination was primarily referred to by the Latin term *imaginatio* (dream, imagination, fantasy), which

Publishing Company, 1997), 244a–257a.

202   See the section "Plato and Aristotle" in the present chapter.

203   Plato, *Protagoras*, trans. S. Lombardo and K. Bell, in *Plato: Complete Works*, eds. J.M. Cooper and D.S. Hutchinson (Indianapolis and Cambridge, MA: Hackett Publishing Company, 1997), 320c–322a.

204   Plato, *Protagoras*, 321d.

205   In English, what in Danish is termed *erkendelse* (German *Erkenntnis*) is translated not only as 'cognition' but also, for example, as 'knowledge,' though 'knowledge' literally means *viden* (German *Wissen*), not *erkendelse*. Likewise, *at erkende* (German *Erkennen*) is often translated as 'to know,' not as 'to cognize.' For the sake of precision I usually prefer to write 'cognition' or 'to cognize,' when I mean *erkendelse* or *at erkende*, but for the sake of convention, linguistic variation, and readability I do sometimes abstain from this rule.

the modern word 'imagination' points back to. *Imaginatio* stems from *imago* (copy, likeness), which originally reflected the Greek word *eikon* (image, copy). The word 'imagination' corresponds in this way to *eikasia* (to make or see images, likelihoods, and conjectures), which stems from *eiko* (to be like).[206] Traditionally, however, philosophers have primarily used the word *phantasia*—not *eikasia*—as a Greek synonym for *imaginatio*, and thus many now say not only that 'imagination' stems from *imaginatio* but also that *imaginatio* is a translation of *phantasia*. In fact, 'imagination' and *phantasia* are often simply equated, even though *phantasia* stems from *phantazo* (to cause to appear, make visible), which is a derivative of *phaino* (to bring forth into the light, shine, appear, be apparent), and even though *phantasia* is thus also connected to *phos* (light) and *phanos* (torch).[207] The two terms are even equated when a rather different quality of imagination is the focus—which is often the case—namely that which corresponds to *eikasia*, that is, that which has to do with images, imitation, and similarities.

Plato and Aristotle

In dialogues such as the *Phaedrus* and the *Symposium*, Plato showed how a meeting with the beautiful in the world can provide the soul with wings and the possibility of again contemplating the ideas in the heavens that had been forgotten.[208] These dialogues can be read as stories about how the experience of beauty can awaken *phantasia*, which, when assisted by the appearance of beauty, can contrib-

---

206   Murray Wright Bundy, *The Theory of Imagination in Classical and Mediaeval Thought*, University of Illinois Studies in Language and Literature Vol. 12, No. 2–3 (May-August 1927) (Urbana: The University of Illinois Press, 1927), 11.

207   Bundy, *The Theory of Imagination*, 12; *New Testament Greek Lexicon—King James Version*, http://www.biblestudytools.com/lexicons/greek/kjv, accessed July 30, 2015.

208   Plato, *Symposium*, trans. A. Nehamas and P. Woodruff, in *Plato: Complete Works*, eds. J.M. Cooper and D.S. Hutchinson (Indianapolis and Cambridge, MA: Hackett Publishing Company, 1997).

ute to the healing of the soul and lead to true knowledge.[209] In the *Republic*, however, *eikasia* is placed at the bottom of the allegory of cognition known as the Analogy of the Divided Line; because of its illusionary character, *eikasia* resides far below the boundary of true knowledge.[210] And in the *Sophist*, *phantasia* is understood—in conjunction with a distinction between "speech"/"thought" (*logos/dianoia*), "opinion" (*doxa*), and "seeming" or "fancy" (*phantasia*)—as "a mixture of sensation and opinion," that is, opinion brought about through sensation.[211] This combination of sensation and opinion, however, also implies that *phantasia* is a form of judgment, evaluation, or interpretation, but different in kind from pure judgment (logical or rational judgment, free of sensation). *Eikasia*'s world of objects consists of the 'illusions' (dreams, shadow figures, and mirror images, as well as paintings) produced by the 'image-making' in both nature and culture, that is, the image-making of both God and humans. *Eikasia* is simply the term that describes the comprehension of such images (without interpreting them qualitatively). The objects of *phantasia*, on the other hand, are the 'things themselves' in their appearance, that is, everything originating in God's or man's 'making of real things' (natural objects and crafted objects), and *phantasia* does not merely sense things but understands them as the appearances they are. It can be deceptive, but if guided by reason and its 'love of wisdom' (*philosophia*), *phantasia* can also

---

209 According to Leonard Brandwood, *A Word Index to Plato* (Leeds: W.S. Maney and Son, 1976), 933, Plato only uses the word *phantasia* in seven places, however; these are: *Republic*, II 382e 10; *Theaetetus*, 152c 1, 161e 8; *Sophist*, 260c 9, 260e 4, 263d 6, 264a 6. For Plato's works in both Greek and English, see *Perseus Digital Library*, ed. G.R. Crane, Tufts University, http://www.perseus.tufts.edu, accessed July 27, 2020.

210 Plato, *Republic*, trans. G.M.A. Grube, rev. C.D.C. Reeve, in *Plato: Complete Works*, eds. J.M. Cooper and D.S. Hutchinson (Indianapolis and Cambridge, MA: Hackett Publishing Company, 1997), 509d–511e.

211 Plato, *Sophist*, 263d–264b. It is *phainetai* that are said to be "a mixture of sensation and opinion," but this also means that the reference is to *phantasia* rather than *logos* or *doxa*. I follow Harold N. Fowler's translation of the *Sophist* in *Perseus Digital Library* instead of Nicholas P. White's in *Plato: Complete Works*, as the former is more consistent with the general terminology of the present chapter. White translates *logos/dianoia*, *doxa*, and *phantasia* as 'speech/thought,' 'belief,' and 'appearance'; he thus identifies phantasia as a "blending of perception and belief," that is, belief brought about by perception.

serve the development of true knowledge and high moral character—which is also the case with poetry, if it is inspired, and the beautiful, if we contemplate it.

Unlike Plato, Aristotle was not interested in imagination's connection with the divine. His treatment was psychological rather than metaphysical and he was more occupied with its epistemological role than with its nature as inspired intuition. Thus, in *On the Soul*, in which he investigates the various powers of the soul, imagination—which he terms *phantasia*—is one of these powers.[212] He differentiates between "sense," "imagination," and "thought," or in Greek: *aisthesis, phantasia,* and *noein*.[213] Furthermore, he distinguishes between *phantasia logistike* (calculative imagination), which is specific to human beings, and *phantasia aisthetike* (sensitive imagination), which is common to humans and animals.[214] According to Aristotle, imagination is "that in virtue of which an image arises for us."[215] In the imagination, *phantasmata* (images) emerge that emanate from sensation, but which are then independent, and, in this way, imagination mediates between sense and thought. The imagination thus represents the ability in both animals and humans to create, store, and retrieve images, which are part of various cognitive activities. This ability is to thought what sense is to imagination, for "images are like sensuous contents except in that they contain no matter," and the soul never thinks without images.[216] Though conceptions of thought (*noemata*) are not images, they do

---

[212] Aristotle, *On the Soul*, trans. J.A. Smith, in *The Complete Works of Aristotle: The Revised Oxford Translation, Volume 1*, ed. J. Barnes (Princeton: Princeton University Press, 1984).

[213] Aristotle, *On the Soul*, III.3, 428a 4ff. For *aisthesis*, see III.2; for *phantasia*, see III.3. In Smith's English translation of Aristotle's work, *aisthesis* understood as a faculty is termed 'sense,' whereas *aisthesis* understood as an activity is termed 'sensation,' and the products of this activity are called 'sensations.' *Aisthesis* means not only physical sense or sensation but also sense and sensation of a more comprehensive nature. *Noein* is actually thinking understood as activity, that is, as in 'to think.'

[214] Aristotle, *On the Soul*, III.10, 433b 29–30.

[215] Aristotle, *On the Soul*, III.3, 428a 1–2.

[216] Aristotle, *On the Soul*, III.8, 432a 9–13.

not exist without images, and because Aristotle thinks that what can be thought is contained in that which can be sensed, it is not possible to think without sensation and images.

Philosophy before Kant

Plato's and Aristotle's understandings of the imagination were diligently reproduced in the Middle Ages, the Renaissance, and the philosophies of the seventeenth and eighteenth centuries, and there are still traces of them in contemporary philosophy. At the beginning of the medieval period, Augustine carried forward the suspicion of images (*phantasmata*) found in Plato and the Bible, but also Aristotle's consideration that the imagination (*phantasia*) is of essential cognitive importance.[217] He identified the will's central role in imagination, and his use of not only *phantasia* but also *imaginatio* laid the groundwork for posterity's use of the Latin term.[218] Later, Thomas Aquinas considered the imagination to be one of the four "inner senses" (*sensus interiores*), which are "common sense," "imagination," "memorative powers," and "estimative powers" (*sensus communis, imaginatio/phantasia, memoria, vis cogitativa*).[219] Analogous to Aristotle, he considered imagination to be a link between sense and intellect ('thought,' in Aristotle's terms), which is necessary for cognition, but its images must be processed intellectually.[220] Contrary to this, Bonaventure, in his *Journey of the Mind*

---

[217] Augustine, *On Music (De musica)*, trans, R.C. Taliaferro, in *The Immortality of the Soul; The Magnitude of the Soul; On Music; The Advantage of Believing; On Faith in Things Unseen* (Washington: The Catholic University of America Press, 2002), VI, 11 [32], and *The Trinity*, trans. S. McKenna, in *The Fathers of the Church: A New Translation, Volume 45*, eds. H. Dressler et al. (Washington: The Catholic University of America Press, 2002), XI. 1–2; see also M. Djuth, "Veiled and Unveiled Beauty: The Role of the Imagination in Augustine's Esthetic," *Theological Studies* Vol. 68 (2007): 79–83.

[218] Todd Breyfogle, "Imagination," in *Augustine through the Ages: An Encyclopedia*, eds. A.D. Fitzgerald et al. (Grand Rapids and Cambridge, UK: William B. Eerdmans Publishing Company, 1999), 443.

[219] Thomas Aquinas, *The Summa Theologica: Complete Edition*, trans. The Fathers of the English Dominican Province (London: Catholic Way Publishing, 2014), I, q. 78, art. 4.

[220] Thomas Aquinas, *Summa Theologica*, I, q. 84, art. 7; I, q. 85, art. 1.

to God (Itinerarium Mentis in Deum) described the imagination as a source of mystical insight, which, however, must be controlled by reason, as both Plato and Augustine had pointed out. Thought must move from sensation to illumination via six stages (*sensus, imaginatio, ratio, intellectus, intelligentia, synderesis*)—conveyed by imagination and reason, among other things.[221]

Dante Alighieri gathered these different traditions with his portrayal in *The New Life* (La Vita Nuova) of the images of imagination as sensory reproductions,[222] which were also independent of sensation. The latter is illustrated in the statement in the seventeenth canto of *Purgatorio* that the imagination (*fantasia*) receives its images as "rain from high heavens."[223] Because they come from above—from a higher power, not from sensation—the imagination is not in need of guidance from reason, even though, according to Dante, it still cannot represent the divine.[224] It was, however, not until Gianfrancesco Pico della Mirandola's *On the Imagination* (De Imaginatione), written in the year 1500, that a text focused exclusively on the imagination.[225] Pico synthesized the positions of the ancients, the medieval period, and his own time (the new Platonism of the Renaissance and Girolamo Savonarola). Referring to Aristotle, he considered imagination to be a power to produce forms, which is set in motion by sensations, but the productivity of which is not controlled by them.[226] Imagination makes the sensed

---

221   Bonaventure, *Itinerarium Mentis in Deum*, in *Works of St. Bonaventure, Volume 2*, eds. Ph. Boehner and Z. Hayes (New York: The Franciscan Institute, St. Bonaventure University, 2003), I, 6.

222   Dante Alighieri, *Vita nuova*, trans. D.S. Cervigni and E. Vasta (Notre Dame: The University of Notre Dame Press, 1995).

223   Dante Alighieri, *Purgatorio*, trans. J. Hollander and R. Hollander (New York: Doubleday, 2003), 17.25.

224   Dante Alighieri, *Paradiso*, trans. J. Hollander and R. Hollander (New York: Doubleday, 2007), 19.9; 24.19–27.

225   Gianfrancesco Pico della Mirandola, *On the Imagination*, trans. H. Caplan (New Haven: Yale University Press, 1930).

226   Pico, *On the Imagination*, IV, 32/33. "A power of the soul which out of itself produces

available for cognition—it links the material and immaterial—but can also be a source of distortion and can thus corrupt the soul.[227] Therefore, its images must be processed by reason (*ratio*) and intellect (*intellect*).[228]

With Aristotle as their starting point, the philosophical rationalists of the seventeenth and eighteenth centuries also gave imagination cognitive significance, understood as the mental reproduction of sense data that is necessary for cognition. They, however, considered the imagination and its images to be considerably lower than the understanding and its concepts; as they saw it, the imagination is a necessary but completely insufficient condition for true cognition. This is precisely what Vico and Baumgarten objected to. Even though they had roots in rationalism, they called into question its 'scientism,' that is, its prioritization of the 'higher' cognitive faculties (intellect and reason) at the expense of the 'lower' cognitive faculties (including imagination), and its associated ideal of science (according to which truth is limited to that for which rational proof can be given).[229] In Vico's case, this questioning was manifest in a rehabilitation of myth and imagination, which was formulated within the framework of a historicist philosophy of science. With Baumgarten, it appeared with his introduction of the concept of 'sensitive cognition,' which took place within the framework of a systematic theory of cognition termed 'aesthetics.'

In *The New Science* (La Scienza Nuova, 1725), Vico described the oldest—mythological—thinking as characterized by "poetic wisdom" (*sapienza poetica*).[230] This thinking was sensuous but also

forms," he writes. But although imagination is productive in itself, it is not creative: it reproduces and combines what it receives from the senses.

227   Pico, *On the Imagination*, II, 28/29f.; VI–VII.

228   Pico, *On the Imagination*, X–XI.

229   As mentioned in the chapter "Experience, Metaphysics, and Immanent Transcendence," footnote 102, the word 'faculty' applies to both the cognitive faculty as such with its two parts and the specific faculties constituting the dispositions of those parts.

230   Giambattista Vico, *The New Science of Giambattista Vico: Unabridged Translation of the Third Edition (1744) with the Addition of "Practice of the New Science,"* trans. T.G. Bergin

interpretive, because human sensation is imaginative. Both animals and humans register external stimuli and react mechanically to them (for example, they are naturally afraid of fire), but humans also interpret what they register (for instance, they read fire as an expression of divine rage). The latter is due to our capacity to imagine, which according to Vico includes *fantasia* (imagination—the ability to alter or imitate things), *ingegno* (ingenuity or invention—the ability to create correspondence between things), and *memoria* (memory—the ability to remember things).[231] This mythological interpretation, which is carried out by sensation and spoken of as 'poetic' by Vico, is different, thanks to its imaginative character, from the intellectual interpretation that we employ when we think rationally. It results not in rational intelligible universals, which are abstract, but in "poetic universals" (*universali poetici*), also called "imaginative universals" (*universali fantastici*).[232] While rational and intelligible universals arise through a naming of things, imaginative poetic universals arise through an imitation of events.

Mythological thought, which is the source of poetic universals, can still be seen in children, according to Vico, as they think mimetically: they try to understand what happens around them by imitating it.[233] Children imagine just as ancient people did when they began to use language. The earliest people to use language imitated that which they experienced with actions accompanied by one-syllable words. Their words were "onomatopoeia" (phonetic imitations of sounds) and products of "interjections" ("sounds articulated under the impetus of violent passions," that is, outbursts

---

and M.H. Fisch (Ithaca and London: Cornell University Press, 1984). The second part of this work is titled "Book Two: Poetic Wisdom."

231 Vico, *The New Science*, §§ 699, 819. Vico actually states that *memory* includes fantasia, ingegno, and memoria, but "memory is the same as imagination" (§ 819).

232 Vico, *The New Science*, §§ 209, 460, 933–934. In the English translation of Vico's work, universals are also referred to as "class concepts."

233 Vico, *The New Science*, §§ 215–217.

of emotion);[234] they were metaphors created in order to understand what they experienced and in order to express themselves.[235] Since that time, mythological thought and poetic language have been replaced by rational thought and its abstract conceptual language, but according to Vico, we miss essential knowledge if we only think rationally and speak abstractly. He thus thought there was a need for a 'new science'—with a better feel for the significance of myth and imagination.

In *Reflections on Poetry* (Meditationes Philosophicae de Nonnullis Ad Poema Pertinentibus, 1735) and *Aesthetica* (Aesthetics, 1750–1758), Baumgarten introduced a theory of cognition that broke with the rationalistic dogma that true cognition is necessarily identical with intellectual cognition, that is, logical (conceptual) cognition.[236] He described another form of cognition, the source of which is the lower rather than the higher cognitive faculties, but which is true, nonetheless. This "sensitive cognition" (*cognitio sensitiva*) is different from both sheer physical sensation and ordinary intellectual cognition. It constitutes a *third* way of accessing the world, which gives insight into wider contexts—rather than merely delivering sense impressions or simply acting to determine objects. This insight is the product of an especially successful interplay of the faculties encompassed by sensitivity, that is, "the senses" (*sensus*), "imagination" (*phantasia*),[237] "perspicaciousness" (*perspicacia*), "memory" (*memoria*), "the faculty of invention" (*facultas*

---

234 Vico, *The New Science*, §§ 447–448.

235 Vico, *The New Science*, § 456.

236 Alexander Gottlieb Baumgarten, *Reflections on Poetry: Alexander Gottlieb Baumgarten's Meditationes Philosophicae de Nonnullis Ad Poema Pertinentibus*, trans. K. Aschenbrenner and W.B. Holter (Berkely and Los Angeles: University of California Press, 1954), and *Ästhetik, Volume 1–2*, trans D. Mirbach (Hamburg: Felix Meiner Verlag, 2007).

237 Baumgarten wrote in Latin, but translated *facultas imaginandi* (for him, the same thing as *phantasia*) as *Einbildungskraft*. See Alexander Gottlieb Baumgarten, *Metaphysica. Editio VII. Reprographischer Nachdruck der Ausgabe Halle 1779* (Hildesheim: Georg Olms Verlagsbuchhandlung, 1963), § 571. For an English translation of this work, see *Metaphysics: A Critical Translation with Kant's Elucidations, Selected Notes, and Related Materials*, eds. and trans. C.D. Fugate and J. Hymers (London: Bloomsbury Academic, 2014).

fingendi), "foresight" (*praevisio*), "judgment" (*iudicium*), "anticipation" (*praesagitio*), and "the faculty of characterization" (*facultas characteristica*).[238]

It was with this new theory of cognition—this philosophy about sensitive cognition—that Baumgarten introduced aesthetics as an independent philosophical discipline.[239] Originally, aesthetics was thus neither theory of sensation nor philosophy of art, let alone theory about 'aestheticism' or 'aestheticization.' On the contrary, aesthetics was the philosophy of a sensitive form of true cognition, the cognitive value of which is due to the play among the lower cognitive faculties that is its source. In this new theory of cognition called 'aesthetics,' the imagination and other lower cognitive faculties were no longer considered to be something that can only be a contributor to cognition carried out by a higher faculty. Instead, the lower faculties of cognition were now considered to produce an independent form of true cognition, which does not rank lower than the intellectual cognition of the higher faculties but, on the contrary, is analogous to that cognition and potentially even stronger than it.[240]

---

238   This is the formulation of the first of Baumgarten's two specifications in *Metaphysics* (§§ 534–623; 640), which is the foundation for his treatment in *Ästhetik* §§ 30–37 of the interplay of the lower cognitive faculties that characterizes 'the lucky aesthete' (*felix aestheticus*, the beautifully thinking person). See Dorthe Jørgensen, *Den skønne tænkning: Veje til erfaringsmetafysk. Religionfilosofisk udmøntet* (Beautiful Thinking: Pathways to the Metaphysics of Experience. Religio-Philosophically Implemented) (Aarhus University Press, 2014), 827–833.

239   Baumgarten, *Reflections on Poetry*, § CXVI; *Ästhetik*, § 1. Art theory and the metaphysics of beauty had existed since antiquity, but they were not independent philosophical disciplines, and their central object of study was not sensitive cognition (aesthetic experience), but art and the beautiful, respectively. See Dorthe Jørgensen, "The Relevance of Aesthetics," in *Poetic Inclinations: Ethics, History, Philosophy* (Aarhus: Aarhus University Press, 2021), and the chapter "The Metamorphosis of Beauty" in the present volume.

240   For a developed presentation of this interpretation of aesthetics, see Jørgensen, *Den skønne tænkning*, 83–158 (English summary of book, 947–965). See also the chapters "Experience, Metaphysics, and Immanent Transcendence" and "Sensuousness and Transcendence" in the present volume for more on the significance of imagination for sensitive cognition.

Facultas Imaginandi

For Plato, Aristotle, and their successors, it was a given that it is the object that is determinate for cognition. The images proceed from the object, so to speak; they are its replica in the mind. This way of thinking lasted all the way to the end of the eighteenth century, even though cognition was partially moved toward the subject with Baumgarten's aesthetics.[241] However, in his *Critique of Pure Reason* Kant entirely inverted the mode of thinking so that it was now the mind that determined the cognition.[242] This 'Copernican revolution' also altered the understanding of imagination, which Kant called *Einbildungskraft*.[243] In analogy with the mediation of imagination between sense and thought in Aristotle's philosophy, for Kant imagination mediated between sensibility and understanding, but this mediation happened on another basis.[244] Hitherto, it had been assumed that we can know things as they are 'in themselves.' According to Kant, however, we can only know them as they 'appear to us.' That which is known is always influenced by the subject because cognition presupposes this appearance and the appearance is determined by the framework that is given with the consciousness for which it appears.

According to Kant, all cognition needs both intuition and concept, for "thoughts without content are empty, intuitions with-

---

241   Jørgensen, *Den skønne tænkning*, 127–128.

242   Immanuel Kant, *Critique of Pure Reason*, eds. and trans. P. Guyer and A.W. Wood (Cambridge, UK: Cambridge University Press, 1998).

243   Rudolf Eisler, "Einbildungskraft," in *Kant-Lexikon: Nachschlagewerk zu Kants sämtlichen Schriften, Briefen und handschriftlichen Nachlass*, 1930, http://www.textlog.de/rudolf-eisler.html, accessed July 22, 2015.

244   Kant differentiated between 'sensation' (*Empfindung*) and 'sensibility' (*Sinnlichkeit*) (*Critique of Pure Reason*, A19–20/B33–34). 'Sensibility' is the ability to have 'intuitions' (*Anschauungen*). (The meaning of the Kantian term 'intuition' is very different from contemporary everyday usage of this word. In a Kantian context, intuition has nothing to do with insight but may loosely be called 'perception.') 'Sensation' is the stimulation of the senses by the real presence of an object affecting them. It always expresses the empirical moment in sensibility, while intuition can be either empirical or pure.

out concepts are blind."[245] All cognition, therefore, involves both sensibility and understanding, receptivity and spontaneity, the faculty of receiving impressions and the faculty of producing and using concepts. Of these faculties, sensibility is receptive and therefore it is also spoken of by Kant as 'passive.'[246] Sensibility is the source of our intuitions, which arise in the meeting with the world of objects, and which are already beforehand (*a priori*) structured in time and space. In the form of intuition, sensibility delivers the material of cognition while understanding, in return, gives the cognition form by processing conceptually what is intuited. The understanding thinks about that which sensibility has made available. It determines it with the help of the concepts that it itself produces and so it is active; Kant therefore speaks of it as 'spontaneous.'[247]

It is the imagination, as noted, that links sensibility and understanding, and it is described as "the faculty for representing an object even *without its presence* in intuition."[248] The imagination is initially part of sensibility, but because it is spontaneous (determining), it belongs to the understanding too. The imagination is the understanding's "first application (and at the same time the ground of all others) to objects of the intuition that is possible for us."[249] Therefore, it does not just mediate between sensibility and understanding; it has a dual character itself, with both a sensible and a conceptual side. This is why it is possible to differentiate between "reproductive imagination" and "productive imagination," as Kant does in the *Critique of Pure Reason*.[250]

---

245 Kant, *Critique of Pure Reason*, A51/B75.

246 Kant, *Critique of Pure Reason*, A51/B75.

247 Kant, *Critique of Pure Reason*, A51/B75.

248 Kant, *Critique of Pure Reason*, B151.

249 Kant, *Critique of Pure Reason*, B152.

250 Kant, *Critique of Pure Reason*, B152.

The reproductive imagination is empirical; it makes empirical syntheses, and thus it belongs to psychology.[251] It assimilates the object (perhaps without its presence) in the representation and binds it together by following the same rule to which the appearances are subject and which ensures that they are not arbitrary.[252] The productive imagination, on the other hand, which is transcendental, must be investigated transcendentally; it produces transcendental syntheses with which it makes possible the reproductive imagination's reproduction of the appearances.[253] But this also means that the two sides of imagination are connected: its productivity is a condition for its ability to reproduce, and the distinction between reproductive and productive imagination is thus only analytical.

This last point is also evidenced by Kant's deliberations over what he calls "images" and "schemata," respectively.[254] With the term 'images,' he refers to representations that intuitively present (*veranschaulichen*) the understanding's concepts; "if I place five points in a row, ..., this is an image of the number five."[255] Schemata, on the other hand, are rules for the application of the understanding's concepts to empirical intuitions. One can, for instance, simply think a number in general, regardless which one; "this thinking is more the representation of a method for representing a multitude (for example, a thousand) in accordance with a certain concept than the image itself."[256] And this representation of a general procedure of the imagination for providing a concept with its image is the schema for this concept. But even though images are products of imagination's empirical faculty, the source of both im-

---

251 Kant. *Critique of Pure Reason*, B152.

252 Kant, *Critique of Pure Reason*, A100–101.

253 Kant, *Critique of Pure Reason*, A101–102.

254 See Kant's schematism chapter, *Critique of Pure Reason*, A137–147/B176–187.

255 Kant, *Critique of Pure Reason*, A140/B179.

256 Kant, *Critique of Pure Reason*, A140/B179–180.

ages and schemata is found in its productivity.[257] The imagination is fundamentally productive; from a transcendental philosophical point of view, this is what makes it distinctive.

Aesthetic Imagination

Kant's investigations were transcendental. In the *Critique of Pure Reason* (1781), the *Critique of Practical Reason* (1788), and the *Critique of Judgment* (1790), he investigated not only cognition, morality, and taste but also their *conditions of possibility*.[258] Regarding imagination, Kant thus focused on its productive rather than its reproductive aspect. Moreover, the productive imagination treated in the *Critique of Judgment* is of a freer kind than the one dealt with in the *Critique of Pure Reason*. In the cognitive judgments that Kant analyzed in the latter, the imagination served the acquisition of knowledge and was thus in the service of understanding. It was subjected to the demand to make the intuitions correspond to the concepts of understanding. The judgments of taste investigated in part one of the *Critique of Judgment* are different from these cognitive judgments in the sense that, initially at least, there is no concept involved in them. In judgments of taste, there is no concept given beforehand, so here the power of judgment functions "reflectively" rather than "determining"—it is "aesthetic" as opposed to "logical."[259] Because the aesthetic reflecting power of judgment lacks a concept that corresponds to the intuition, it does not use but rather seeks an adequate concept (which it does not find, at least not in the form of one of understanding's concepts). This searching rather than determining reflection sets imagination free; in judg-

---

257 Kant, *Critique of Pure Reason*, A141/B181.

258 Immanuel Kant, *Critique of Practical Reason*, ed. and trans. M.J. Gregor (Cambridge, UK: Cambridge University Press, 1999), and *Critique of the Power of Judgment*, eds. and trans. P. Guyer and E. Matthews (New York: Cambridge University Press, 2000).

259 Kant, *Critique of Judgment*, 15 (20: 211), 89 (5: 203). The adverb 'reflectively' does not appear in Kant's text, but he speaks of "reflecting judgment" and "determining judgment."

ments of taste, imagination does not serve the understanding but, on the contrary, plays along with it.

It is this free productive imagination that is the *aesthetic* imagination. It 'plays' with the wealth of impressions that understanding must abstract from during its identification of objects and its production and employment of concepts. This aesthetic imagination Kant also speaks of as "spirit, in an aesthetic significance," and he describes it as 'life-giving.'[260] It is "the animating [*belebende*] principle in the mind," which consists in "the faculty for the presentation of aesthetic ideas."[261] These *aesthetic* ideas are imagination's counterpart to the *intellectual* ideas of reason. Ideas are concepts of reason (not concepts of understanding), for which no intuition (representation of the imagination) can be adequate.[262] They are "indemonstrable," which means precisely that they are concepts that cannot be intuitively presented;[263] 'God,' 'the soul,' and 'the world as a whole' are examples of ideas of reason. But the *aesthetic* ideas function in an inverse manner. They are representations of the imagination that "occasion much thinking" for which no concept can be adequate.[264] Aesthetic ideas are thus "inexponible."[265] They are representations that cannot be presented with the help of concepts, and thus which no language fully attains or can make intelligible.[266]

Kant's analysis of the judgments of taste, in which the free aesthetic play of imagination manifests itself, shows that it is "the indeterminate idea of the supersensible in us" that is the subjec-

---

260 Kant, *Critique of Judgment*, 192 (5: 313).

261 Kant, *Critique of Judgment*, 192 (5: 313–314).

262 Kant, *Critique of Judgment*, 192 (5: 314).

263 Kant, *Critique of Judgment*, 218 (5: 342).

264 Kant, *Critique of Judgment*, 192 (5: 314).

265 Kant, *Critique of Judgment*, 218 (5: 342).

266 Kant, *Critique of Judgment*, 192 (5: 314).

tive foundation for the universal validity of these judgments.[267] The foundation is something that cannot be made comprehensible, which also means that imagination is a power that is "hidden to us even in its sources."[268] Likewise, in the *Critique of Pure Reason*, Kant wrote that the productive imagination is "a blind though indispensable function of the soul."[269] And the schematism of theoretical reason he described as "a hidden art in the depths of the human soul, whose true operations we can divine from nature and lay unveiled before our eyes only with difficulty."[270] It was through his analysis of the *practical* reason that Kant had come closest to a determination of the supersensible, which is in principle indeterminate.[271] However, now it became evident from his analysis of taste that the actualization of practical reason presupposes the reflecting power of judgment and aesthetic imagination. For ideas of reason are, as noted, about something that can only be thought but not intuitively presented, that is, something transcendent. Therefore the very thinking of an idea of reason requires that, in thought, one can get beyond the sensible in the direction of something supersensible. It presupposes the ability to transcend, which is what imagination or, more precisely, free productive imagination, is. Conceiving of the good life—a central idea for reason—requires *aesthetic* imagination, and this imagination is also necessary in order to actualize this idea in praxis.

This last point appears from § 40 of the *Critique of Judgment*, where this issue is thematized as a question about *expanded thinking*. The expanded way of thinking is the power of judgment's—that

267   Kant, *Critique of Judgment*, 217 (5: 341).

268   Kant, *Critique of Judgment*, 217 (5: 341).

269   Kant, *Critique of Pure Reason*, A78/B103.

270   Kant, *Critique of Pure Reason*, A141/B180–181.

271   To Kant, everything supersensible is indeterminate, that is, not accessible to understanding. Reason, on the other hand, can think of something supersensible, which it does when it creates its ideas of, for instance, the 'thing in itself' (*Critique of Pure Reason*), 'freedom' (*Critique of Practical Reason*), and 'the good' understood as 'the common weal,' that is: what is universally good (*Critique of Judgment*).

is, the aesthetic reflecting power of judgment's—way of thinking; understanding and reason, on the other hand, think 'without prejudice' and 'consistently,' respectively.[272] While understanding's and reason's ways of thinking are 'intellectual,' that is, conceptual (each in its own way), the expanded way of thinking, by contrast, is 'aesthetic,' that is, sensitive. The expanded and as such aesthetic way of thinking is that in which imagination freely plays together with understanding and thus contributes to sympathetic insight, transcendence, and integration—rather than barren abstraction.[273] Precisely *imagination's* contribution to the expanded way of thinking is the condition for that which characterizes this way of thinking, namely, the ability to empathize with other human beings without giving up one's own perspective, and the ability to transcend toward an idea of 'the common weal,' which is necessary in order to be able to integrate a respect for both one's own desires and the desires of others in what one does in praxis. Thus, morality and ethics depend on taste and aesthetics. The actualization of practical reason presupposes aesthetic reflecting judgment. It demands aesthetic imagination, which freely plays together with the understanding, and thus not only makes thought more lively but also makes active life more thoughtful.

Fantasy and Fanaticism

The discussion, however, has not yet addressed *fantasy*, for in Kant's terminology this word denotes not only something other than productive/reproductive imagination but also something other than aesthetic imagination. This is clear from a number of different texts from his hand, including the *Critique of Judgment* and *Anthropolo-*

---

272 Kant, *Critique of Judgment*, 174–175 (5: 294–295). Paul Guyer and Eric Matthews translate Kant's German term *die erweiterte Denkungsart* as 'the broad-minded way of thinking,' but for reasons stated in the chapter "The Significance of Sensitivity," footnote 21, I prefer 'the expanded way of thinking.'

273 This does not mean that no abstraction is taking place. On the contrary, when we think in the expanded way we abstract from what is just private and arbitrary. See Kant, *Critique of Judgment*, 173–175 (5: 293–295).

gy from a Pragmatic Point of View (1798).²⁷⁴ Just as in the *Critique of Pure Reason*, Kant also distinguishes in his anthropology between productive and reproductive imagination, which are also spoken of here as the "inventive" and the "recollective."²⁷⁵ At the same time, he categorizes them together now, as they both serve cognition because they are regulated by understanding, which also means that they can both be viewed as *voluntary* (intended) imagination. This joint categorization is related to the fact that, in his anthropology, Kant is concerned with distinguishing between this form of imagination, which is bound to understanding, and another form that is neither regulated by understanding (as is the case for voluntary imagination) nor plays together with it (as the aesthetic imagination does). Imagination that completely lacks understanding, or at least one in which it is indiscernible, Kant categorizes as *involuntary* (unintended) imagination, and it is this form he refers to when he uses the word *fantasy*.²⁷⁶

Not equated with aesthetic imagination, fantasy is the involuntary and, as such, ruleless form of imagination that is manifest in dreams and dementia. To dream is natural, according to Kant,²⁷⁷ but to fantasize while awake reveals a diseased condition,²⁷⁸ and if a person confuses his daytime fantasies with real experiences, he is being a "visionary" (*Phantast*), a state related to "dementia" and "insania" (*Wahnsinn* and *Wahnwitz*).²⁷⁹ The problem with fantasizing while awake is precisely its characteristic absence of the

---

274   Immanuel Kant, *Anthropology from a Pragmatic Point of View*, ed. and trans. R.B. Louden (New York: Cambridge University Press, 2006).

275   Kant, *Anthropology*, 61 (7: 167). The word 'inventive' must not be confused with the word 'creative.' The productive imagination is not creative, for it is "not capable of producing a sense representation that was *never* given to our faculty of sense; one can always furnish evidence of the material of its ideas." Kant, *Anthropology*, 61 (7: 168).

276   Kant, *Anthropology*, 60 (7: 167).

277   Kant, *Anthropology*, 60, 68 (7: 167, 175).

278   Kant, *Anthropology*, 68 (7: 175).

279   Kant, *Anthropology*, 60, 96–97 (7: 167, 202–203).

understanding (its rulelessness),[280] which, according to Kant, does *not* characterize the work of aesthetic imagination (despite the aforementioned absence of understanding's concepts). Though the aesthetic imagination does not serve the understanding, it plays along with it. Without this interplay, no aesthetic ideas would be produced; nor would expanded thinking be possible, and art would not exist. Spirit is characterized *not* merely as aesthetic imagination in free play, but also as the ability to give expression to the aesthetic ideas produced by this play. As mentioned, the latter cannot be done adequately by using concepts, but it nonetheless requires understanding, and the result is beautiful art.[281]

Kant was aware from very early on of the ambivalent nature of fantasy and thus also of the problems associated with it. In his article "Essay on the Maladies of the Head" (Versuch über die Krankheiten des Kopfes, 1764), he distinguished between *enthusiasm* and *fanaticism*, understood, respectively, as a positive and a negative expression of fantasy.[282] The word 'enthusiasm' denotes the kind of fantasy that can be seen in the ambitions of moral people, and without which nothing great would be accomplished in the world. Fanatics, on the other hand, are deranged people who claim to have received immediate inspiration and to be familiar with divine powers, and "human nature knows no more dangerous illusion."[283] Kant also describes this fanaticism as *Schwärmerei*, a word that is used in his *Critiques* to describe the transcending of the boundaries of human reason.[284] According to him, it is *moral Schwärmerei*

---

280   Kant, *Anthropology*, 74–75 (7: 181).

281   Kant, *Critique of Judgment*, 194–195 (5: 316–317).

282   Immanuel Kant, "Essay on the Maladies of the Head," in *Observations on the Feeling of the Beautiful and Sublime and Other Writings*, eds. and trans. P. Frierson and P. Guyer (New York: Cambridge University Press, 2011), 213 (2: 267).

283   Immanuel Kant, "Essay on the Maladies of the Head," 213 (2: 267).

284   For the meaning of this Kantian notion, see Rudolf Eisler, "Schwärmerei," in *Kant-Lexikon*. *Schwärmerei* is often translated as 'enthusiasm,' which is also the case in the English translation of Kant's *Anthropology*. But in that work Kant refers to something else when he writes *Schwärmerei* than the *Enthusiasmus* described in his text on the maladies

when one allows one's morals to be driven by an infatuation with noble, dignified actions rather than the moral law.[285] And it is *religious Schwärmerei* to think that by striving for an alleged intimacy with God one can justify oneself before him—to think that something like that can have a moral (*sittlich*) effect.[286]

Those given to *Schwärmerei* are exalted and eccentric people who believe in powers revealed to them alone—fantasts with a proclivity for illusions they confuse with genuine experiences—and *Schwärmerei* is thus associated with insania, which is consistent with the previous description of fantasy.[287] Kant accused many of his contemporaries of *Schwärmerei*, for example Johan Gottfried von Herder; they promoted not *expanded* thinking, but *unclear* thinking.[288] This critique did not rest on a demand from Kant's side that understanding must reign alone. On the contrary, understanding needs imagination (to make cognitive judgments), and it even needs the liberation of imagination from this service (when making the judgments of taste that are necessary for reason's actualization). Thus, Kant's point was not to entrust everything to understanding. His point was, on the contrary, that cognition, morality, and taste are all lost if imagination does not play together with understanding, that is, if it does not infuse understanding's concepts with life and thus expand thinking, but just gives itself free rein.

---

of the head. I therefore abstain from translating *Schwärmerei* as 'enthusiasm.' The word 'fanaticism' would be a better choice (and was chosen for the title of this section of the present chapter). However, Kant's term *Schwärmerei* encompasses more than the word 'fanaticism' does in our contemporary usage. Hence, in general I keep the word *Schwärmerei* untranslated, in order not to nourish further confusion.

285 Kant, *Critique of Practical Reason*, 72ff. (5: 84ff.).

286 Immanuel Kant, *Religion Within the Boundaries of Mere Reason and Other Writings*, eds. and trans. A. Wood and G.D. Giovanni (Cambridge, UK: Cambridge University Press, 1998), 169–170 (6: 174).

287 Kant, *Anthropology*, 96–97, 36 (7: 202–203, 145).

288 See, for example, Immanuel Kant, "Reviews of Herder's Ideas on the Philosophy of the History of Mankind," in *Political Writings*, ed. H.S. Reiss, trans. H.B. Nisbet (New York: Cambridge University Press, 1991) (8: 43–66).

Similarly, Georg Wilhelm Friedrich Hegel criticized early German Romantics such as Friedrich Schlegel for preferring fragmented aesthetic expressions of particular feelings as opposed to "the labor of the concept," which, as he saw it, philosophical knowledge requires.[289] Søren Kierkegaard reproached "Romantic irony" and "the aesthete" for being self-deceptive, removed from reality, void of content, inconsistent, and irresponsible.[290] And many twentieth-century philosophers and theologians have formulated critiques cut from the same cloth, arguing against 'the Romantics' and 'aesthetics,' though it was, in fact, *Schwärmerei* that was their target.

Philosophy after Kant

Kant was Baumgarten's immediate intellectual descendent but he rejected his concept of sensitive cognition and his effort to formulate a philosophy about this form of knowledge.[291] There were several reasons for this rejection, but only one will be mentioned here, namely, Kant's own definition of cognition. According to him, cognition is per definition a product of the understanding; as noted earlier, it presupposes not only intuition, but also concepts. It was thus impossible for Kant to use the word 'cognition' about something like Baumgarten's 'sensitive cognition,' which was not guided by conceptual thought. He could not understand judgments of taste as cognitive judgments, and that was exactly what Baumgarten did. This was possible for Baumgarten because of his realization that

---

289 Georg Wilhelm Friedrich Hegel, *The Phenomenology of Spirit*, ed. and trans. T. Pinkard (Cambridge, UK: Cambridge University Press, 2018), 44. Hegel's criticism of the early German Romantics is articulated in, for example, the introduction to his *Aesthetics*. See Georg Wilhelm Friedrich Hegel, *Aesthetics: Lectures on Fine Art, Volume 1*, trans. T.M. Knox (Oxford: Clarendon Press, 1988), 63ff.

290 This criticism can be found, for example, in the second part of Kierkegaard's dissertation *The Concept of Irony, with Continual Reference to Socrates*, in the section titled "Irony After Fichte," and in the first part of his *Either/Or: Part I–II*; see volumes 2 and 3 in *Kierkegaard's Writings*, eds. H.V. Hong and E.H. Hong (Princeton: Princeton University Press, 1992 and 1988).

291 Kant, *Critique of Pure Reason*, A21/B35 footnote.

with judgments of taste, there is *another* form of cognition at work, different from intellectual cognition, and this second form of cognition qualified as *cognition* for him because he considered it to be *sensitive*, rather than merely sensuous. Kant overlooked this distinction between sensitivity and sensuousness and thus believed that Baumgarten had simply inverted the traditional hierarchy of sense and intellect. According to Kant, the aesthetics introduced by Baumgarten would thus necessarily result in *Schwärmerei*.

As shown previously, however, Kant himself contributed to the novel interpretation of imagination that Baumgarten made possible when he conceived of the lower cognitive faculties as independent from the higher faculties. With time, Kant even formulated an aesthetics—a critique of taste, in his own words—in which he considered the aesthetic judgment of taste to be *emotional* (that is, sensitive, rather than sensuous), and, as noted, he linked it to *aesthetic ideas*, *expanded thinking*, and even *insight* (in the form of a feeling of assurance, associated with beauty, of fitting into the world). In the years following the publication of the *Critique of Judgment*, Kant's new interpretation of imagination was radicalized by German idealists and Romantics such as Friedrich Wilhelm Joseph von Schelling and Novalis (Friedrich von Hardenberg); and more than a century later it was further developed by philosophical phenomenologists such as Bachelard and Martin Heidegger.[292] Kant's transcendental treatment of the imagination and his aesthetic focus on this faculty in its most potent form—considered not only as a requirement for experience and cognition but also as what

---

292 See, for example, Novalis, *The Novices of Sais*, trans. R. Manheim (New York: Archipelago Books, 2005), and Friedrich Wilhelm Joseph von Schelling, *Philosophical Investigations into the Essence of Human Freedom*, trans. J. Love and J. Schmidt (Albany: State University of New York Press, 2007). Before finishing those works, both Novalis and Schelling had grappled with Johann Gottlieb Fichte's interpretation of Kant's concept of productive imagination. It was also this concept—rather than that of aesthetic imagination—that was reinterpreted by Heidegger in *Kant and the Problem of Metaphysics*, trans. R. Taft (Bloomington: Indiana University Press, 1997). However, Heidegger's phenomenology was in actuality a philosophical aesthetics (Jørgensen, *Den skønne tænkning*, 343–357), and in time the aesthetic imagination did indeed become more prominent in his thinking (Christopher Yates, *The Poetic Imagination in Heidegger and Schelling* [London and New York: Bloomsbury Academic, 2013]). In Bachelard's case, several of his works are in the tradition of philosophical aesthetics in an indisputably aesthetic sense; here, however, only *The Poetics of Space*, trans. M. Jolas (New York: Penguin Books, 2014), will be singled out.

creatively produces aesthetic ideas and as the necessary condition for thinking in an expanded way—was an important presupposition for the *de*subjectification of imagination that the German idealists and early Romantics sought, and which hermeneutic phenomenologists such as Heidegger and Hans-Georg Gadamer wanted as well.

The notion that imagination is creative—not just productive—that can be seen today is generally considered to be a product of the eighteenth century, that is, of Idealism and Romanticism. If imagination is creative, it does not simply reproduce and combine representations received from the senses, as it did for Aristotle and all his successors. On the contrary, it generates its own representations and it does so potentially independently of all sensation. Even though our current interest in the creative imagination can be considered a child of its times—modernity and postmodernity—it shares traits with what, in antiquity and medieval times, was said to 'rain down from high heavens' and called 'divine inspiration.' The interest of our day in the creative imagination is precisely directed toward something that is experienced as beyond our control and thus feels like something that is not located in us, but intervenes from the outside. That is, its products give the impression that they are not planned by us but, on the contrary, unexpectedly accrue to us as gifts. Such experiences of 'outside intervention' and 'unexpected rain of gifts' are desubjectifying: they remove the command from the conscious subject or, more accurately, they show that it has already lost control. If these experiences are taken seriously within the framework of modern philosophical thinking, the result is precisely some of the philosophies of imagination that have been formulated in recent times and, not least, the phenomenological philosophies.

The Situation Today

Philosophical phenomenology can be traced back to Hegel's *The Phenomenology of Spirit* (1807)—or even back to Baumgarten's aesthetics.[293] As early as *The Phenomenology of Spirit*, imagination played an important though tacit role.[294] Later on, Edmund Husserl spoke of the imagination as "the vital element" of phenomenology, Heidegger interpreted it in *Being and Time* as "the ecstatic nature of Dasein," and Jean-Paul Sartre called it "an essential and transcendental condition of consciousness."[295] Imagination has also been a key issue for many other phenomenologists and hermeneutic thinkers—for example, Bachelard, Maurice Merleau-Ponty, Paul Ricoeur, Cornelius Castoriardis, Edward S. Casey, and Richard Kearney.[296] These philosophers have typically shown a great interest in art and literature (and in some cases religion too), and they have formulated thoughts that can be categorized as philosophical aesthetics (thoughts on insight procured sensitively). These philosophers, however, have not *themselves* understood their thoughts as expressions of aesthetic theory. On the contrary, they have spo-

293   For this interpretation of the relationship between aesthetics and phenomenology, which is developed in *Den skønne tænkning*, see the book's five parts on philosophical aesthetics, pp. 83–550, including the chapters "Fænomenologi er æstetik (Phenomenology is Aesthetics) and "Æstetikfilosofisk afrunding" (Closing Chapter on Philosophical Aesthetics). See also the "Indledning" (Introduction), pp. 21–82.

294   Jennifer Ann Bates, *Hegel's Theory of Imagination* (Albany: State University of New York Press, 2004).

295   Edmund Husserl, *Ideas Pertaining to a Pure Phenomenology and to a Phenomenological Philosophy, First Book: General Introduction to a Pure Phenomenology*, trans. F. Kersten, in *Collected Works, Volume 2*, ed. R. Bernet (Dordrecht: Kluwer Academic Publishers, 1983), 160; Jean-Paul Sartre, *The Imaginary: A Phenomenological Psychology of the Imagination*, trans. J. Webber (London and New York: Routledge, 2004), 188; Julia Jansen, "Phenomenology, Imagination and Interdisciplinary Research," in *Handbook of Phenomenology and Cognitive Science*, eds. S. Gallagher and D. Schmicking (Dordrecht: Springer Science+Business Media, 2010), 142.

296   See, for example, Maurice Merleau-Ponty, *Phenomenology of Perception*, trans. D.A. Landes (London and New York: Routledge, 2012); Paul Ricoeur, *The Rule of Metaphor: The Creation of Meaning in Language*, trans. R. Czerney, K. McLaughlin, and J. Costello (London and New York: Routledge, 2004); Cornelius Castoriadis, *The Imaginary Institution of Society* (Cambridge, UK: Polity Press, 1997) and *World in Fragments: Writings on Politics, Society, Psychoanalysis, and the Imagination* (Stanford: Stanford University Press, 1997); Edward S. Casey, *Imagining: A Phenomenological Study* (Bloomington: Indiana University Press, 1976); Richard Kearney, *The Wake of Imagination: Toward a Postmodern Culture* (Minneapolis: University of Minnesota Press, 1991), *Poetics of Imagining: From Husserl to Lyotard* (London: HarperCollins Academic, 1991), and *Poetics of Modernity: Toward a Hermeneutic Imagination* (Atlantic Highlands: Humanities Press, 1995).

ken of them as phenomenological, failing to recognize phenomenology's debt to aesthetics. The reason for this is, not least, that they have confused aesthetics with the philosophy of art and/or the study of art, which is why especially the hermeneutic philosophers among them have rejected aesthetics (misunderstood as the modern scientification of the approach to art and literature). But at the same time, they have 'reinvented' aesthetics under the title 'phenomenology,' which, however, was done without an eye for phenomenology's kinship with the original philosophical aesthetics.[297]

The philosophical aesthetics introduced by Baumgarten in the mid-eighteenth century contains essential potentials for a philosophy of experience. However, if these potentials are to be realized (made real), it is necessary to actualize aesthetics because not only in phenomenology but also generally it is confused with the philosophy of art and/or the study of art (for instance, this also happens in contemporary analytic philosophy and in various academic disciplines dealing with artworks or other artifacts), and because the potentials in aesthetics for developing a philosophy of experience thus fade out of sight.[298] However, because of its appearance in the eighteenth century, the original aesthetics also took the form of a philosophy of faculties, which it is *not* suitable to pursue today. The desubjectification of imagination, which was mentioned previously, was precisely an early attempt to get beyond the philosophy of faculties, and the same goes for the predilection of many current philosophers for *imagining* (a process) rather than *imagination* (understood as a faculty). This preference can be seen, for instance, in the thought of Casey, who, more specifically, has emphasized "merely imagining" (understood as common to all acts of imagining proper), which includes reverie, daydreaming, and more controlled acts such as artistic creation.[299] This form of imagining is "the conscious projection and contemplation of objects posited as

---

[297] Jørgensen, *Den skønne tænkning*.

[298] See Jørgensen, "The Relevance of Aesthetics."

[299] Edward S. Casey, "Imagination: Imagining and the Image," *Philosophy and Phenomenological Research* Vol. 31, No. 4 (1971): 475.

pure possibilities," whereas we operate with hypothetical possibilities (as opposed to pure possibilities) when we formulate scientific hypotheses.[300] But merely imagining and its pure possibilities also have significance for scientific work; this is evidenced, according to Casey, by the use of thought experiments by modern scientists.

Despite the widespread desire today to avoid philosophizing about faculties, imagining is often portrayed as a subjective production of images, and the results of this production are frequently described as mental copies. To take an example, Tamar Gendler writes in a lexicon entry that to imagine something is to "form a particular sort of mental representation of that thing," and she categorizes imagining as a "mental state" that is usually distinguished from other mental states, such as perceiving, remembering, and believing.[301] However, by virtue of this comparison, imagining is also looked on as similar to such states. Gendler's article concentrates on recent investigations into imagination in Anglo-American philosophy, which variously see imagination as an element in the subject's cognitive processing of sense impressions, as an element in its production of art, and as an element in its development of self-understanding and understanding of the world. Despite this diversity and the current reluctance to reproduce the way of thinking known from the philosophy of faculties, it is, however, a constant feature of these sorts of academic philosophical studies that the source of imagining is seen as something within us. Likewise, a majority of all the other humanists and social scientists who also study the imagination treat it as a psychological phenomenon, and they often work with a foundation in cognitive studies as well (for instance, Gilles Fauconnier, Mark Turner, Scot Barry Kaufman, Jim Davies, and Alexander A. Schlegel). Thus, most contemporary imagination studies are not only distant from Plato's 'religious' theory of imagination but also a long way from Kant's aesthetic in-

---

300   Casey, "Imagination: Imagining and the Image," 476.

301   Tamar Gendler, "Imagination," in *Stanford Encyclopedia of Philosophy*, March 14, 2011, https://plato.stanford.edu, accessed May 23, 2015.

terpretation of the free productive imagination and the desubjectification of imagination that other thinkers have sought.

The protagonists of desubjectification have appreciated imagination for its power to transcend the given and to create something new. They have taken imagination to be something that either is greater than us (analogous to Plato) or puts us in contact with something that is greater than us (analogous to Kant). As mentioned, this way of thinking lives on in the contemporary hermeneutic phenomenological research in imagination, which typically takes the form of interpretations of texts by thinkers such as Novalis, Schelling, Heidegger, Bachelard, Sartre, and Ricoeur. There are also traces of the desubjectifying approach to the imagination in postmodern thought (not least, thought inspired by literary studies), which can be found in works by, for example, Kearney. Moreover, the desubjectifying approach has played an important role in the most recent decades of theological thinking about imagination,[302] for instance when Mark C. Taylor (inspired by the Romantics) equates God with the imagination understood as the both form-productive and form-destructive power in everything there is.[303]

Despite the internal differences, in all these cases of desubjectification, imagination is taken to be both asubjective and transcending the subject; something that cannot be studied empirically but must be discovered in philosophical or theological reflection. Contrariwise, within the framework of the previously mentioned scientific model of research, imagination is considered to have its source in and be limited to the subject—something psychological that can and ought to be studied with the tools of (cognitive) science.

It is the latter sort of research that dominates the field today—research characterized by the duality of scientism and subjectivism beyond which hermeneutic phenomenologists such as

---

302 Jørgensen, *Den skønne tænkning*, 731, footnote 748.

303 Jørgensen, *Den skønne tænkning*, 727–757; Taylor, *After God*, xvii–xviii, 117, 122, 307.

Heidegger, Gadamer, and Ricoeur tried to move.[304] At the same time, however, it is in large part the creative aspect of imagination that attracts attention in our times—this is the case on a popular level, among educators, in artistic circles, but also among academics, including psychologists. It is therefore relevant to actualize the critical attempt of hermeneutic phenomenology—in order both to get beyond scientism (which itself implies subjectivism, according to Gadamer in the first part of *Truth and Method*) and to avoid replacing the attitude of scientism with a subjectivist attitude (which can be the result at the popular level, among educators, in artistic circles, and also in psychological research).[305] It is relevant to actualize the critical attempt of hermeneutic phenomenology, first, because the scientific approach to imagination only gives limited insight into it, inasmuch as that sort of approach only acknowledges conclusions based on what can be studied experimentally; and secondly, because the subjectivist approach to imagination, which follows the scientific approach around like its shadow, is also limiting inasmuch as its sentimental celebration of imagination clouds an understanding of it. However, the mobilization of the hermeneutic phenomenological attempt to get beyond the prevailing duality of scientism and subjectivism must happen within the horizon of a philosophy of experience that is liberated from the aversion to aesthetics that limited the otherwise broad thought of, for example, Heidegger and Gadamer. Therefore, the mobilization of hermeneutic phenomenology presupposes the previously mentioned actualization of philosophical aesthetics.

Imagination, Interpreted through the Philosophy of Experience

It has been argued previously that, from the beginning, the philosophy of imagination treated both the human and something greater

---

304 For a more general discussion of this problem, see, in *Poetic Inclinations*, the chapter "Philosophy at a Crossroads" on the current state of philosophical thought.

305 Hans-Georg Gadamer, *Truth and Method*, trans. J. Weinsheimer and D.G. Marshall (London and New York: Bloomsbury Academic, 2013).

than the human. The latter was a priority in the 'Platonic' tradition, the former in the 'Aristotelian.' With Baumgarten, however, the old question about the nature of the human being was asked again. He raised the question indirectly, as he problematized the traditional identification of cognition with intellectual cognition, and thus challenged the associated understanding of the human being as the *animal rationale*, 'the rationally thinking animal.' Baumgarten asked and answered the question from the point of view of a theory of aesthetics, and the result was his recognition of the human being as a creature that excels thanks to its sensitive rather than its intellectual dispositions. Despite his rejection of Baumgarten's aesthetics, Kant developed Baumgarten's insight inasmuch as he portrayed the faculty of imagination as the animating and thus life-giving principle in human beings. Since then, many phenomenologists and hermeneutic philosophers have regarded their own positions as criticisms of the dualist philosophy of mind, not least the way Kant conceived of it. Their understanding of the imagination as an asubjective power, which works in human beings but also transcends them, nonetheless has roots in Kant's conception of imagination and thus also in Baumgarten's philosophy of sensitive cognition.

These considerations may be considered a brief summary of the historical presentation formulated in the previous sections of this chapter. We should not forget the history, but if we now take our point of departure in *both* traditions—both philosophical aesthetics and hermeneutic phenomenology—we have the opportunity to reformulate the question about the human being in our own way. The answer that such a point of departure makes possible refers not only to the sensitivity 'unveiled' by Baumgarten—its cognitive and moral potential—understood as something that is characteristic of us as human beings, and which we thus share with each other; it also has a clear path to understanding the human being as *existence* as opposed to *subject* (an understanding that harmonizes with the hermeneutic phenomenological mode of thought), and for interpreting this existence (thanks to the additional integration of philosophical aesthetics) as characterized by a threefold structure of *sensation, faith,* and *comprehension*.[306]

Such an understanding of the human being is formulated in the book *Den skønne tænkning* (Beautiful Thinking), in which philosophical aesthetics and hermeneutic phenomenology are presented as pathways to a philosophy of experience termed the *metaphysics of experience*.[307] For this purpose, the book contains detailed interpretations of the philosophies of Baumgarten, Kant, Benjamin, Heidegger, and Gadamer, as well as contemporary thinkers such as Hermann Schmitz, Gernot Böhme, Martin Seel, Jean-Louis Chrétien, Eugenio Trías, Christoph Menke, Wolfgang Welsch, Richard Shusterman, and Hans-Ulrich Gumbrecht.

Walter Benjamin plays a prominent role in the book, which shows that with his proposal for a philosophy of "higher experience" (*höhere Erfahrung*) he offered a new interpretation of the metaphysics that had been handed down.[308] Benjamin did not wish to reproduce traditional metaphysics understood as what is today often referred to as 'essentialism,' but he was also reluctant to give up the possibility of formulating a philosophical understanding of our experiences of transcendence (traditionally termed metaphysical, religious, or aesthetic experiences). With his proposal for a philosophy of 'higher experience' he offered a new type of meta-

---

306 Jørgensen, *Den skønne tænkning,* 791–804. 'Sensation, faith, and comprehension' is a translation of the Danish 'fornemmelse, tro og forståelse,' which in German would be 'Empfindung, Glauben und Verstehen.' The word 'sensation' (*fornemmelse, Empfindung*) is used here in another sense than in Kant's philosophy—with a wider meaning inspired by contemporary philosophical aesthetics. It denotes not just sense impression/perception, but also and not least sensitive experience containing insight. Likewise, the word 'faith' is not used here to signify religious confession, but merely *trust*. This trust may be the source of faith in a religious sense, but this presupposes a religious interpretation of that in which one has 'faith.' Furthermore, 'forståelse' is translated as 'comprehension' (not 'understanding,' though the adequate German translation would be 'Verstehen'), in order not to confuse it with the faculty called 'understanding' and its intellectual reasoning.

307 Concerning this metaphysics of experience, see, for example, the chapter "Experience, Metaphysics, and Immanent Transcendence." See also "English Summary" in *Den skønne tænkning*, 947–965.

308 See Walter Benjamin, "On the Program of the Coming Philosophy," trans. M. Ritter, in *Selected Writings, Volume 1: 1913–1926,* eds. M. Bullock and M.W. Jennings (Cambridge, MA and London: The Belknap Press of Harvard University Press, 2002), 102.

physics, instead of rejecting philosophical thinking that does not ape modern scientism. In similar fashion, Heidegger also formulated a new metaphysics that was more deeply rooted in experience than traditional metaphysics was, though he is better known for his criticism of metaphysics. He criticized in order not to reject but instead to develop. According to Heidegger, the problem is not that the metaphysicians of the past went too far; it is that they did not go far enough. They aspired to wise insight but only reached rational knowledge, as they confused thinking with reasoning. Although Benjamin never referred to Baumgarten, and Heidegger reproached aesthetics, they both took over where Baumgarten had left off, wording philosophical aesthetics for the twentieth century. Benjamin and Heidegger brought philosophical aesthetics into the topical realm, thereby reinterpreting metaphysics for their own day and age instead of rejecting it. Their philosophies thus contain many elements of relevance for a new kind of metaphysics understood as a contemporary philosophy of experience that suspends the dogmatism of both essentialism and scientism.[309]

Even on a more general level, it is observable that philosophical aesthetics and hermeneutic phenomenology put behind them the hope of traditional metaphysics, that is, the hope of being able to fathom or provide proof of something transcendent—though they did not deny the possibility of experiencing transcendence, but were, rather, deeply involved in precisely this kind of experience and in its significance for us as human beings. Accordingly, *Den skønne tænkning* shows how the sensitive cognition dealt with in philosophical aesthetics can be interpreted as a metaphysical insight into our possibility of experiencing transcendence, and as an insight into what this possibility means for us as human beings. The book further shows that philosophical investigations into this experiential sphere can promote new development in many differ-

---

309 This interpretation of Benjamin and Heidegger is from the parts "Benjamins metafysik" (Benjamin's Metaphysics) and "Heideggers fænomenologi" (Heidegger's Phenomenology) of *Den skønne tænkning*, 175–255 and 275–357. See the chapter "Experience, Metaphysics, and Immanent Transcendence" in the present volume for a presentation that is more detailed than the one it is possible to offer here.

ent fields—theology, pedagogy, and the philosophy of science, for instance—by contributing an experiential dimension that otherwise remains lacking.

This latter point, however, makes it necessary to revise the current understanding of experience. The word 'experience' is most often used to denote sensory experience, empirical experience, or, at best, life experience. Furthermore, such experiences are usually considered to be mental acts performed by a subject who thus perceives or cognizes something that has the status of an object. But experiences of transcendence exist at a level prior to the constituting of subject and object. If this experiential sphere is to be investigated philosophically, we must necessarily enlarge the concept of experience. This concept must be made applicable to something that *occurs*—that happens to someone who, in this situation, is not the subject of something, but is rather the object of the event this experience constitutes.

The philosophy of experience proposed in *Den skønne tænkning* is precisely about types of experience that have no subject, and which therefore have no object either. These experiences occur, and they do not occur in the subject but rather in an *intermediate world*, where things are not the object of an experience, but are solely occasions of experience.[310] In other words, these experiences take place before any subject or object is constituted; they do not depend on any subject as such, but on subjectivity understood as *presence*. Thanks to hermeneutic phenomenology this kind of experience can be understood as an *event*, but thanks to philosophical aesthetics it is also possible to profile the *sensitive* aspect (as opposed to the sensuous aspect) of the event in question. Furthermore, the aesthetic as well as phenomenological anchoring of this philosophy of experience nourishes an understanding of the investigated experiences as ones of *transcendence*—and of experiences of transcendence as ones of a *surplus of meaning*. The experiences surpass the material and the immanent without leaving it, and they

---

310   See both the chapter "The Intermediate World" in the present volume, and, for example, pp. 727–774 and 805–818 in *Den skønne tænkning* for the concept of the 'intermediate world.'

transcend in both time and space; the result is a world giving the impression of being multilayered, and phenomena appearing to be loaded with a 'more,' a surplus of meaning, that is, meaning not accessible to understanding.

Such is the background on which 'sensation,' 'faith,' and 'comprehension' are identified, in *Den skønne tænkning*, as equiprimordial aspects of the same *basic experience*. The experience containing these three aspects is the book's term for that which was referred to earlier as 'existence.' Consequently, the basic experience is no particular singular experience but rather the attentive beginning of all perception, without which we would have no experience, nor would we have any knowledge, be it sensory, sensitive, or intellectual. This level, called 'basic experience,' is our very being-there-in-the-universe-together-with-whatever-else-there-is, and it is this attentive beginning of everything that is of a sensitive, a faithful, and a comprehensive character. Hence, at the most basic level we sensitively sense the presence of that which is. This sensitive experience contains knowledge, though not of a rational kind, and it delivers this insight not only because of its sensitivity but also because of the trust with which we respond to it.

In our *sensations* we sensitively comprehend ourselves, each other, and the world around us, and we spontaneously have faith in what we *comprehend*: we trust the insight we receive in our sensitive experience. We sense, comprehend, and have faith in what we comprehend when our experience is something that *happens* to us (instead of being something we, ourselves, *accomplish*—which is the case with rational thought). Comprehendingly and trustingly we transcend the given (the merely material and the truistic), if our comprehension of and trust in what is comprehended are sensitive. These examples of transcendence take place in the *intermediate world* that sensitivity makes out: the sphere of 'feeling, sensation, and presentiment,' in which no subject and no object have yet crystallized.[311] The transcendences thus happen in the sphere

---

311 In *Den skønne tænkning*, the sensitivity that constitutes the intermediate world and thus basic experience is referred to as "feeling, sensation, and presentiment" ("følelse, fornemmelse og anelse"), understood not as subjective faculties or psychological phenome-

modern philosophers, such as Heidegger, K.E. Løgstrup, and Gernot Böhme, call "the space of attunement (*Befindlichkeit, stemthed*) or atmosphere," and which others before them called "the world of fantasy and imagination."[312]

Our dual point of departure in both philosophical aesthetics and hermeneutic phenomenology, which provides the possibility of thinking of a fundamental threefold structure of human existence, thus lets *sensitivity* appear as a central philosophical issue—understood not as a faculty within the subject, but as an *existentiale* (a dimension in life that we do not control, and which constitutes a point of departure for everything we think and do). Furthermore, with this sensitive threefold structure, *imagination* is also central—not in the sense of a subjective capacity, but as an asubjective and in a way quasi-objective condition for the lives we lead as human beings. The argument for the latter is found in the *openness* so characteristic of the intermediate world, because it is not merely "a fluid field between or beyond subject and object, physical sensation and conceptual thought; it is also that layer or space in which we, in thought, can be in more than one place at the same time."[313] The argument is found in the link between openness and imagination that is evidenced by the fact that transcendence of the subject/object-structured world of understanding presupposes *imagination.*

The intermediate world is the sphere of our experiences of transcendence; experience of a 'surplus of meaning' is the content of this sphere. The openness of the intermediate world is thus a transcendence within thought, which makes possible experience and cognition that go beyond the given without postulating anything about another world somewhere else. "The openness is our entryway into the transcendent, but as it discloses itself in the at-

na but as an existential dimension. To be more specific, the phrase 'feeling, sensation, and presentiment' is a specification of the component in basic experience that is abbreviated as 'sensation' in the full description of the experience as 'sensation, faith, and comprehension.' That is, 'feeling, sensation, and presentiment' is a specification of the *sensitive* dimension of the experience.

312   Jørgensen, *Den skønne tænkning*, 728, 729.

313   Jørgensen, *Den skønne tænkning*, 729.

tunement or atmosphere, that is, in the intermediate world—not as it exists for itself in a distant and foreign world."[314] This openness is the result of *imagination*; it is a consequence of imagination's work within sensitivity. We know this work—the play of imagination— from our sensitive experiences, in modern times most often called 'aesthetic experiences,' which are precisely experiences in which we transcend the given (mere physical sensation and the truisms resting on the dogma that only empirical experience and logical thinking can be true). The openings these experiences make out— toward something that transcends the intermediate world without moving into something transcendent—must thus be considered products of *imagination*. Without the element in sensitivity represented by imagination, there would be no comprehension (insight), nor would there be faith (trust in that which is given by insight). If imagination did not play tricks on understanding, we would not have any culture—no art, no philosophy, no religion—and we would have no community understood as a life of fellowship. Life with each other requires an eye for more than ourselves, namely, the common weal, and we need imagination in order to 'see' what cannot be seen. It takes imagination to think and orient oneself toward an idea, such as that of the common weal.

---

314   Jørgensen, *Den skønne tænkning*, 742.

The Intermediate World

Introduction

The expression 'beautiful thinking' derives from the opening section of Alexander Gottlieb Baumgarten's *Aesthetica*.[315] Aesthetics is "the science of sensitive cognition," Baumgarten writes, and in a parenthesis he lists the following synonyms for aesthetics: "the theory of the liberal arts," "gnoseology of the lower faculties," "the art of beautiful thinking," and "the art of thinking analogous to reason."[316] In my book *Den skønne tænkning* (Beautiful Thinking), I presented and interpreted Baumgarten's philosophical aesthetics, Immanuel Kant's critique of reason, Walter Benjamin's modern metaphysics, Martin Heidegger's hermeneutic phenomenology, and a number of current aesthetic theories as *pathways to the metaphysics of experience*.[317] The term 'metaphysics of experience' I originally coined to describe a philosophy dealing with experiences that are commonly described as, for example, 'aesthetic' or 'religious.' It indicates a philosophy that in its exploration of such experiences attempts to surpass the way they are treated by dualist philosophies of mind. The metaphysics of experience is thus the philosophy of a realm of

315 Alexander Gottlieb Baumgarten, *Ästhetik, Volume 1-2*, trans. D. Mirbach (Hamburg: Felix Meiner Verlag, 2007).

316 Baumgarten, *Ästhetik*, § 1.

317 See Dorthe Jørgensen, *Den skønne tænkning: Veje til erfaringsmetafysik. Religionsfilosofisk udmøntet* (Beautiful Thinking: Pathways to the Metaphysics of Experience. Religio-Philosophically Implemented) (Aarhus: Aarhus University Press, 2014), 12. This section in its totality refers to pp. 12–14.

experience that, viewed from the perspective of the subject/object-structured way of thinking still reproduced by the majority, constitutes what in *Den skønne tænkning* I call 'the intermediate world'; an experiential level at which subject and object are connected in an original way before they are separated intellectually.[318]

As early as the eighteenth century, Baumgarten initiated a philosophical exploration of the intermediate world by introducing philosophical aesthetics. With this invention, he founded a new epistemology that anticipated the hermeneutic phenomenological philosophy of experience of the twentieth century, and he thus also founded a new metaphysics that, unlike traditional metaphysics, revolved around 'sensitive cognition,' 'beautiful thinking,' and 'aesthetic truth.' However, Baumgarten's thought still originated in rationalism; essentially, his aesthetics therefore belonged to the dualist philosophy of mind. It was formed as a philosophy of human faculties that, thanks to its notion of sensitive cognition, which bridges sense perception and abstract thinking, tended to burst the subject/object paradigm, but was prevented by its rationalist origins from conducting a proper exploration of the intermediate world. Furthermore, Baumgarten's definition of aesthetics as the philosophy of sensitive cognition was soon forgotten by posterity, and aesthetics was replaced first by the philosophy of art and later by the study of art.[319]

As a consequence of this scenario, for many years, my work was motivated by the idea that philosophical aesthetics represents an as yet unfulfilled possibility that must be fulfilled, since it is con-

---

318 Consequentially, 'intermediate' does not mean 'mediated' (by, for instance, the subject and its faculties), and it only means 'in-between' if approached intellectually (that is, from a dualist and thus less original point of view).

319 I distinguish between 'the metaphysics of beauty,' 'art theory,' 'philosophy of art,' and 'philosophical aesthetics' (see "English Summary" in *Den skønne tænkning*, 947–965, and the chapter "The Metamorphosis of Beauty" in the present volume). The metaphysics of beauty and philosophical aesthetics focus on *beauty* and *aesthetic experience*, respectively, whereas art theory and the philosophy of art both focus on *art*. However, art theory deals with the formal aspects of art, whereas the philosophy of art is concerned with questions concerning the nature of art. 'The study of art' is an academic approach to art that was developed in the nineteenth and twentieth centuries, and which is empirical and analytical and thus based on art theory rather than philosophical aesthetics.

cerned with something that is dealt with in far less detail in other parts of philosophy. However, such a fulfillment cannot take the form of a simple reproduction of the original aesthetics. Instead, it must actualize certain aspects of aesthetics, including its concepts of 'sensitive cognition,' 'beautiful thinking,' and 'aesthetic truth'; the result of this effort is what I call the 'metaphysics of experience.' Between aesthetics and the metaphysics of experience, there is thus kinship, but not identity. The metaphysics of experience is a philosophy that is meta-physical, but in a modern way. It is *not* an essentialist philosophy of epistemological objects, that is, of something whose nature can be determined by thought because that nature is a static given. On the contrary, it is a nonessentialist philosophy of the not only aesthetic but also religious dimension of our experiences, and of the not yet actualized volatile-indeterminate possibilities offered by this dimension. The metaphysics of experience discloses no hidden objects behind the world in which we live, but opens a neglected dimension of it: the intermediate world.

With 'intermediate world' as its key term, this chapter addresses the following questions: 1) In which dimension of the world does transcendence occur? 2) Which faculties are involved when we are present in this dimension, that is, the intermediate world? 3) How might we conceive of the limit implied in all ideas of transcendence, and thus also in the notion of an intermediate world associated with experiencing transcendence? 4) What is the intermediate world, if it is not a locatable domain of the empirical world or a container for experience? 5) How can philosophy access the poetic dimension of the world with which the intermediate world is synonymous when interpreted as sensitive subjectivity?

Entering the Intermediate World

Aesthetic and religious experiences are experiences of transcendence; they surpass both empirical experience and rational understanding. Such experiences bring insight and qualify as experiences of a surplus of meaning, because they are sensitive rather than sensuous, and because they occur to us rather than being controlled by us. Since ancient times, artists, philosophers, and priests have shown great interest in the possibility of our experiencing transcendence, regardless of how they interpreted it, but the approach to our experiences of transcendence and thus also their interpretations have changed throughout history. Furthermore, there was not always such a clear focus on the experience as *experience*—let alone on the experience as sensate and yet full of insight—as that which was introduced by philosophical aesthetics, that is, in the eighteenth century.[320]

It is also worth noticing that the designation 'the intermediate world' for the 'place' where transcendence occurs is a relatively new phenomenon. The painter Paul Klee used this term, or rather its German equivalent *die Zwischenwelt*, in the early twentieth century. To give only one of several possible examples, in an interview, he said that "in our time worlds have opened up which not everybody can see into, although they too are a part of nature. Perhaps it's really true that only children, madmen and savages see into them. I mean, for example, the realm of the unborn and the dead, the realm of what can be, might be, but need not necessarily be. An in-between world [*Zwischenwelt*]. At least for me, it's an in-between world. I call it that because I feel that it exists between the worlds our senses can perceive, and I absorb it inwardly to the extent that I can project it outwardly in symbolic correspondences. Children, madmen and savages can still, or again, look into it. And what they see and picture is for me the most precious kind of confirmation."[321]

In English translations of Klee's terminology, the 'Zwischenwelt' mentioned by him is often translated as 'the in-between

---

320   The word 'sensate' here refers to 'sensation' as in the 'feeling, sensation, and presentiment' mentioned in footnote 323. 'Sensate' connotes sensitivity rather than sensuousness; expressed in German/Danish, it means *empfindend/fornemmende* rather than *sinnend/sansende*. What is sensitive is emotional, whereas what is sensuous is physical. This is why sensitive experiences such as aesthetic and religious experiences do not simply stimulate our senses but provide insight.

321   The conversation is rendered in Felix Klee, *Paul Klee: His Life and Work in Documents* (New York: George Braziller, 1962), and the quoted passage appears pp. 183–184 in a rather free translation. Felix Klee's rendering of the conversation quotes Lothar Schreyer, *Erinnerungen an Sturm und Bauhaus* (München: Albert Langen and Georg Müller, 1956).

world,' but I prefer to translate the German word 'Zwischenwelt' and the Danish word 'mellemverden' with the phrase 'the intermediate world.' As an artist, Klee explored this intermediate world, and he left behind a wealth of symbolic expressions of its morphology. As stated earlier, Klee regarded the intermediate world as invisible to the physical eye, but he also thought that art could make it visible. "Art does not reproduce the visible; rather, it makes visible," said Klee in his "Creative Confession."[322] Art does not show the world as we know it, but as it is; art presents *natura naturans* rather than *natura naturata*, being rather than the beings. However, unlike others, Klee did not conceive a systematic philosophy of the intermediate world; and those who attempted to do so did not make use of his term. I refer to the philosophies, among others, of 'attunement,' 'mood,' and 'atmosphere' introduced by Martin Heidegger, K.E. Løgstrup, Hermann Schmitz, and Gernot Böhme, but I also allude to both older and newer philosophies of 'imagination.' My concept of the intermediate world originates not in Klee's terminology or his interpretation of the realm by him called 'die Zwischenwelt,' but rather in inspiration acquired from philosophies of the aforementioned sort, especially philosophical aesthetics and hermeneutic phenomenology.

In *Den skønne tænkning*, I state that the sensitive cognition mentioned by Baumgarten is of a 'feeling, sensate, and presentimental' character, and this is because it is neither simply sensuous nor intellectual, but sensitive.[323] The philosophies that surround the attunement, mood, or atmosphere mentioned by Heidegger, Løgstrup, Schmitz, and Böhme also present us with a level of experience and a dimension of existence in which what happens is of a sensitive character. However, unlike Baumgarten's approach to this level of experience, the hermeneutic phenomenological approach is not marked by a philosophy of faculties; hermeneu-

---

322 Paul Klee, "Creative Confession, 1920," in *Creative Confession and Other Writings* (London: Tate Publishing, 2013), 7.

323 'Feeling, sensation, and presentiment' is a translation of the Danish expression 'følelse, fornemmelse og anelse' (which, in German, would be 'Gefühl, Empfindung und Ahnung') used in *Den skønne tænkning* to describe what I also refer to as 'sensitive subjectivity.'

tic phenomenology focuses on experience defined as something that occurs, not experience defined as something a subject in the sense of an ego or a person has and controls.[324] In order to obtain better insight into the experiences occurring in the intermediate world, the metaphysics of experience also aims to surpass the subject/object-structured way of thinking appertained to dualist philosophies of mind. Therefore, the actualization performed by the metaphysics of experience of the possibility that philosophical aesthetics remains—the possibility of developing a philosophy of experiences of transcendence defined as sensitive experiences of a surplus of meaning—includes the further development of aesthetics that hermeneutic phenomenology represents, despite its reluctance toward aesthetics.[325]

Phantasia and Imagination

According to Baumgarten, sensitive cognitions are the products of an interplay between what in his time were called the 'lower' cognitive faculties, and which included *phantasia*, or in German: *die Einbildungskraft*.[326] Of all the lower cognitive faculties, it was precisely imagination that Kant took up in his *Critique of Judgment* when he wished to determine the pure judgment of taste, that is, the experience of beauty.[327] Baumgarten's concept of phantasia refers, among other things, to Aristotle, who, in *On the Soul*, distin-

---

324 For the mood, the atmosphere, and the attunement, respectively, see the chapters "Tanken om stemthed" (The Idea of Being in a Mood), "Ny fænomenologi, ny æstetik" (New Phenomenology, New Aesthetics), and "Fænomenologi er æstetik" (Phenomenology is Aesthetics) in *Den skønne tænkning*.

325 This reluctance is apparent in, for example, Heidegger's lectures on Friedrich Nietzsche. See Martin Heidegger, *Nietzsche, Volume 1: The Will to Power as Art; Volume 2: The Eternal Recurrence of the Same*, ed. and trans. D.F. Krell (San Francisco: HarperSanFrancisco, 1991), Vol. 1, 77–91 (in particular).

326 In English, both 'phantasia' and 'Einbildungskraft' are usually referred to as 'imagination.' For a detailed presentation and discussion of a wide range of notions of imagination from antiquity to our day, see the chapter "The Philosophy of Imagination."

327 Immanuel Kant, *Critique of the Power of Judgment*, eds. and trans. P. Guyer and E. Matthews (New York: Cambridge University Press, 2000).

guished between "sense" (*aisthesis*), "imagination" (*phantasia*), and "thought" (*noein*).[328] When Baumgarten introduced philosophical aesthetics as the philosophy of sensitive cognition, that is, the philosophy of a third power compared to physical sensation and intellectual cognition, he did more than is usually acknowledged. Not only the fact that Baumgarten actualized aisthesis but also the way in which he did this—his eye for the sensitive rather than the merely sensuous—implied the emergence of new ways to approach phantasia. It created new opportunities for developing philosophy that did not just reproduce the traditional notion of phantasia defined as the representation in mind of aisthesis and as something that can only be prereflective. It was now possible to regard imagination as an aspect, perhaps even the core, of the third power (compared to physical sensation and intellectual cognition), for the exploration of which Baumgarten introduced new terms such as 'sensitive cognition,' 'aesthetic truth,' and 'beautiful thinking.'[329]

Aristotle considered phantasia to be reproductive, but Baumgarten regarded "the faculty of invention" (*facultas fingendi*) related to imagination as creative.[330] This thought was continued by Kant, who, in his *Critique of Pure Reason*, depicted the imagination as both reproductive and productive, and, in his *Critique of Judgment*, highlighted the productive side of it.[331] Accord-

---

328 Aristotle, *On the Soul*, trans. J.A. Smith, *The Complete Works of Aristotle: The Revised Oxford Translation, Volume 1*, ed. J. Barnes (Princeton: Princeton University Press, 1984). For *aisthesis*, see book III.2; for *phantasia*, see book III.3. In Smith's English translation of Aristotle's work, *aisthesis* understood as a faculty is termed 'sense,' whereas *aisthesis* understood as an activity is termed 'sensation,' and the products of this activity are called 'sensations.' *Aisthesis* means not simply physical sense or sensation, but sense and sensation of a more comprehensive nature. *Noein* is actually thinking understood as activity, that is, as in 'to think.'

329 Baumgarten, *Ästhetik*, §§ 1 and 423.

330 Alexander Gottlieb Baumgarten, *Metaphysics: A Critical Translation with Kant's Elucidations, Selected Notes, and Related Materials*, eds. and trans. C.D. Fugate and J. Hymers (London: Bloomsbury Academic, 2014), §§ 589–594. For Baumgarten's view of the relationship between imagination and the faculty of invention, see Dagmar Mirbach, "Alexander Gottlieb Baumgarten: Fantasia, facultas fingendi og phantasmata/fictions," trans. S. Liisberg, *Slagmark* Vol. 46 (2006): 33–47.

331 Immanuel Kant, *Critique of Pure Reason*, eds. and trans. P. Guyer and A.W. Wood (Cam-

ing to Kant, it is not only as reproductive imagination but also as productive or rather creative imagination that the imagination is one of two faculties—understanding is the other faculty—whose free and harmonious interplay is the source of pure judgments of taste, which represent a unifying and transcending way of thinking that Kant referred to as "expanded."[332] Later, Heidegger approved the thesis he identified in Kant's first *Critique* that imagination is the common root of sensibility and understanding, an idea that, in Heidegger's interpretation of it, meant that imagination is the basic prerequisite for understanding.[333] According to Heidegger, imagination opens the horizon without which understanding (in the sense of knowledge) would not be possible.[334] Likewise, many other modern philosophers have awarded imagination great importance, and some contemporary theologians regard it as a major theological issue.[335]

Nevertheless, theology's attempt to rehabilitate the notion of imagination encounters problems if it implies that humans are

bridge, UK: Cambridge University Press, 1998), A 100–102, and *Critique of Judgment*, part one on the aesthetic judgment.

332   Kant, *Critique of Judgment*, 173–176 (5: 293–296). Paul Guyer and Eric Matthews translate the German word *erweitert* as 'broad-minded,' but for reasons stated in the chapter "The Significance of Sensitivity," footnote 21, I prefer 'expanded.'

333   For Heidegger's interpretation of Kant, see Martin Heidegger, *Kant and the Problem of Metaphysics*, trans. R. Taft (Bloomington: Indiana University Press, 1997).

334   The 'understanding' here referred to is not the faculty that in German is termed *Verstand* but the activity termed *Verstehen*, which also includes the result of this activity.

335   This theological interest is not completely new. For example, imagination already played an important though negative role for Friedrich D.E. Schleiermacher, as he warned against defining religion as "nur Fantasie und Dichtung" (mere imagination and poetry). See his *Über die Religion: Reden an die Gebildeten unter ihren Verächtern (1799)*, in *Kritische Gesamtausgabe I/2: Schriften aus der Berliner Zeit 1796–1799*, ed. G. Meckenstock (Berlin and New York: Walter de Gruyter, 1984), 312. In the second edition, 'Fantasie' was replaced by 'Einbildungskraft,' see *Kritische Gesamtausgabe I/12: Über die Religion (2.-)4. Auflage, Monologen (2.-)4. Auflage*, 278. For an English translation of the work, see Friedrich Schleiermacher, *On Religion: Speeches to Its Cultured Despisers*, ed. R. Crouter (Cambridge, UK: Cambridge University Press, 1996). However, parallel to the emergence of new disciplines such as theological aesthetics, the theological interest in imagination has become more intense. See, for example, footnotes 1499 and 1748 in *Den skønne tænkning* for numerous examples from recent decades of studies of the importance of imagination in and for theology.

equipped with a creativity that should only be ascribed to God—that is, if the consequence of the attempt is that humans cannot only depict something given but can also create anew without an original. In this case, theology violates the biblical idea of an essential dissimilarity between God and human. However, it is possible to overcome this obstacle by abolishing the traditional notion of imagination as a subjective faculty and by replacing it with a broader one. For this purpose, theology can find inspiration in philosophical aesthetics, because imagination has been an aesthetic concept since the introduction of aesthetics, and because, since the Romantics, aesthetics has attempted to transcend the way of thinking appertained to dualist philosophies of mind. Theology and aesthetics thus have a common agenda, and theology might find a model in aesthetics, for example, in early German Romanticism and its expanded notion of imagination, including its concept of 'progressive universal poetry.'[336]

Marc C. Taylor took advantage of the aforementioned possibility when, in 2009, he wrote *After God*, in which an expanded notion of imagination plays an important role.[337] Taylor regards the imagination as the power and activity in all beings that produces all existing figures, right from the empirical forms of nature to our ideas and concepts.[338] The imagination is an infinite process of change that is both figuring and disfiguring or both creative and destructive, namely "the activity through which the figures that

---

336 See, for example, footnote 260 and the end of the chapter "Sandheden sker" (Truth Happens), as well as the chapter "Aisthesis- eller kraftæstetik" (Aesthetics Focusing on Aisthesis or on Force), in *Den skønne tænkning*.

337 Mark C. Taylor, *After God* (Chicago: University of Chicago Press, 2007), 19. My presentation of Taylor refers in particular to the chapter "Åbenheden i mellemverdenen" (The Openness of the Intermediate World) in *Den skønne tænkning*. Taylor himself refers largely to Kant, G.W.F. Hegel, other German idealists, and, among others, Nietzsche, Heidegger, and Maurice Blanchot, besides early German Romanticism. In the case of imagination, he refers to Kant in particular, but his interpretation is strongly influenced by the early Romantics. This is most likely because Taylor reads Kant through the aforementioned thinkers and because their philosophies—for example, those of Nietzsche, Heidegger, and Blanchot—are marked by and actualize ideas of an early Romantic origin.

338 Taylor, *After God*, 125.

pattern the data of experience emerge, are modified, and dissolve."[339] According to Taylor, the figures referred to by him are not representations, but presentations. They do not represent the existent but put forward something that would not be present without this presentation of it. Imagination is thus the ground of all that exists—it is the source of it—but, because imagination is spontaneous, it itself exists without ground. Imagination is a "groundless ground," and it is also an "unfathomable ground."[340] As imagination is the prerequisite for knowledge, we cannot know imagination itself: it is an "abyss" of incomprehensibility.[341]

On the Limit

Imagination is the "no-thing on which every foundation founders," and which creates "freely out of nothing," says Taylor.[342] It is not a subjective faculty but God; or vice versa: God is imagination in the sense of life and death, the power to create and to destroy. Thus, although Taylor's argument is unconventional, his conclusion is not—except for one important aspect: according to him, imagination is entirely immanent and immanence is opaque. There is no trace in the immanent of anything transcendent, except for the transcendence that imagination itself represents by being transcendent to the concept (but not to experience). We may experience God's presence as a creative and destructive power, but we cannot understand him, and only in immanence is he present. Immanence thus contains no fissures. The realm of concepts is fissured, it opens up to experience, but the realm of experience is not. In *After God*, Taylor thus seems to claim that immanence closes in on itself.

Compared with Taylor's, Eugenio Trías's view on the relationship between the immanent and the transcendent is more

---

339   Taylor, *After God*, 307.

340   Taylor, *After God*, 117.

341   Taylor, *After God*, 116.

342   Taylor, *After God*, 117.

uplifting, even in a literal sense. Since Taylor does not regard the imagination as a human faculty, the problem is not that he allots immense power to the imagination but that he takes the aforementioned absolutism of immanence for granted. It is because of Taylor's radical immanentism—not his romanticism—that I now, to critique his view, include Trías's notion of the limit in my discussion. In the philosophy of Trías, the transcendent is not made something entirely immanent, though it can only be studied in the form of an experience and thus in an immanent form.[343] He refers to the transcendent as "the holy," and believes that it is only if the holy reveals itself that it can be experienced by us.[344] Such revelation takes place on the *limit*, which is Trías's term for what I call the intermediate world, and which is not just a border between the immanent and the transcendent. The limit is also, or more specifically, a space where what is immanent meets what is transcendent, referred to by Trías as a "symbolic event."[345] This event is made possible by the subject's encounter on the limit with his or her "*daimon*," interpreted platonically by Trías as an erotic power.[346] In his philosophy, we thus also find a power the format of which is 'expanded,' but without Taylor's depreciation of the transcendent as transcendent.

Trías's conception of the daimon and his definition of it as an erotic power rest on his notion of 'being' as a three-pronged whole consisting of *existence* (the dimension of being that reveals itself),

---

343 Concerning Trías, see besides the chapter "Åbenheden i mellemverdenen" also the chapters "Efter Guds død" (After the Death of God) and "Det sublime ved det skønne" (The Sublime in the Beautiful) in *Den skønne tænkning*. My presentation here and in what follows rests primarily, however, on "Åbenheden i mellemverdenen."

344 However, we never experience the holy as such, but only its incomplete self-manifestation in the form of "the sacred." For more concerning the relationship between the holy and the sacred, see footnote 350. See also the chapter "Limit and Threshold" in Dorthe Jørgensen, *Poetic Inclinations: Ethics, History, Philosophy* (Aarhus: Aarhus University Press, 2021).

345 Eugenio Trías, *Pensar la religión* (Barcelona: Ediciones Destino, 1997), 21, 152ff.

346 Trías, *Pensar la religión*, 227ff.; for Trías' definition of the daimon as erotic power, see 233. Later I will resume this interpretation.

the holy (a dimension of being that does not show itself), and *the being of the limit* (in the sense of "a being that highlights the duality and the asymmetry between two areas," the areas of what appears and what is hermetical).[347] Whenever one says 'being,' one also says 'God' (or vice versa), Trías thinks, and therefore the concept of the *being of the limit* must be supplemented by an analogous concept of the *god of the limit*. This does not mean that God and being are identical, but that they are linked dialectically. Similarly, philosophy and religion are not about the same thing, but about things that are related, for which they have different names, and to which they relate in different ways. According to Trías, the internal connection between God and being consists in the fact that God is being in a personal form and that being is the impersonal substrate of the divine. This is why he says that the being of the limit "assumes *personal* form as the God of the limit."[348] Moreover, this is Trías's own notion of God, for he also writes that "God is God of the limit: a God who from the limit, which designs and constitutes him, retains an intrinsic substrate while thanks to the caesura (and the passion that might define this) opens himself toward the existential revelation."[349]

For Trías, God reveals himself in the symbolic event that occurs in the intermediate world constituted by the limit, and he lets us feel a presence we can bear witness to, although God as such is out of reach.[350] Admittedly, today, all visible traces of such symbolic

---

347   Trías, *Pensar la religión*, 166.

348   Trías, *Pensar la religión*, 170–171.

349   Trías, *Pensar la religión*, 188.

350   Trías also describes this duality of the holy by distinguishing between *santo* and *sagrado* (Greek *hagion* and *hieron*, Latin *sanctus* and *sacer*), or in English: 'the holy' and 'the sacred.' The word 'sacred' refers to the dimension of the holy that appears and can be experienced and even used, while 'holy' denotes a dimension of it that is and will remain unavailable. Although it is possible to distinguish them, we are dealing with "two dimensions articulated by a single *phenomenon* (the holy-and-sacred)." See p. 106, endnote 7, in Trías's article "Thinking Religion: the Symbol and the Sacred," in *Religion*, eds. J. Derrida and G. Vattimo (Stanford: Stanford University Press, 1998). Here Trías also presents Rudolf Otto's *mysterium tremendum et fascinans* as structured in a similar way. For Otto, see *The Idea of the Holy*, trans. J.W. Harvey (New York: Oxford University Press, 1970); the German original

events have disappeared; gone are all concrete signs of any presence of the holy, that is, such symbolic events no longer occur as visionary experiences; to use Trías's words, the daimon no longer acts as a manifested presence. However, the consequence of this change is *not* that nobody meets a daimon anymore—that nobody exceeds what Trías calls "the personal subject."[351] The consequence is rather that the surpassing and the encounter occur "in secret," that is, without vision and manifestation, and thus most likely in the form of what in *Skønhedens metamorfose* (The Metamorphosis of Beauty) I meant by *experience of immanent transcendence* (as distinct from religious experience traditionally defined).[352]

As examples of 'secret' experiences of the presence of the holy, Trías mentions love, the painful experience of loss, the proximity of death (the death both of others and of oneself), that is, "all the harrowing and transformative experiences that force existence to seek a change from its *ethos*, its position, its actions."[353] These examples represent "experience that exceeds calculation and 'rational' computing," and which thus transcends rationality.[354] Therefore, they also exemplify experience that transcends the personal subject and shows openness toward the self in the sense of the daimon of the individual. Despite the nowadays often unformed and thus seemingly empty nature of the experience, the outcome of such a surpassing of rationality and of the subject is not empty, according to Trías's own interpretation of it: we do encounter something, even when we think that we do not since we are no longer able to visualize it. We meet our daimons, the powers that open us up and accomplish ex-

---

first appeared in 1917.

351 Trías, *Pensar la religión*, 228.

352 Trías, *Pensar la religión*, 227; Dorthe Jørgensen, *Skønhedens metamorfose: De æstetiske idéers historie* (The Metamorphosis of Beauty: History of Aesthetic Ideas) (Odense: Odense University Press, 2001).

353 Trías, *Pensar la religión*, 228.

354 Trías, *Pensar la religión*, 227–228.

pansions of the horizons we ourselves constitute—surpassings we do not master, but can try to express.

Sensitive Subjectivity

Klee instructed the artist to visualize what occurs invisibly in the intermediate world—to create a visual language for the processes and the forms of this world. However, according to him, expression is not the only purpose of the effort. If an artist symbolizes what, in the words of Trías, occurs on the limit between the immanent and the transcendent, both the artist and the rest of us might be able to *think* about what is otherwise invisible, and to *consider* how to explain the fact that it becomes visible. The artistic symbolization gives food for thought on the 'thinking eye' and its 'creative thinking' that, besides being at work in the viewer, already unfolds in the image and the artist's production of it.[355] The artistic visualization of something invisible also offers an opportunity to consider art as a way of comprehending what the understanding cannot understand. One must not, therefore, be surprised by the fact that some contemporary philosophers of science propose resorting to the arts in order to escape deficiencies experienced in modern science that are caused by the understanding's way of thinking.[356] As early as in the days of Klee, philosophy was advised to do something similar, namely to engage with the arts.[357]

In *Den skønne tænkning*, I explain the relationship between art, philosophy, and science considered by both philosophers of science and philosophers of art with reference to a common ori-

---

355 *Das bildnerische Denken* is the title of a book by Klee published in English as *Paul Klee Notebooks 1: The Thinking Eye*, ed. J. Spiller, trans. R. Manheim (London: Lund Humphries, 1961).

356 See, for example, Alfred I. Tauber (ed.), *The Elusive Synthesis: Aesthetics and Science* (Dordrecht, Boston, and London: Kluwer Academic Publishers, 1996).

357 The proponents of this idea include, among others, Benjamin, Heidegger, Theodor W. Adorno, and Hans-Georg Gadamer.

gin of art, philosophy, and science called 'basic experience.'[358] The intermediate world, which in the book is also referred to as 'sensitivity' (as distinct from the senses) and 'subjectivity' (as opposed to the subject), is unlocatable and indefinite; it is not a container for but rather consists of experiences of transcendence, for example, aesthetic or religious experiences. *Basic experience*, on the other hand, is the common source of these experiences. Unlike our individual experiences of transcendence, basic experience is *not* a particular single experience, but our very sensitively sensuous 'being-there-in-the-universe-together-with-whatever-else-there-is.' This source called 'basic experience' we experience only in its phenomenal manifestations; we only 'know' it thanks to our single experiences and the cultural phenomena in which they manifest themselves, that is, in the form of art and religion, for example. In order to approach the basic experience, one must thus enter the intermediate world—the realm of experience of transcendence, that is, sensitive subjectivity different from the subject. It is only in this way that one can comprehend inner connections between what is otherwise separated analytically; for example, the immanent and the transcendent. If we wish to come closer to an understanding of the relationship between art, philosophy, and science, we must approach basic experience, which itself requires that we enter the intermediate world. Philosophy can take this step by opening itself toward the arts, and the art world can take this step by opening itself toward philosophy (in the sense of *philosophia*).

    This intermediate world is not the same as life; it is not identical to human existence between birth and death, on earth under the sky. The expression 'the intermediate world' is *not* a (possibly theological) term for the 'geography' of existence, from here to there in time and space. This is *not* what I envisage when I use this expression in *Den skønne tænkning*. Nor is the intermediate world identical to the arts only, viewed as a realm reserved for spe-

---

358 See the chapter "Fornemmelse, tro og forståelse" (Sensation, Faith, and Comprehension) in *Den skønne tænkning*, in which I describe the basic experience as characterized by a trinity of sensation, faith, and comprehension—a trinity itself characterized by equiprimordiality (not hierarchy).

cial individuals who clearly envision something that others cannot see, and whose reality is thus different from other people's reality. This is also *not* what I have in mind when I use the expression 'the intermediate world' in *Den skønne tænkning*. Moreover, the intermediate world is *not* a universe created by individual people's subjective fantasies, without a connection to anything beyond fantasy itself. It is not a psychological phenomenon, although imagination is indeed part of it, for, in *Den skønne tænkning*, imagination is not a subjective faculty but a power in total being. Similarly, the expression 'the intermediate world' does *not* simply refer to the relationship between the human being and the world, although the realm it denotes does consist of experience, for, as previously shown, it is not just about any kind of experience. The word 'experience' here refers *not* to physical sensation, mere impression, empirical experience, life experience, or rational understanding, but to something that by its transcending nature truly qualifies as *experience*.

So what *is* the intermediate world? It is the sensitive subjectivity in which experiences of transcendence—aesthetic or religious experiences, for example—occur before any crystallization of subject and object has taken place. To be more specific, the intermediate world is the totality of experiences occurring in this realm of experience. The 'place' for the event that the intermediate world is thus considered to be must therefore be found outside what is generally meant by 'time and place.' Furthermore, it appeared earlier that the intermediate world is not a container for, but identical to, the experiences occurring in it; these are experiences of transcendence and therefore the intermediate world is characterized by *openness*. It is open to what cannot be sensed physically or explained by the understanding, and which is thus called 'suprasensuous.' This openness is what Taylor cannot see but Trías (like Klee) is aware of; Taylor regards immanence as opaque, regardless of how much he cares for immanent transcendence (which he interprets as imagination's transcendence of rationality), whereas the limit referred to by Trías is porous, as it is the place where the immanent and the transcendent meet.

Philosophical 'Method'

The intermediate world is distinguished not only by openness. In the experiences of transcendence that constitute it, a production of meaning takes place, since, to use Baumgarten's terminology, these experiences are characterized not by 'unity' or 'diversity,' but 'unity in diversity.' Furthermore, despite the fact that experiences of transcendence qualify as events, they can happen anywhere and at any time. Even in the most everyday situations, the world might unfold in experience thanks to which meaning of a different order—that is, a surplus—appears. Furthermore, events are by definition transformative, wherever they occur; no one leaves unaltered the space of experience constituted by events. Even in entirely ordinary situations, a person's view of the world might suddenly change, and the one to whom this happens is thus also transformed. The sensitive possibility of insight, to which the incidence of such experience testifies, can be regarded a poetic dimension of the world. It is this 'world poetry'—the poetry of the intermediate world—that has attracted attention in both philosophical aesthetics and hermeneutic phenomenology.[359] This world poetry is also what the metaphysics of experience illuminates, but in its own way: without aesthetics' point of departure in a philosophy of faculties and without phenomenology's reluctance toward aesthetics.

Philosophy only has access to the world poetry if it opens itself up to the dimension of 'feeling, sensation, and presentiment' in the realm of experience, that is, the dimension by aesthetics dubbed the 'aesthetic' side of that realm. It requires open-mindedness to reflect on what is happening in the intermediate world; it demands receptivity to the *meaningfulness* that distinguishes experiences of transcendence as experiences of a surplus. The intellectual ethos thus demanded is a precondition for any attempt by philosophy to cherish the world poetry, and the gentle handling of the beauty of the world poetry that is associated with this ethos is a prerequisite

---

359 The notion of 'world poetry' applied in *Den skønne tænkning* derives from Dorthe Jørgensen and Bettina Winkelmann, *Verdenspoesi: Malerier og tankebilleder* (World Poetry: Paintings and Thought-Images) (Aarhus: Women's Museum, 2011). See also the chapter "Hospitality and World Poetry" in Jørgensen, *Poetic Inclinations*.

for understanding the value of experiencing transcendence. For the sake of the beauty bestowed in the intermediate world, philosophy itself must thus undergo a 'beautification.' It must become more *sensitive* (not just sensuous) and more in search of *insight* (not just knowledge), as well as more *accurate* (in order, for example, not to confuse semiotic and existential meaning). In the realm of conceptual thinking, philosophy must strive for what Klee sought as an artist, namely, "exactitude winged by intuition."[360]

---

360   Paul Klee, "Exact Experiments in the Realm of Art, 1928," in *Creative Confession and Other Writings* (London: Tate Publishing, 2013), 18. This text was first published in *Bauhaus: Zeitschrift für Bau und Gestaltung* Vol. 2, No. 2–3 (1928): 17–17.

The Aesthetics of Prayer

"Without prayer, religious sensibility would likely atrophy and perhaps die," write Bruce Ellis Benson and Norman Wirzba in *The Phenomenology of Prayer*.[361] Praying is of paramount importance because it "connects us to the divine, to something beyond ourselves and beyond immediate reality."[362] Furthermore, in his book *Prayer*, Hans Urs von Balthasar writes that "most Christians are convinced that prayer is more than the outward performance of an obligation, in which we tell God things he already knows."[363] Although this is often how prayer functions—as a kind of accounting, or a request for something—most people know, nonetheless, or at least they have an obscure intimation, that there should be more to it. The latter is related, von Balthasar thinks, to the fact that a prayer is not a monologue but a conversation, namely between God and the soul, and that this conversation takes place in God's language.[364] According to von Balthasar, all speech is ultimately conversation, for speaking implies reciprocity; it is an exchange of thoughts in a common spirit, and it demands an I and a Thou.[365] "In prayer,

---

[361] Bruce Ellis Benson and Norman Wirzba, "Introduction," in *The Phenomenology of Prayer*, eds. B.E. Benson and N. Wirzba (New York: Fordham University Press, 2005), 1.

[362] Benson and Wirzba, "Introduction," 1.

[363] Hans Urs von Balthasar, *Prayer*, trans. G. Harrison (San Francisco: Ignatius Press, 1986), 13.

[364] Von Balthasar, *Prayer*, 14.

[365] Von Balthasar, *Prayer*, 14.

moreover, man speaks to a God who has long since revealed Himself to him in a Word which is so stupendous and all-embracing that it can never be 'past tense'; this Word resounds through all times as a present reality." Therefore, von Balthasar concludes that "the better a man learns to pray, the more deeply he finds that all his stammering is only an answer to God's speaking to him."[366] But this also means that "any understanding between God and man must be on the basis of God's language," which perhaps explains why it is so difficult to pray.[367] Over the years, many thinkers have said that we do not really know how to pray; a thought that may give rise to the idea that prayer is a constant learning process.[368] In this case, the question is which position one must adopt to best learn how to pray, which is the same as asking which position to adopt in prayer. The answer could well be *kenosis*, which means striving to empty oneself. Phenomenologically, such an emptying appears as a decentering because an opening of the subject takes place when one's focus is moved from oneself to God. To use the terminology from my book *Den skønne tænkning* (Beautiful Thinking), with this emptying, a movement from subject into subjectivity occurs, through which the divine can access and find a place in the individual.[369]

Among the proponents of kenosis seen as a path to God one finds Merold Westphal and James Mensch, who both contributed to *The Phenomenology of Prayer*.[370] Mensch takes his point of departure in questions previously discussed by Plato and Jacques Derrida (among others): how can prayer connect us with the sacred,

---

366 Von Balthasar, *Prayer*, 14.

367 Von Balthasar, *Prayer*, 14.

368 Benson and Wirzba suggest this idea on page four of their introduction to *The Phenomenology of Prayer*, and, in the passage quoted earlier, von Balthasar invites a similar conclusion.

369 Dorthe Jørgensen, *Den skønne tænkning: Veje til erfaringsmetafysik. Religionsfilosofisk udmøntet* (Beautiful Thinking: Pathways to the Metaphysics of Experience. Religio-Philosophically Implemented), Aarhus: Aarhus University Press, 2014.

370 Merold Westphal, "Prayer as the Posture of the Decentered Self," and James Mensch, "Prayer as Kenosis," both in *The Phenomenology of Prayer*.

and how can we ask for something without getting caught up in the "'earthly economy'"?[371] Considering these questions, Mensch regards prayer as an attempt to create a space for the appearance of the sacred, which involves a kenosis by which the sacred can incarnate in our bodily presence. According to him, we have a model for this in the form of the New Testament description of God's incarnation as his kenosis: his gradual emptying of himself, culminating on the cross. For Mensch, this emptying took place because it was the only way that God could manifest himself in the secular as non-secular; only thus could he appear *in* the world as being *outside* the world, that is, outside its 'economy.'[372] Just as God is in the world thanks to his kenosis, we must also empty ourselves, according to Mensch, in order to create a space in which God can appear to us and in which we ourselves are receptive to him.[373] However, Westphal believes that this kenosis, which is also a kind of receptivity, is not only what happens in prayer; it is also a prerequisite for truly being able to pray. The reason for this is that, according to Westphal, prayer holds five aspects in the form of praise, thanksgiving, confession, petition (for self), and intercession (for others), and he regards praise as the essence of prayer, even though the majority of us today find it most difficult to deal with this particular form of prayer.[374] Praise is fundamental because it is when one praises

---

371 Mensch, "Prayer as Kenosis," 63. In the chapter "The Intermediate World" it appeared that Eugenio Trías distinguishes between the 'holy' and the 'sacred.' Mensch distinguishes, instead, between two notions of the sacred: either it stays out of the world by hiding itself, or it comes into the world by incarnating itself. For the discussions by Plato and Derrida of the questions reexamined by Mensch, see Plato, "Euthyphro," trans. G.M.A. Grube, in *Plato: Complete Works*, eds. J.M. Cooper and D.S. Hutchinson (Indianapolis and Cambridge, MA: Hackett Publishing Company, 1997), and Jacques Derrida, *The Gift of Death*, trans. D. Wills (Chicago and London: The University of Chicago Press, 1996).

372 Mensch, "Prayer as Kenosis," 65. Gianni Vattimo already profited postmetaphysically from the New Testament construction of God's incarnation as kenosis, interpreted by Vattimo as his 'weakening' (*indebolimento*), in *Credere di credere*, published in 1996. See Gianni Vattimo, *Belief*, trans. L. D'Isanto and D. Webb (Stanford: Stanford University Press, 1999).

373 Mensch, "Prayer as Kenosis," 67.

374 Westphal, "Prayer as the Posture of the Decentered Self," 13. Westphal's contribution takes its point of departure in the estrangement he himself feels from praise, even though he is familiar with the other aspects of prayer.

that one truly disregards the interpersonal relationships that dominate social life and are reproduced by religion, and which are often structured by the exchange logic. But, for Westphal, this emancipation from the exchange logic requires the earlier mentioned kenosis, which he presents as a gesture that, since it precedes praise, also precedes the other aspects of prayer. However, this relationship between prayer and kenosis is probably best understood ontologically rather than genealogically: it is not according to the clock of historical temporality that the emptying of the self occurs before the actual praying. Kenosis is rather something that takes place through prayer and is thus happening in prayer's temporality; in turn, it is only when this emptying does in fact occur that anyone is truly praying.

In the preface to *The Phenomenology of Prayer*, Benson and Wirzba state that prayer is not, however, simply about a connection to the divine; it is also about us, since we pray to get what we request from God.[375] In claiming this, they are alluding to petitionary prayer, but there is also the prayer of thanks, and thanking is perhaps more fundamental to prayer than requesting is. For instance, it appears from Dieter Henrich's *Gedanken zur Dankbarkeit* (Thoughts of Gratitude) that it is the feeling of gratitude that is both the driving force of prayer and the source of philosophical thinking.[376] However, when Benson and Wirzba mention that praying is not just a matter of connecting God and human, they also refer to something else, namely that, in prayer, we learn who we are and how we relate to God, and that prayer can change our passions and existence in general, making us live in better harmony with faith. By extension, they ask what it is that gives prayer its force, and answer with reference to the idea that prayer is an *experience*

---

375   Benson and Wirzba, "Introduction," 1.

376   Dieter Henrich, "Gedanken zur Dankbarkeit," in *Bewusstes Leben: Untersuchungen zum Verhältnis von Subjektivität und Metaphysik* (Stuttgart: Philipp Reclam jun., 1999). This publication is an enlarged version of another text by Henrich with the same title, published in *Oikeiosis: Festschrift für Robert Spaemann*, ed. R. Löw (Weinheim: Acta Humaniora, 1987).

at the limit and an *intensification of the experience*.[377] In their view, prayer removes all pretension and eventually leads into a wordless mysterious dark night or blinding light, where the person at prayer is totally enclosed by the transcendent, which both exceeds and maintains the being of the person. In this sense, prayer is an experience at the limit, but, as mentioned, it can also be described as an intensification of the experience because, by opening up the mind in existentially transformative ways, it allows for recognition of a depth and breadth of existence—"life's gratuity, fragility, terror, blessing, and interdependence"—we otherwise overlook or take for granted.[378] The *normal experience* is thus what prayer intensifies, by which prayer itself takes shape as an *experience at the limit*, and this is not intellectually controlled, but emotional. Prayer is an emotional action that opens up the subject, that is, the one controlled by understanding, and leads to a movement into a subjectivity that in *Den skønne tænkning* I refer to as 'the intermediate world.'[379] There, I describe the intermediate world as the sphere of experience that exists before the constitution of any subject and object—a sphere that, in the eighteenth century, was dubbed the world of aesthetic experiences. I therefore add to Benson and Wirzba's presentation the idea that, if praying is an emotional act, and, if it takes place in what I call the intermediate world, it is an *aesthetic* phenomenon: it springs from, opens up for, regulates, and produces feeling, sensation, and presentiment.

The interpretations of prayer presented earlier concern more than various aspects of the phenomenology of prayer; they also touch upon classical positions in prayer's history of ideas. As Christoph Klein says in *Das grenzüberschreitende Gebet* (The Limit-Transcending Prayer), Christianity nourished two interpretations in particular of what it means to pray: the traditional Western understanding of prayer as a conversation with God per-

---

377 Benson and Wirzba, "Introduction," 2.

378 Benson and Wirzba, "Introduction," 2.

379 See also the chapter "The Intermediate World."

ceived as a person before oneself; and the traditional Eastern understanding of prayer as a mystical connection to or becoming one with God.[380] Despite the various qualities of these traditions, Klein regards their interpretations of prayer as one-sided, and he therefore argues for a third option, according to which prayer is both a "speaking" and a "connecting" with God: it is "a total happening."[381] Klein's concept of 'limit-transcending experience' is intended to describe this more comprehensive understanding of prayer, as he joins Paul Tillich in arguing that "being 'at the limit'" is "'the truly fertile place for cognition,' which allows us to stand between the positions and thus absorb both positions in a tense, but helpful 'mutuality,' through which the contradictions can be overcome."[382] In other words, Klein wants not only to develop a third perception of what it means to pray, but to do so by unifying the existent understandings without blurring their differences so as to benefit from their respective qualities. Inspired by Hans-Martin Barth's *Wohin—woher mein Ruf?* (To Whom—Wherefrom My Call?), the result is a *Trinitarian-koinonian* interpretation of prayer that is both different from the theistic conception of prayer as a dialogue and the nonpersonal interpretation that results from the 'death of God' theology.[383] Klein believes that, by ourselves, we are not able to pray, and that, in prayer, we do not enter into a direct and unmediated relationship with God. Trinitarian-koinonially understood prayer is rather something that occurs thanks to an initiative that

---

380   Christoph Klein, *Das grenzüberschreitende Gebet: Zugänge zum Beten in unserer Zeit* (Göttingen: Vandenhoeck and Ruprecht, 2004).

381   Klein, *Das grenzüberschreitende Gebet*, 14. It is obvious that the 'happening' referred to by Klein is not just an incident, but an occurrence and event; this is confirmed in footnote 383.

382   Klein, *Das grenzüberschreitende Gebet*, 14.

383   Hans-Martin Barth, *Wohin—woher mein Ruf? Zur Theologie des Bittgebets* (München: Chr. Kaiser Verlag, 1981). The term 'Trinitarian' indicates that Klein actualizes the Christian doctrine of the trinity of God with the result that, in prayer, there is not only an I in front of a Thou. Furthermore, it is evidenced by the name 'koinonian' (derived from the Greek *koinonia*, that is, connection through intimate involvement) that prayer gives birth to community, and that it is characterized by occurrence, not by mysterious union.

stems from God and is mediated by the Son—an initiative that enables the individual's prayer in the Spirit. According to this understanding, petitionary prayer is more fundamental than prayer of thanks; but the interpretation of petitionary prayer now referred to is different from that described previously.[384] Petitionary prayer is of such fundamental importance not as a result of the exchange logic but as an expression of an experience and acceptance of one's own distress and dependence. "He who prays in the Spirit professes his distress and admits that he is dependent on something happening to him," writes Klein.[385] In prayer, the person at prayer becomes "aware that he cannot pray by himself, but that his praying accomplishes itself as he articulates it, and even before he says anything."[386] Therefore, when someone prays, he or she is not in control of their praying, but *it prays in them*.[387]

Traditionally, oral and contemplative prayers were given priority, but, after Klein's clarification of these forms of prayer, he highlights the prayer of the heart. *Oral prayer* is discursive and dialogical; the word mediates between God and human, and the result is named conversation.[388] *Contemplative prayer* is more comprehensive in that it "makes use of thought, imagination, emotionality, and longing," and it is not discursive but affective.[389] The *prayer*

---

384 According to Barth, praise (or worship, *Anbetung*, as he actually writes) was traditionally regarded as the most weighty form of prayer, followed by thanksgiving and finally by petitionary prayer. But Barth inverts this hierarchy as he thinks that it demands more from us, especially from us as modern people, to request than to praise; see pp. 12–15 in *Wohin—woher mein Ruf?* As it appears from what follows, Klein shares this opinion.

385 Klein, *Das grenzüberschreitende Gebet*, 74.

386 Klein, *Das grenzüberschreitende Gebet*, 74.

387 Klein, *Das grenzüberschreitende Gebet*, 74. "'It prays in him,'" Klein himself writes, referring to "the experience of the great praying persons."

388 Klein, *Das grenzüberschreitende Gebet*, 96. Oral prayer dates from the time of Jesus, but it has been cultivated by Protestant Churches in particular.

389 On page 102 in *Das grenzüberschreitende Gebet* Klein quotes Ecclesia Catholica, *Katechismus der Katholischen Kirche* (München, Wien, Leipzig, Freiburg, and Linz: Oldenbourg, Benno. Paulusverlag, and Veritas, 1993), 679. In the Catholic Church, the contemplative prayer has a particularly strong position.

of the heart, however, is neither a "prayer of the lips" nor a "prayer of the spirit."[390] It is neither just verbal nor just contemplative, neither simply discursive nor simply affective, but includes and exceeds both possibilities since the word 'heart' refers to "the human person as a whole."[391] The heart is the "middle," the midst of consciousness, unconsciousness, soul, spirit, body, the intelligible and the unintelligible, that is, "the absolute center," and praying is about entering this center.[392] Here it prays in you, and this is similar to breathing: "One breathes without being conscious of it, but can always become aware of it."[393] One can become aware of how one is covered and carried by one's breath. Likewise prayer is something that happens; but through prayer one can become aware that it occurs and aware of the existential importance of it. If in prayer we enter the center called the heart, in which praying with all of us is taking place, we have, however, already made the previously mentioned move from being subjects to being in subjectivity, that is, we have entered the intermediate world—yet without turning off all consciousness and without suspending all thought. Although Klein does not offer an explanation of this sort, his study of prayer and the interpretation of it he presents confirm prayer's aesthetic nature. Prayer is not aesthetic in the currently dominant hollowed sense of the word 'aesthetic,' where it only means sensuous. On the contrary, it is aesthetic in the full philosophical sense: it is sensitive and therefore both bodily and mental—or rather *lived-bodily* (leiblich). The heart is lived-bodily, which is why it can be "the place of the meeting between God and man," which neither the brain nor

---

390   Klein, *Das grenzüberschreitende Gebet*, 111. The prayer of the heart began among the desert fathers. The first monk to write about this form of prayer rooted in the New Testament was Evagrius Pontikus, who died in 399, Klein writes on page 106.

391   Klein, *Das grenzüberschreitende Gebet*, 111.

392   Klein, *Das grenzüberschreitende Gebet*, 111. Klein quotes Antonie Plamadeala, *Traditie si libertate in spiritualitatea ortodoxa* (Sibiu, 1983), 281f.

393   Klein, *Das grenzüberschreitende Gebet*, 74.

consciousness can ever be.[394] It is precisely because the heart is lived-bodily that it has theological significance but also points to the fundamentally aesthetic quality of religious experiences.

In the philosophy of Jean-Louis Chrétien, it is in the intermediate world—in other words, aesthetically—that we perceive the call he has contemplated for years. Not only does Chrétien think of the beautiful as a response to God's induction of the being to being and as a calling of us; he considers our aesthetic experiential relationship to the world as what, essentially, enables us to perceive God's call. This is evidenced, for example, by Chrétien's analysis of the senses, in which he argues that sight and hearing are closely related—the eye listens, the voice is visible—and also that the sense of touch is the foundation of the other senses.[395] According to him, it is the sense of touch—which by nature requires the 'lived body'—that enables the physical body to listen; ultimately, this sense is thus what allows us to perceive God's call. For "nor does the ear alone listen; the eye also listens and responds. The possibility of their listening, however, ultimately takes root in the totality of the flesh. The flesh listens. And the fact that it listens is what makes it respond."[396] According to Chrétien, the sense of touch explains how the call can reverberate throughout all of our substance and thus all our senses. To be touched by God is "to listen with one's whole being, body and soul, without anything in us that escapes hearing and stands outside of it."[397] Against this background, in his essay "The Wounded Word," Chrétien thinks of our recitation of the words of prayer as "the breath drawn in and blown out," and he regards

---

394 Klein, *Das grenzüberschreitende Gebet*, 111. For a discussion of this religious use of the word 'heart,' see Troels Nørager, "Heart as Metaphor in Religious Language," in *Metaphor and God-talk*, eds. I. Boeve and K. Feyaerts (Bern: Peter Lang, 1999), 215–232.

395 See the second and fourth chapters of Jean-Louis Chrétien, *The Call and the Response*, trans. Anne A. Davenport (New York: Fordham University Press, 2004).

396 Chrétien, *The Call and the Response*, 130. The word 'flesh' translates Chrétien's French term *la chair*, different from *la viande* (meat). Having the aforementioned distinction between the physical and the lived body in mind, we could also translate 'la chair' as 'lived body' (different from 'physical body,' *le corps*).

397 Chrétien, *The Call and the Response*, 130.

prayer, as such, as "the event wherein what is invisible to myself illuminates me."[398] In traditional thought, illumination was also considered a feature of philosophical cognition, which in turn, according to Chrétien, was usually considered a result of the thoughtful person's conversation with herself, the so-called *soliloquy*, or of the study of consciousness. Like von Balthasar's description of prayer as a dialogue rather than a monologue, Chrétien thinks, however, that the illumination of someone in prayer differs phenomenologically from the illumination of philosophical cognition by having an addressee outside the individual herself. One does not pray to nothing, but, in prayer, one approaches and addresses another; however, it is we who are taught by what is uttered, and it is on us that it acts.[399] The words we utter when we pray have no influence on God and do not change him but rather us. Prayer has formative power and effect, and, because praying is an aesthetic phenomenon of the intermediate world, *aesthetic formation* is what takes place when we pray. Prayer cultivates our ability to receive the divine in lived-bodily experience.

The formation brought about by prayer is a learning process that takes a detour around the body. Depending on our churches, we fold our hands or kiss icons, light candles, inhale incense, let rosaries slip between our fingers, or burst into song. However, it is to open up the *lived* body for the divine that the *physical* body is mobilized. It is as something aesthetic—not just sensuous—that the formation brought about by prayer takes place in the intermediate world. Although the physical body contributes, and consciousness is affected by its actions, the aesthetic formation brought about by prayer occurs neither in the physical body nor in consciousness, but in the lived body. As mentioned earlier, this formation that cultivates our ability to receive the divine in a lived-bodily way is an opening of the subject; and, considered a phenomenon of forma-

---

398 Jean-Louis Chrétien, "The Wounded Word: The Phenomenology of Prayer," trans. B.G. Prusak, in *Phenomenology and the "Theological Turn": The French Debate*, eds. D. Janicaud et al. (New York: Fordham University Press, 2000), 154.

399 Chrétien, "The Wounded Word," 152–153.

tion, it is thus essentially a development of *open-mindedness*. Albeit indirectly, Chrétien himself touches upon this when he writes that prayer is the religious phenomenon par excellence, *because* it is "the sole human act that opens the religious dimension and never ceases to underwrite, to support, and to suffer this opening."[400] Considered a radically opening phenomenon, prayer is also essentially undogmatic, which is also consistent with its aesthetic nature: it is open and undogmatic *because* it is aesthetic, that is, sensitively emotional, sensate, and presentimental, including all the unprejudiced receptivity that this implies.[401] This kind of openness is reflected in a statement about prayer from Walter Benjamin, by which he also indirectly confirmed the aesthetic nature of prayer.[402] Benjamin stated that "even if Kafka did not pray—and this we do not know—he still possessed in the highest degree what Malebranche called 'the natural prayer of the soul': attentiveness."[403] As I write in *Den skønne tænkning*, Benjamin regarded this attentiveness as crucial to the perception that is an indispensable condition for experience. Along with habit, it is prayer as Benjamin describes it that, according to him, is a precondition for being able to 'read' the world. However, as I also explain in *Den skønne tænkning*, it appears that, nowadays, our attention has become lethargic. We have lost the ability to pray and are therefore confronted with an expe-

---

400   Chrétien, "The Wounded Word," 147.

401   Here the word 'undogmatic' is used in its contemporary everyday meaning, not in its philosophical meaning derived from Immanuel Kant's definition of 'dogmatic.' From Kant's preface to the second edition of the *Critique of Pure Reason* (B XXXV), it appears that he applied different meanings to the words 'dogmatic' and 'dogmatism.' He considered dogmatism to be the opposite of criticism, but regarded 'dogmatic' as identical to 'systematic' and 'scientific.' Therefore, he rejected dogmatism, but highlighted the need for dogmatic investigation. For the latter, see Immanuel Kant, *Critique of Pure Reason*, eds. and trans. P. Guyer and A.W. Wood (Cambridge, UK: Cambridge University Press, 1998), BXXXV.

402   For Benjamin's construction of prayer, and for a number of related phenomena and concepts, also see Carolin Duttlinger, "Studium, Aufmerksamkeit, Gebet: Walter Benjamin und die Kontemplation," in *Profanes Leben: Walter Benjamins Dialektik der Säkularisierung*, ed. D. Weidner (Frankfurt am Main: Suhrkamp Verlag, 2010).

403   Walter Benjamin, "Franz Kafka: On the Tenth Anniversary of his Death," trans. H. Zorn, in *Selected Writings, Volume 2: 1927–1934*, eds. M.W. Jennings, H. Eiland, and G. Smith (Cambridge, MA and London: The Belknap Press of Harvard University Press 2001), 812.

rience issue that involves far more than the question of whether we believe in (a particular) god. It is our conscious life as such that is at stake, since someone who cannot pray like Kafka is also unable to find his place in the world, because he sees nothing and understands nothing. He lacks the *aesthetic sensitivity* that is the source of understanding.

Prayer not only includes an aesthetic formation through which we develop our ability to receive the divine in lived-bodily experience. It also allows us to gain access to, sharpen, and refine our aesthetic sensitivity—our attentive openness to the world—without which we might survive (perhaps satisfy our physical needs and calculate sufficiently) but we would not *think*, and we would therefore not live as *human* beings. Aristotle defined the human as 'the thinking being,' the *zoon logon echon* or *animal rationale*, but Martin Heidegger stated that human being-there in the world is distinguished by something other than rational knowledge.[404] What is peculiar to being-there is rather a sensitive thoughtful openness—to the world, and also to the Being (without which there would be nothing to be open to). It is a similar mindset that is expressed—albeit theologically—by von Balthasar when he refers to the human as "created to be a hearer of the word" and claims that "it is in responding to the word that it attains its true dignity."[405] Humans are created to listen to something that does not come from them, but which they become, namely truly human, von Balthasar, the *theologian*, states. His statement is indirectly confirmed by the *philosopher* Heidegger, who does not say that we should listen to God but who does encourage us to lend an ear to more than our monologues with ourselves. The human's "innermost constitution has been designed for dialogue," von Balthasar also claims in *Das betrachtende*

---

[404] Heidegger problematized the usual Latin-based interpretation of Aristotle's notion of the human being rather than this notion itself. According to Heidegger, the Latin translation of *zoon logon echon* as *animal rationale* implied a transformation of the being that thinks because it speaks and listens into the merely rationally thinking being. See Martin Heidegger, "Letter on 'Humanism,'" trans. F.A. Capuzzi, in *Pathmarks*, ed. W. McNeill (Cambridge, UK: Cambridge University Press, 1998), 245 ff.

[405] Von Balthasar, *Prayer*, 22. Translation modified.

Gebet. "Human reason is equipped with as much light of its own as it needs to apprehend God speaking to it."[406] This light of its own, which is not the announcement as such, but what makes it possible to apprehend the announced, is in the words of philosophical aesthetics the aforementioned aesthetic sensitivity. It is because reason is nourished by a sensitivity that is of a feeling, sensate, and presentimental nature that it is capable of the transcendence that allows it to connect what the understanding divides analytically; for example, the immanent and the transcendent. This is also why a conversation is taking place, even though the person at prayer appears to be talking to herself—a conversation between the soul that is aesthetically sensitive (: it has heart) and the God who appears for the soul in the openness to divinity included by sensitivity (: God appears in the heart).

In a time like ours, however, it is easy to doubt that a person at prayer can have contact with anything other than herself. When we see someone praying, we see "a man who speaks alone," writes Chrétien in *The Wounded Word*, and Immanuel Kant was misled by this observation to regard prayer as a conversation that one has with *oneself*.[407] In *Religion within the Boundaries of Mere Reason*, Kant thus refers to the praying person as someone who appears to be talking to God but is really talking to herself.[408] He also compares the person at prayer with someone who is caught speaking aloud although she is alone, and who is therefore suspected of being crazy. According to Kant, it is not even wrong to consider a person at prayer as disturbed, since she behaves in a way that implies there is somebody in front of her even though she is the only person present.[409] Kant actually regarded this conception of prayer—namely, as an expression of the belief in the presence of another—as a "su-

406 Von Balthasar, *Prayer*, 22. Translation modified.

407 Chrétien, "The Wounded Word," 150.

408 Immanuel Kant, *Religion within the Boundaries of Mere Reason: And Other Writings*, eds. and trans. A. Wood and G.D. Giovanni (Cambridge, UK: Cambridge University Press, 1998), 188 (6: 197).

409 Kant, *Religion within the Boundaries of Mere Reason*, 186 (6: 195, footnote)

perstitious illusion" and "fetish-making."[410] He therefore wished to save the "spirit of prayer" from the "address"; he wished to free faith understood as sheer moral sense from any mythological costume.[411] However, talking *alone* is not the same as talking to *oneself*, Chrétien notes, and he further states that Kant misunderstood and distorted prayer because he did not study it phenomenologically but simply equated prayer and soliloquy. "To collapse prayer into pure soliloquy, into dialogue with oneself, is not to describe but to interpret and construct by doing violence to the phenomenon," writes Chrétien.[412] But if we study prayer phenomenologically, we learn that another being actually appears for the praying person, and that this other being, called God, appears as an emotional, sensate, and presentimental—that is, an aesthetic and thus lived-bodily—reality.

Phenomenologically considered, a person at prayer is thus not talking to herself but to God, who, in prayer, manifests himself lived-bodily for those who are open to such an appearance. However, according to von Balthasar, there is a shortage of such openness today although, essentially, human being is "the creature with a mystery in its heart that is bigger than itself. It is built like a tabernacle around a most sacred mystery."[413] The latter means that we do not actually need to do anything in order to approach God. No one needs to "take deliberate action to open up his or her innermost self" because "it is already there, its very nature is readiness, receptivity, the will to surrender to what is greater."[414] However, von Balthasar believes that, in our day, the bond between God and human is broken, and there is therefore a need to pray, that is, to once again open the mind. It is necessary to carry out the aesthetic for-

---

410   Kant, *Religion within the Boundaries of Mere Reason*, 186 (6: 194).

411   Kant, *Religion within the Boundaries of Mere Reason*, 186 (6: 195 and the footnote same page). I have omitted the italics for the sake of my own emphases in the sentence that follows.

412   Chrétien, "The Wounded Word," 151.

413   Von Balthasar, *Prayer*, 22–23. Translation modified.

414   Von Balthasar, *Prayer*, 23. Translation modified.

mation through prayer that is the work of prayer. However, this formative aspect of prayer is precisely what Klein hints at by using the word *koinonia* when he refers to prayer as something Trinitarian-koinonian, even though he does this without any attention to its aesthetic nature, and thus also without reaching a complete understanding of it. Thanks to its roots in *koinos*, the word 'koinonia' denotes, among other things, community and common participation, and the verb *koinonein* means 'to share something,' be it materially or spiritually.[415] Similarly, a *koinonos* is someone who, through active participation, shares something with others, be it in the form of joint ownership or sharing a belief.

In Greek thought, this koinonia can be linked to the formative ideal called *kalokagathia*, beauty-and-goodness, in so far as the latter not only includes a person's physical appearance, but also his or her moral behavior and way of participating in the community.[416] Later, the first Christians developed an understanding of koinonia as the Church's community of faith in God carried by the Holy Spirit; and, over the years, koinonia has referred, in particular, to the supper communion with Christ described as an event. In koinonia, the individual transcends herself, without herself being in control of what is happening, and she participates in the actualization of something larger, be it the Greek ethos or the Christian faith. In spirit and action, a unity in diversity is koinonially formed that exceeds the individual's own interests in favor of the common good. However, since antiquity, unity in diversity was regarded and discussed as something *beautiful*. Furthermore, Kant showed that

---

415 For the meaning of the word 'koinonia,' see, for example, Heinrich Seesemann, *Der Begriff 'Koinonia' im Neuen Testament* (Giessen: Verlag von Alfred Töpelmann, 1933), and Verna Lewis-Elgidely, *Koinonia in the Three Great Abrahamic Faiths: Acclaiming the Mystery and Diversity of Faiths* (South Bend: Cloverdale Books, 2007).

416 Alex García-Rivera states such a connection in his "Communion and Community: The Language of the Sacraments," in *Languages of Worship/El lenguaje de la liturgia*, ed. R. Gómez (Chicago: Liturgy Training Publications, 2004). In Christianity, the beautiful-and-good becomes the beautiful-and-sacred, says García-Rivera. He therefore regards the language of the sacraments as the language of kalokagathia, that is, an aesthetic language in which the beautiful and the sacred are one (p. 44). This is the reason why this language is not dead, but alive.

the *sensus communis* in the form of which he himself themed such nonreductive transcendence is *aesthetic* by nature, as it is neither the understanding's nor the reason's way of thinking but rather the aesthetic judgment's that enables such transcendence.[417] According to Kant, it is thus actually aesthetic judgment that is the common sense, because the free reflexivity unfolded by judgment does not simply replace one with the other but rather seeks what is common. The consequence of this is that koinonia is in fact aesthetic: koinonein historically anticipated what later was thematized as *aesthetic thinking*.

Prayer is room for the aesthetic thinking with which we lived-bodily address and approach God—both listening and speaking, being present with all of us, not just sensuously or mentally, but sensitively and lived-bodily, that is, emotionally, perceptively, and forebodingly, or in other words: aesthetically. Prayer *presupposes* aesthetic sensitivity—the openness and receptivity that sensitivity represents—but it also *sharpens* the aesthetic sensitivity of the person who actually tries to pray. Prayer thus has a forming effect in the true sense of the word 'formation:' it unfolds a possibility that already exists in us, but is most often ignored and dries out, namely the possibility of hearing and responding to what Chrétien describes as the call—a possibility implied by the sensitivity that characterizes being-there. The listening and speaking that is practiced in prayer—not only with the ears and the voice, but with all the physical-spiritual presence in the world of someone who is praying—does not lead into the mysterious dark night or blinding light referred to by Benson and Wirzba. Or, as far as it darkens, this is something that only happens to the subject controlled by understanding; it is the subject but not subjectivity that is blinded. For, as described earlier, prayer requires and brings about a kenosis, but this emptying of the self does not clear the person at prayer of everything. It is only the subject controlled by understanding that is emptied, stripped of its governance, which happens in favor of the

---

417 Immanuel Kant, *Critique of the Power of Judgment*, eds. and trans. P. Guyer and E. Matthews (New York: Cambridge University Press, 2000), § 40 (5: 293–296).

free and as such aesthetic reflexivity of subjectivity that is open and receptive. From this, it also follows that no mystical union with the divine is taking place at prayer, that is, the praying person does not become one with God. Such an elimination of all differences would not be aesthetic, but as stated previously, prayer is exactly room for aesthetic thinking. Nevertheless, when we pray, we do indeed encounter something other than ourselves, as was described by Chretien and von Balthasar: we are part of a 'dialogue' that is not just a conversation with ourselves, and which, as described by Klein, allows us to feel that we are united with something greater. Prayer encourages the feeling of entering a community of not only other worshippers, but also the God we worship, and this community is by nature an occurrence: it is so close and intimate, so detached from all exchange logic—all ideas of 'one thing for another,' all instrumentalism—that it is confusingly similar to mysterious unity, but it is different. Both of these—both the resemblance and the difference—confirm the aesthetics of prayer: that it is beautiful when it is successful, meaning that it happens.

Bibliography

Adorno, Theodor W. *Aesthetic Theory*. Edited by G. Adorno and R. Tiedemann, translated by R. Hullot-Kentor. London: Athlone Press, 1997.

Aquinas, Thomas. *The Summa Theologica: Complete Edition*. Translated by The Fathers of the English Dominican Province. London: Catholic Way Publishing, 2014.

Aristotle. *Metaphysics*. Translated by W.D. Ross. In *The Complete Works of Aristotle: The Revised Oxford Translation, Volume 2*, edited by J. Barnes, 1552–1728. Princeton: Princeton University Press, 1984.

Aristotle. *On the Soul*. Translated by J.A. Smith. In *The Complete Works of Aristotle: The Revised Oxford Translation, Volume 1*, edited by J. Barnes, 641–692. Princeton: Princeton University Press, 1984.

Aristotle, *Poetics*. Translated by I. Bywater. In *The Complete Works of Aristotle: The Revised Oxford Translation, Volume 2*, edited by J. Barnes, 2316–2340. Princeton: Princeton University Press, 1984.

Augustine. *On music (De musica)*. Translated by R.C. Taliaferro. In *The Immortality of the Soul; The Magnitude of the Soul; On Music; The Advantage of Believing; On Faith in Things Unseen*, 153–379. Washington: The Catholic University of America Press, 2002.

Augustine. *The Trinity*. Translated by S. McKenna. In *The Fathers of the Church: A New Translation, Volume 45*, edited by H. Dressler et al. Washington: The Catholic University of America Press, 1963.

Bachelard, Gaston. *Earth and Reveries of Will: An Essay on the Imagination of Matter*. Translated by K. Haltman. Dallas: The Dallas Institute Publications, 2002.

Bachelard, Gaston. *The Poetics of Reverie: Childhood, Language, and the Cosmos*. Translated by D. Russell. Boston: Beacon Press, 1971.

Bachelard, Gaston. *The Poetics of Space*. Translated by M. Jolas. New York: Penguin Books, 2014.

Balthasar, Hans Urs von. *Prayer*. Translated by G. Harrison. San Francisco: Ignatius Press, 1986.

Barth, Hans-Martin. *Wohin—woher mein Ruf? Zur Theologie des Bittgebets*. München: Chr. Kaiser Verlag, 1981.

Barth, J. Robert. "Imagination." In *New Dictionary of the History of Ideas, Volume 3*, edited by M.C. Horowitz, 1102–1109. New York: Charles Scribner's Sons, 2005.

Bates, Jennifer Ann. *Hegel's Theory of Imagination*. Albany: State University of New York Press, 2004.

Baumgarten, Alexander Gottlieb. *Ästhetik, Volume 1–2*. Translated by D. Mirbach. Hamburg: Felix Meiner Verlag, 2007.

Baumgarten, Alexander Gottlieb. *Die Vorreden zur Metaphysik*. Edited and translated by U. Niggli. Frankfurt am Main: Vittorio Klostermann, 1998.

Baumgarten, Alexander Gottlieb. *Metaphysica. Editio VII*. Reprographischer Nachdruck der Ausgabe Halle 1779. Hildesheim: Georg Olms Verlagsbuchhandlung, 1963.

Baumgarten, Alexander Gottlieb. *Metaphysics: A Critical Translation with Kant's Elucidations, Selected Notes, and Related Materials*. Edited and translated by C.D. Fugate and J. Hymers. London: Bloomsbury Academic, 2014.

Baumgarten, Alexander Gottlieb. *Reflections on Poetry: Alexander Gottlieb Baumgarten's Meditationes philosophicae de nonnullis ad poema pertinentibus*. Translated by K. Aschenbrenner and W.B. Holther. Berkeley and Los Angeles: University of California Press, 1954.

Benjamin, Walter. *Berlin Childhood around 1900*. Translated by H. Eiland. In *Selected Writings, Volume 3: 1935–1938*, edited by H. Eiland and M.W. Jennings, 344–413. Cambridge, MA and London: The Belknap Press of Harvard University Press, 2002.

Benjamin, Walter, "'Experience.'" Translated by L. Spencer and S. Jost. In *Selected Writings, Volume 1: 1913–1926*, edited by M. Bullock and M.W. Jennings, 3–5. Cambridge, MA and London: The Belknap Press of Harvard University Press, 2002.

Benjamin, Walter. "Franz Kafka: On the Tenth Anniversary of his Death." Translated by H. Zorn. In *Selected Writings, Volume 2: 1927–1934*, edited by M.W. Jennings, H. Eiland, and G. Smith, 794–818. Cambridge, MA and London: The Belknap Press of Harvard University Press, 2001.

Benjamin, Walter. "Little History of Photography." Translated by E. Jephcott and K. Shorter. In *Selected Writings, Volume 2: 1927–1934*, edited by M.W. Jennings, H. Eiland, and G. Smith, 507–530. Cambridge, MA and London: The Belknap Press of Harvard University Press, 2001.

Benjamin, Walter. "On Language as Such and on the Language of Man." Translated by E. Jephcott. In *Selected Writings, Volume 1: 1913–1926*, edited by M. Bullock and M.W. Jennings, 62–74. Cambridge, MA and London: The Belknap Press of Harvard University Press, 2002.

Benjamin, Walter. "On Some Motifs in Baudelaire." Translated by H. Zohn. In *Selected Writings, Volume 4: 1938–1940*, edited by H. Eiland and M.W. Jennings, 313–355. Cambridge, MA and London: The Belknap Press of Harvard University Press, 2003.

Benjamin, Walter. "On the Concept of History." Translated by H. Zohn. In *Selected Writings, Volume 4: 1938–1940*, edited by H. Eiland and M.W. Jennings, 389–400. Cambridge, MA and London: The Belknap Press of Harvard University Press, 2003.

Benjamin, Walter. "On the Program of the Coming Philosophy." Translated by M. Ritter. In *Selected Writings, Volume 1: 1913–1926*, edited by M. Bullock and M.W. Jennings, 100–110. Cambridge, MA and London: The Belknap Press of Harvard University Press, 2002.

Benjamin, Walter. "Surrealism: The Last Snapshot of the European Intelligentsia." Translated by E. Jephcott. In *Selected Writings, Volume 2: 1927–1934*, edited by M.W. Jennings, H. Eiland, and G. Smith, 207–221. Cambridge, MA and London: The Belknap Press of Harvard University Press, 2001.

Benjamin, Walter. *The Origin of German Tragic Drama*. Translated by J. Osborne. London and New York: Verso, 2009.

Benjamin, Walter. "The Work of Art in the Age of Its Technological Reproducibility: Second Version." Translated by E. Jephcott and H. Zohn. In *Selected Writings, Volume 3: 1935–1938*, edited by H. Eiland and M.W. Jennings, 101–133. Cambridge, MA and London: The Belknap Press of Harvard University Press, 2002.

Benson, Bruce Ellis and Norman Wirzba. "Introduction." In *The Phenomenology of Prayer*, edited by B.E. Benson and N. Wirzba, 1–9. New York: Fordham University Press, 2005.

Böhme, Gernot. *Aisthetik: Vorlesungen über Ästhetik als allgemeine Wahrnehmungslehre*. München: Wilhelm Fink Verlag, 2001.

Böhme, Gernot. *Ethik leiblicher Existenz: Über unseren moralischen Umgang mit der eigenen Natur*. Frankfurt am Main: Suhrkamp Verlag, 2008.

Böhme, Gernot. "The Concept of Body as the Nature We Ourselves Are." *The Journal of Speculative Philosophy* Vol. 24, No. 3 (2010): 224–238.

Boileau-Despréaux, Nicolas. *The Art of Poetry*. Translated by W. Soames. Richmond: Alma Books, 2008.

Bonaventura. *Itinerarium Mentis in Deum*. In *Works of St. Bonaventure, Volume 2*. Edited by Ph. Boehner and Z. Hayes. New York: The Franciscan Institute, St. Bonaventura University, 2003.

Breyfogle, Todd. "Imagination." In *Augustine Through the Ages: An Encyclopedia*, edited by A.D. Fitzgerald et al., 442–443. Grand Rapids and Cambridge, UK: William B. Eerdmans Publishing Company, 1999.

Bundy, Murray Wright. *The Theory of Imagination in Classical and Mediaeval Thought*. University of Illinois Studies in Language and Literature Vol. 12, No. 2–3 (May–August 1927). Urbana: The University of Illinois Press, 1927.

Burkert, Walter. *The Orientalizing Revolution: Near Eastern Influence on Greek Culture in the Early Archaic Age*. London and Cambridge, MA: Harvard University Press, 1992.

Casey, Edward S. "Imagination: Imagining and the Image." *Philosophy and Phenomenological Research* Vol. 31, No. 4 (1971): 475–490.

Casey, Edward S. *Imagining: A Phenomenological Study*. Bloomington: Indiana University Press, 1976.

Cassirer, Ernst. *An Essay on Man: An Introduction to a Philosophy of Human Culture*. New Haven and London: Yale University Press, 1974.

Castoriadis, Cornelius. *The Imaginary Institution of Society*. Cambridge, UK: Polity Press, 1997.

Castoriadis, Cornelius. *World in Fragments: Writings on Politics, Society, Psychoanalysis, and the Imagination*. Stanford: Stanford University Press, 1997.

Chrétien, Jean-Louis. *Hand to Hand: Listening to the Work of Art*. Translated by S.E. Lewis. New York: Fordham University Press, 2003.

Chrétien, Jean-Louis. *The Call and the Response*. Translated by A.A. Davenport. New York: Fordham University Press, 2004.

Chrétien, Jean-Louis. "The Wounded Word: The Phenomenology of Prayer." Translated by B.G. Prusak. In *Phenomenology and the "Theological Turn": The French Debate*, edited by D. Janicaud et al., 147–175. New York: Fordham University Press, 2000.

Cornford, Francis MacDonald. *From Religion to Philosophy: A Study in the Origins of Western Speculation*. Princeton: Princeton University Press, 1991.

Dante Alighieri. *Purgatorio*. Translated by J. Hollander and R. Hollander. New York: Doubleday, 2003.

Dante Alighieri. *Vita nuova*. Translated by D.S. Cervigni and E. Vasta. Notre Dame: The University of Notre Dame Press, 1995.

Deleuze, Gilles, and Félix Guattari. *What Is Philosophy?*. Translated by H. Tomlinson and G. Burchell. London and New York: Verso, 1995.

Derrida, Jacques. *The Gift of Death*. Translated by D. Wills. Chicago and London: The University of Chicago Press, 1996.

Djuth, Marianne. "Veiled and Unveiled Beauty: The Role of the Imagination in Augustine's Esthetic." *Theological Studies* Vol. 68 (2007): 77–91.

Duttlinger, Carolin. "Studium, Aufmerksamkeit, Gebet: Walter Benjamin und die Kontemplation." In *Profanes Leben: Walter Benjamins Dialektik der Säkularisierung*, edited by D. Weidner, 95–119. Frankfurt am Main: Suhrkamp Verlag, 2010.

Ecclesia Catholica. *Katechismus der Katholischen Kirche*. München, Wien, Leipzig, Freiburg, and Linz: Oldenbourg, Benno, Paulusverlag, and Veritas, 1993.

Eisler, Rudolf. "Einbildungskraft." In *Kant-Lexikon: Nachschlagewerk zu Kants sämtlichen Schriften, Briefen und handschriftlichen Nachlass*. 1930, digitized 2004. http://www.textlog.de/rudolf-eisler.html. Accessed July 22, 2015.

Eisler, Rudolf. "Schwärmerei." In *Kant-Lexikon: Nachschlagewerk zu Kants sämtlichen Schriften, Briefen und handschriftlichen Nachlass*. 1930, digitized 2004. http://www.textlog.de/rudolf-eisler.html. Accessed July 22, 2015.

Foucault, Michel. "On the Genealogy of Ethics: An Overview of Work in Progress." In *The Foucault Reader*, edited by P. Rabinow, 340–372. London: Penguin Books, 1991.

Gadamer, Hans-Georg. "Aesthetics and Hermeneutics." Translated by D.E. Linge. In *The Gadamer Reader: A Bouquet of the Later Writings*, edited by R.E. Palmer, 123–131. Evanston: Northwestern University Press, 2007.

Gadamer, Hans-Georg. *Praise of Theory: Speeches and Essays*. Translated by C. Dawson. New Haven and London: Yale University Press, 1998.

Gadamer, Hans-Georg. *Truth and Method*. Translated by J. Weinsheimer and D.G. Marshall. London and New York: Bloomsbury Academic, 2003.

García-Rivera, Alex. "Communion and Community: The Language of the Sacraments." In *Languages of Worship/El lenguaje de la liturgia*, edited by R. Gómez, 38–44. Chicago: Liturgy Training Publications, 2004.

Gendler, Tamar. "Imagination." *Stanford Encyclopedia of Philosophy*. March 14, 2011. https://plato.stanford.edu. Accessed May 23, 2015.

Gordon, Cyrus H. *The Common Background of Greek and Hebrew Civilizations*. New York and London: W.W. Norton and Company, 1965.

Greenaway, Peter. *The Cook, the Thief, His Wife, and Her Lover*. DVD. 1989; London: Fabulous Films, 2016.

Greenaway, Peter. *The Pillow Book*. DVD. 1996; Stockholm: Atlantic Film AB, 2006.

Greenaway, Peter. *The Pillow Book*. Movie script. Paris: Éditions Dis Voir, 1996.

Gross, Steffen W. *Felix Aestheticus: Die Ästhetik als Lehre vom Menschen. Zum 250. Jahrestag des Erscheinens von Alexander Gottlieb Baumgartens "Aesthetica."* Würzburg: Verlag Königshausen and Neumann, 2001.

Hawthorne, Christopher. "Flesh and Ink." *Salon Magazine* June 6, 1997. https://www.salon.com/1997/06/06/greenaway970606/. Accessed July 21, 2020.

Hegel, Georg Wilhelm Friedrich. *Aesthetics: Lectures on Fine Art, Volume 1*. Translated by T.M. Knox. Oxford: Clarendon Press, 1988.

Hegel, Georg Wilhelm Friedrich. *The Phenomenology of Spirit*. Edited and translated by T. Pinkard. Cambridge, UK: Cambridge University Press, 2018.

Heidegger, Martin. *Being and Time*. Translated by J. Stambaugh, translation revised by D.J. Schmidt. Albany: State University of New York Press, 2010.

Heidegger, Martin. *Kant and the Problem of Metaphysics*. Translated by R. Taft. Bloomington: Indiana University Press, 1997.

Heidegger, Martin. "Letter on 'Humanism.'" Translated by F.A. Capuzzi. In *Pathmarks*, edited by W. McNeill, 239–276. Cambridge, UK: Cambridge University Press, 1998.

Heidegger, Martin. "Memorial Address." In *Discourse on Thinking: A Translation of Gelassenheit*, translated by J.M. Anderson and E.H. Freund, 43–57. New York: Harper and Row, 1966.

Heidegger, Martin. *Nietzsche, Volume 1: The Will to Power as Art; Volume 2: The Eternal Recurrence of the Same*. Edited and translated by D.F. Krell. San Francisco: HarperSanFrancisco, 1991.

Heidegger, Martin. "The Origin of the Work of Art." In *Poetry, Language, Thought*, edited and translated by A. Hofstadter, 15–86. New York: Harper Perennial Modern Thought, 2013.

Heidegger, Martin. "What Is Metaphysics?." Translated by W. Kaufmann. In *Pathmarks*, edited by W. McNeill, 277–290. Cambridge, UK: Cambridge University Press, 1998.

Henrich, Dieter. "Gedanken zur Dankbarkeit." In *Bewusstes Leben: Untersuchungen zum Verhältnis von Subjektivität und Metaphysik*, 152–193. Stuttgart: Philipp Reclam jun., 1999.

Henrich, Dieter. "Gedanken zur Dankbarkeit." In *Oikeiosis: Festschrift für Robert Spaemann*, edited by R. Löw, 69–86. Weinheim: Acta Humaniora, 1987.

Hjarvad, Stig. *En verden af medier: Medialiseringen af politik, sprog, religion og leg* (A World of Media: The Medialization of Politics, Language, Religion, and Play). Frederiksberg: Samfundslitteratur, 2008.

Hofmann, Werner. *Die Moderne im Rückspiegel: Hauptwege der Kunstgeschichte*. München: C.H. Beck Verlag, 1998.

Homer. *The Odyssey*. Edited by L.R. Loomis and translated by S. Butler. Cabin John: Wildside Press, 2007.

Horace. *The Art of Poetry: An Epistle to the Pisos*. Translated by G. Colman. Gloucester: Dodo Press, 2008.

Husserl, Edmund. *Ideas Pertaining to a Pure Phenomenology and to a Phenomenological Philosophy, First Book: General Introduction to a Pure Phenomenology*. Translated by F. Kersten. In *Collected Works, Volume 2*, edited by R. Bernet. Dordrecht: Kluwer Academic Publishers, 1983.

Jansen, Julia. "Phenomenology, Imagination and Interdisciplinary Research." In *Handbook of Phenomenology and Cognitive Science*, edited by S. Gallagher and D. Schmicking, 141–158. Dordrecht: Springer Science+Business Media, 2010.

Joyce, James. *A Portrait of the Artist as a Young Man*. Edited by J. Johnson. New York: Oxford University Press Inc., 2008.

Jüthner, Julius. "Kalokagathia." In *Charisteria: Alois Rzach zum achtzigsten Geburtstag dargebracht*, edited by M. Adler et al., 99–119. Reichenberg: Verlag von Gebrüder Stiepel, 1930.

Jørgensen, Dorthe. *Aber die Wärme des Bluts: Et studium i den romantisk-moderne dialektik imellem vilje til Form og erfaring af faktisk fragmentering. I anledning af G.W.F. Hegels fortrængning af modernitetserfaringen* (Aber die Wärme des Bluts: A Study in the Romantico-Modern Dialectic between the Will to Form and the Experience of Actual Fragmentation. On the Occasion of G.W.F. Hegel's Displacement of the Experience of Modernity). Aarhus: Modtryk, 1996.

Jørgensen, Dorthe. *Aglaias dans: På vej mod en æstetisk tænkning* (Aglaia's Dance: Toward an Aesthetic Thinking). Aarhus: Aarhus University Press, 2008.

Jørgensen, Dorthe. "Bønnens æstetik" (The Aesthetics of Prayer). In *Den skønne tænkning: Veje til erfaringsmetafysik. Religionsfilosofisk udmøntet* (Beautiful Thinking: Pathways to the Metaphysics of Experience. Religio-Philosophically Implemented), 759–774. Aarhus: Aarhus University Press, 2014.

Jørgensen, Dorthe. *Den skønne tænkning: Veje til erfaringsmetafysik. Religionsfilosofisk udmøntet* (Beautiful Thinking: Pathways to the Metaphysics of Experience. Religio-Philosophically Implemented). Aarhus: Aarhus University Press, 2014.

Jørgensen, Dorthe. "Erfahrung von Göttlichkeit in einer modernen Welt." Translated by C. Diehn. In *Gelebte Religionen: Untersuchungen zur sozialen Gestaltungskraft religiöser Vorstellungen und Praktiken in Geschichte und Gegenwart. Festschrift für Hartmut Zinser zum 60. Geburtstag*, edited by H. Piegeler et al., 241–253. Würzburg: Königshausen and Neumann, 2004.

Jørgensen, Dorthe. "Etik og transcendens" (Ethics and Transcendence). *1. Omtanke: Større end kroppen—omskæring* (1. Consideration: Larger than the Body—Circumcision). November 21, 2018. https://omtanke1.tt-eksistensen.dk. Accessed November 29, 2018.

Jørgensen, Dorthe. "Experience, Metaphysics, and Immanent Transcendence." In *Truth and Experience: Between Phenomenology and Hermeneutics*, edited by D. Jørgensen et al., 11–30. Newcastle upon Tyne: Cambridge Scholars Publishing, 2015.

Jørgensen, Dorthe. "Fornemmelsens filosofi" (The Philosophy of Sensitivity). In *Filosofi og kunst* (Philosophy and Art), edited by U. Thøgersen and B. Troelsen, 33–45. Aalborg: Aalborg University Press, 2012.

Jørgensen, Dorthe. "Guddommelighedserfaring i en moderne verden" (Experiencing Divinity in a Modern World). In *Interesse for Gud*, edited by H. Brandt-Pedersen and N. Grønkjær, 98–117. Frederiksberg: Anis, 2002.

Jørgensen, Dorthe. *Historien som værk: Værkets historie* (History as a Work: The Work's History). Aarhus: Aarhus University Press, 2006.

Jørgensen, Dorthe. "Hvad er æstetik?" (What is Aesthetics?). In *Æstetik og pædagogik* (Aesthetics and Pedagogy), edited by M.B. Johansen, 23–38. Copenhagen: Akademisk Forlag, 2018.

Jørgensen, Dorthe. *Hvorfor er vi så fantasiforskrækkede? Om reformationen og æstetikken* (Why Are We Afraid of the Imagination? On the Reformation and Aesthetics). Frederiksberg: Eksistensen, 2017.

Jørgensen, Dorthe. "Krop og bøn" (Body and Prayer). *Kritisk forum for praktisk teologi* (Critical Forum for Practical Theology) Vol. 155 (2019): 62–70.

Jørgensen, Dorthe. "Meningen med kunst" (The Meaning of Art). *Billedkunstneren* Vol. 1 (2014): 20–21.

Jørgensen, Dorthe. "Meningen med kunst" (The Meaning of Art). In *Nærvær og eftertanke: Mit pædagogiske laboratorium* (Presence and Afterthought: My Educational Laboratory), 148–151. Skive: Wunderbuch, 2015

Jørgensen, Dorthe. "Menneskets modtagelighed for tro" (Man's Receptivity to Faith). In *Midt i en medietid: Digitalisering og medialisering i religion, filosofi og kunst* (In a Time of Mass Media: Digitalization and Medialization in Religion, Philosophy, and Art), 49–59. Frederiksberg: Eksistensen, 2020.

Jørgensen, Dorthe. *Nær og fjern: Spor af en erfaringsontologi hos Walter Benjamin* (Near and Far: Traces of an Ontology of Experience in Walter Benjamin). Aarhus: Modtryk, 1990.

Jørgensen, Dorthe. *Nærvær og eftertanke: Mit pædagogiske laboratorium* (Presence and Afterthought: My Educational Laboratory). Skive: Wunderbuch, 2015.

Jørgensen, Dorthe. *Poetic Inclinations: Ethics, History, Philosophy*. Aarhus: Aarhus University Press, 2021.

Jørgensen, Dorthe. "Preface." In *Verdenspoesi: Malerier og tankebilleder* (World Poetry: Paintings and Thought-Images), 73–73. Aarhus: Women's Museum, 2011.

Jørgensen, Dorthe. "Profan metafysik: Om det guddommelige i metafysikken" (Profane Metaphysics: On the Divine in Metaphysics). *Kritisk forum for praktisk teologi* (Critical Forum for Practical Theology) Vol. 78 (1999): 80–94.

Jørgensen, Dorthe. "Protestantism and Its Aesthetic Discontents." In *The Reformation of Philosophy: The Philosophical Legacy of the Reformation Reconsidered*, edited by M.T. Mjaaland, 193–205. Tübingen: Mohr Siebeck, 2020.

Jørgensen, Dorthe. "Sensoriness and Transcendence: On the Aesthetic Possibility of Experiencing Divinity." In *Transcendence and Sensoriness: Perceptions, Revelation, and the Arts*, edited by S.A. Christoffersen et al., 63–85. Leiden: Brill Academic Publishers, 2015.

Jørgensen, Dorthe. "Skær af guddommelighed: Skønhedens aktualitet i æstetikhistorisk perspektiv" (A Glow of Divinity: The Relevance of the Beautiful in Aesthetic-Historical Perspective). *Passepartout: Skrifter for kunsthistorie* (Passepartout: Writings on Art History) Vol. 16 (2000): 11–36.

Jørgensen, Dorthe. *Skønhed—En engel gik forbi* (Beauty—An Angel Passed By). Aarhus: Aarhus University Press, 2006.

Jørgensen, Dorthe. *Skønhedens metamorfose: De æstetiske idéers historie* (The Metamorphosis of Beauty: History of Aesthetic Ideas). Odense: Odense University Press, 2001.

Jørgensen, Dorthe. "Teologisk æstetik i Norden? Den 'æstetiske vending' til diskussion" (Theological Aesthetics in the Nordic Region? Questioning the 'Aesthetic Turn'). In *Kontinuitet og radikalisme* (Continuity and Radicalism), edited by K. Garne and R. Vangshardt, 257–269. Copenhagen: Vartov, 2013.

Jørgensen, Dorthe. "The Intermediate World." *Open Philosophy* Vol. 1 (2018): 50–58.

Jørgensen, Dorthe. "The Philosophy of Imagination." In *Handbook of Imagination and Culture*, edited by T. Zittoun and V.P. Gläveanu, 19–45. New York: Oxford University Press, 2017.

Jørgensen, Dorthe and Bettina Winkelmann. *Verdenspoesi: Malerier og tankebilleder* (World Poetry: Paintings and Thought-Images). Aarhus: Women's Museum, 2011.

Jørgensen, Dorthe. "Æstetik og intuition" (Aesthetics and Intuition). In "Trump-paradigmet" (The Trump Paradigm), edited by H. Laura et al. *Weekendavisen*, Sektion 4 (Ideer), December 29, 2017: 4.

Kandinsky, Wassily. *Concerning the Spiritual in Art*. Translated by M.T.H. Sadler. New York: Dover Publications, 1977.

Kant, Immanuel. *Anthropology from a Pragmatic Point of View*. Edited and translated by R.B. Louden. New York: Cambridge University Press, 2006.

Kant, Immanuel. *Critique of Practical Reason*. Edited and translated by M.J. Gregor. Cambridge, UK: Cambridge University Press, 1999.

Kant, Immanuel. *Critique of Pure Reason*. Edited and translated by P. Guyer and A.W. Wood. Cambridge, UK: Cambridge University Press, 1998.

Kant, Immanuel. *Critique of the Power of Judgment*. Edited and translated by P. Guyer and E. Matthews. New York: Cambridge University Press, 2000.

Kant, Immanuel. "Essay on the Maladies of the Head." In *Observations on the Feeling of the Beautiful and Sublime and Other Writings*, edited and translated by P. Frierson and P. Guyer, 205–220. New York: Cambridge University Press, 2011.

Kant, Immanuel. *Gesammelte Schriften* (Akademie-Ausgabe), I–XXIII. InteLex Past Masters. http://www.nlx.com.

Kant, Immanuel. *Religion within the Boundaries of Mere Reason: And Other Writings*. Edited and translated by A. Wood and G.D. Giovanni. Cambridge, UK: Cambridge University Press, 1998.

Kant, Immanuel. "Reviews of Herder's Ideas on the Philosophy of the History of Mankind." In *Political Writings*, edited by H.S. Reiss and translated by H.B. Nisbet, 201–220. New York: Cambridge University Press, 1991.

Kearney, Richard. *Poetics of Imagining: From Husserl to Lyotard*. London: HarperCollins Academic, 1991.

Kearney, Richard. *Poetics of Modernity: Toward a Hermeneutic Imagination*. Atlantic Highlands: Humanities Press, 1995.

Kearney, Richard. *The Wake of Imagination: Toward a Postmodern Culture.* Minneapolis: University of Minnesota Press, 1991.

Kierkegaard, Søren. *Concluding Unscientific Postscript to Philosophical Fragments.* In *Kierkegaard's Writings, Volume 12/1–2*, edited and translated by H.V. Hong and E.H. Hong. Princeton: Princeton University Press, 1992.

Kierkegaard, Søren. *Either/Or: Part I–II.* In *Kierkegaard's Writings, Volume 3–4*, edited and translated by H.V. Hong and E.H. Hong. Princeton: Princeton University Press, 1988.

Kierkegaard, Søren. *Philosophical Fragments, or a Fragment of Philosophy/Johannes Climacus, or De omnibus dubitandum est.* In *Kierkegaard's Writings, Volume 7*, edited and translated by H.V. Hong and E.H. Hong. Princeton: Princeton University Press, 1987.

Kierkegaard, Søren. *Stages on Life's Way: Studies by Various Persons.* In *Kierkegaard's Writings, Volume 11*, edited and translated by H.V. Hong and E.H. Hong. Princeton: Princeton University Press, 1991.

Kierkegaard, Søren. *The Concept of Irony, with Continual Reference to Socrates/Notes of Schelling's Berlin Lectures.* In *Kierkegaard's Writings, Volume 2*, edited and translated by H.V. Hong and E.H. Hong. Princeton: Princeton University Press, 1992.

Klee, Felix. *Paul Klee: His Life and Work in Documents.* New York: George Braziller, 1962.

Klee, Paul. "Creative Confession, 1920." In *Creative Confession and Other Writings*, 7–14. London: Tate Publishing, 2013.

Klee, Paul. "Exact Experiments in the Realm of Art, 1928." In *Creative Confession and Other Writings*, 18–19. London: Tate Publishing, 2013.

Klee, Paul. "Exakte Versuche im Bereich der Kunst." *Bauhaus: Zeitschrift für Bau und Gestaltung* Vol. 2, No. 2–3 (1928): 17–17.

Klee, Paul. *Paul Klee Notebooks 1: The Thinking Eye.* Edited by J. Spiller, translated by R. Manheim. London: Lund Humphries, 1961.

Klein, Christoph. *Das grenzüberschreitende Gebet: Zugänge zum Beten in unserer Zeit.* Göttingen: Vandenhoeck and Ruprecht, 2004.

Küwen, Roxana. "Circus performer Roxana Küwen." July 25, 2017. https://www.youtube.com/watch?v=BxfHO7dg86o. Accessed November 18, 2018.

Küwen, Roxana. "Roxana Küwen: Jonglieren mit Händen und Füssen." November 30, 2016. https://www.youtube.com/watch?v=b8NKLUvZ7Dk. Accessed November 18, 2018.

Lewis-Elgidely, Verna. *Koinonia in the Three Great Abrahamic Faiths: Acclaiming the Mystery and Diversity of Faiths.* South Bend: Cloverdale Books, 2007.

Longinus, "On the Sublime." In *Aristotle, Poetics. Longinus, On the Sublime. Demetrius, On Style.* Translated by W.H. Fyfe, 143–307. Loeb Classical Library 199. Cambridge, MA: Harvard University Press, 1995.

Løgstrup, K.E. *Kunst og erkendelse: Kunstfilosofiske betragtninger: Metafysik II* (Art and Knowledge: Art Philosophical Considerations. Metaphysics II). Edited by S. Andersen et al. Copenhagen: Gyldendal, 1983.

Løgstrup, K.E. "Min tids tre fromhedsbølger: En smule subjektivt set" (The Three Waves of Piety in My Time: Somewhat Subjectively Seen). In *Solidaritet og kærlighed og andre essays* (Solidarity and Love and Other Essays), edited by O. Jensen et al., 146–157. Copenhagen: Gyldendal, 1987.

Meier, Georg Friedrich. *Anfangsgründe aller schönen Wissenschaften: Part I–III*. Hildesheim and New York: Georg Olms Verlag, 1976.

Mensch, James. "Prayer as Kenosis." In *The Phenomenology of Prayer*, edited by B.E. Benson and N. Wirzba, 63–72. New York: Fordham University Press, 2005.

Merleau-Ponty, Maurice. *Phenomenology of Perception*. Translated by D.A. Landes. London and New York: Routledge, 2012.

Merleau-Ponty, Maurice. *The Visible and the Invisible: Followed by Working Notes*. Translated by A. Lingis. Evanston: Northwestern University Press, 1968.

Mirbach, Dagmar. "Alexander Gottlieb Baumgarten: Fantasia, facultas fingendi og phantasmata/fictions." Translated by S. Liisberg. *Slagmark* Vol. 46 (2006): 33–47.

New Testament Greek Lexicon—King James Version. http://www.biblestudytools.com/lexicons/greek/kjv. Accessed July 30, 2015.

Norton, Robert E. *The Beautiful Soul*. Ithaca: Cornell University Press, 1995.

Novalis, *The Novices of Sais*. Translated by R. Manheim. New York: Archipelago Books, 2005.

Nørager, Troels, "Heart as Metaphor in Religious Language." In *Metaphor and God-talk*, edited by I. Boeve and K. Feyaerts, 215–232. Bern: Peter Lang, 1999.

O'Grady, Patricia. *Thales of Miletus: The Beginnings of Western Science and Philosophy*. Aldershot and Burlington: Ashgate, 2002.

Otto, Rudolf. *The Idea of the Holy*. Translated by J.W Harvey. New York: Oxford University Press, 1970.

Pallasmaa, Juhani. *The Eyes of the Skin: Architecture and the Senses*. Chichester: John Wiley and Sons, 2005.

Pamuk, Orhan. *The Innocence of Objects*. Translated by E. Oklap. New York: Abrams, 2012.

Pamuk, Orhan. *The Museum of Innocence: A Novel*. Translated by M. Freely. London: Faber and Faber, 2010.

Pamuk, Orhan. *The Naive and the Sentimental Novelist*. Translated by N. Dikbas. London: Faber and Faber, 2010.

Perseus Digital Library. Edited by G.R. Crane. Tufts University. http://www.perseus.tufts.edu. Accessed July 29, 2020.

Pico della Mirandola, Gianfrancesco. *On the Imagination.* Translated by H. Caplan. New Haven: Yale University Press, 1930.

Plamadeala, Antonie. *Traditie si libertate in spiritualitatea ortodoxa.* Sibiu, 1983.

Plato, "Euthyphro." Translated by G.M.A. Grube. In *Plato: Complete Works*, edited by J.M. Cooper and D.S. Hutchinson, 1–16. Indianapolis and Cambridge, MA: Hackett Publishing Company, 1997.

Plato. *Phaedrus.* Translated by A. Nehamas and P. Woodruff. In *Plato: Complete Works*, edited by J.M. Cooper and D.S. Hutchinson, 506–556. Indianapolis and Cambridge, MA: Hackett Publishing Company, 1997.

Plato. *Protagoras.* Translated by S. Lombardo and K. Bell. In *Plato: Complete Works*, edited by J.M. Cooper and D.S. Hutchinson, 746–790. Indianapolis and Cambridge, MA: Hackett Publishing Company, 1997.

Plato. *Republic.* Translated by G.M.A. Grube, translation revised by C.D.C. Reeve. In *Plato: Complete Works*, edited by J.M. Cooper and D.S. Hutchinson, 971–1223. Indianapolis and Cambridge, MA: Hackett Publishing Company, 1997.

Plato. *Sophist.* Translated by N.P. White. In *Plato: Complete Works*, edited by J.M. Cooper and D.S. Hutchinson, 235–293. Indianapolis and Cambridge, MA: Hackett Publishing Company, 1997.

Plato. *Sophist.* Translated by H.N. Fowler. In *Plato in Twelve Volumes, Volume 7: Theaetetus; Sophist*, edited by J. Henderson, 259–459. Loeb Classical Library 123. London and Cambridge, MA: William Heinemann and Harvard University Press, 1921. Perseus Digital Library. http://www.perseus.tufts.edu. Accessed, July 29, 2020.

Plato. *Symposium.* Translated by A. Nehamas and P. Woodruff. In *Plato: Complete Works*, edited by J.M. Cooper and D.S. Hutchinson, 457–505. Indianapolis and Cambridge, MA: Hackett Publishing Company, 1997.

Plato. *Theaetetus.* Translated by M.J. Levett, translation revised by M. Burnyeat. In *Plato: Complete Works*, edited by J.M. Cooper and D.S. Hutchinson, 157–234. Indianapolis and Cambridge, MA: Hackett Publishing Company, 1997.

Plotinus, "Ennead I.6: On Beauty." In *Ennead, Volume I: Porphyry on the Life of Plotinus. Ennead I*, translated by A.H. Armstrong, 229–264. Loeb Classical Library 440. Cambridge, MA: Harvard University Press, 1969.

Redeker, Mirjam-Christina. *Wahrnehmung und Glaube: Zum Verhältnis von Theologie und Ästhetik in gegenwärtiger Zeit.* Berlin and New York: De Gruyter, 2011.

Ricoeur, Paul. *The Rule of Metaphor: The Creation of Meaning in Language.* Translated by R. Czerney, K. McLaughlin, and J. Costello. London and New York: Routledge, 2004.

Sartre, Jean-Paul. *The Imaginary: A Phenomenological Psychology of the Imagination.* Translated by J. Webber. London and New York: Routledge, 2004.

Schelling, Friedrich Wilhelm Joseph von. *Philosophical Investigations into the Essence of Human Freedom*. Translated by J. Love and J. Schmidt. Albany: State University of New York Press, 2007.

Schiller, Friedrich. "Naive and Sentimental Poetry." In *Naive and Sentimental Poetry, and On the Sublime: Two Essays*, edited and translated by J.A. Elias, 81–190. New York: Frederick Ungar Publishing Company, 1975.

Schiller, Friedrich. *On the Aesthetic Education of Man in a Series of Letters*. Edited and translated by E.M. Wilkinson and L.A. Willoughby. Oxford: Clarendon Press, 1967.

Schleiermacher, Friedrich. *On Religion: Speeches to Its Cultured Despisers*, edited by R. Crouter. Cambridge, UK: Cambridge University Press, 1996.

Schleiermacher, Friedrich Daniel Ernst. *Über die Religion: Reden an die Gebildeten unter ihren Verächtern (1799)*. In *Kritische Gesamtausgabe I/2: Schriften aus der Berliner Zeit 1796–1799*, edited by G. Meckenstock, 185–326. Berlin and New York: Walter de Gruyter, 1984.

Schleiermacher, Friedrich Daniel Ernst. *Über die Religion: Reden an die Gebildeten unter ihren Verächtern*. In *Kritische Gesamtausgabe I/12: Über die Religion (2.–)4. Auflage, Monologen (2.–)4. Auflage*, edited by G. Meckenstock, 1–321. Berlin and New York: Walter de Gruyter, 1995.

Schmitz, Hermann. *Der unerschöpfliche Gegenstand: Grundzüge der Philosophie*. Bonn: Bouvier Verlag, 1990.

Schmitz, Hermann et al. "Emotions outside the Box—the New Phenomenology of Feeling and Corporeality." *Phenomenology and the Cognitive Sciences* Vol. 10, No. 2 (2011): 241–259.

Schmitz, Hermann. *Kurze Einführung in die Neue Phänomenologie*. Freiburg and München: Verlag Karl Alber, 2009.

Schreyer, Lothar. *Erinnerungen an Sturm und Bauhaus*. München: Albert Langen and Georg Müller, 1956.

Seesemann, Heinrich. *Der Begriff 'Koinonia' im Neuen Testament*. Giessen: Verlag von Alfred Töpelmann, 1933.

Shaftesbury, Lord. *Characteristics of Men, Manners, Opinions, Times*. Edited by L.E. Klein. Cambridge, UK: Cambridge University Press, 1999.

Shonagon, Sei. *The Pillow Book of Sei Shonagon*. Translated by I. Morris. London, Melbourne, and Kuala Lumpur: Oxford University Press, 1967.

Tauber, Alfred I. (ed.). *The Elusive Synthesis: Aesthetics and Science*. Dordrecht, Boston, and London: Kluwer Academic Publishers, 1996.

Taylor, Mark C. *After God*. Chicago and London: The University of Chicago Press, 2007.

The Chicago Manual of Style Online. Seventeenth edition. Chicago: Chicago University Press, 2017. www.chicagomanualofstyle.org.

The Merriam-Webster Dictionary. Springfield: Merriam-Webster Inc., 2020. www.merriam-webster.com.

Theissen, Gerd. *Transparente Erfahrung: Predigten und Meditationen*. Gütersloh: Gütersloher Verlagshaus, 2014.

Trías, Eugenio. *Pensar la religión*. Barcelona: Ediciones Destino, 1997.

Trías, Eugenio. "Thinking Religion: the Symbol and the Sacred." In *Religion*, edited by J. Derrida and G. Vattimo, 95–110. Stanford: Stanford University Press, 1998.

Vattimo, Gianni. *Belief*. Translated by L. D'Isanto and D. Webb. Stanford: Stanford University Press, 1999.

Vattimo, Gianni. *Credere di credere*. Milano: Garzanti, 1996.

Vervoordt, Axel and Daniela Ferretti (eds.). *Intuition*. Gent: AsaMER, 2017.

Vico, Giambattista. *The New Science of Giambattista Vico. Unabridged Translation of the Third Edition (1744) with the addition of 'Practic of the New Science.'* Translated by T.G. Bergin and M.H. Fisch. Ithaca and London: Cornell University Press, 1984.

Wankel, Hermann. *Kalos kai agathos*. Diss. Würzburg. Julius-Maximilians-Universität zu Würzburg, 1961.

Welsch, Wolfgang. *Ästhetisches Denken*. Stuttgart: Reclam Verlag, 1993.

Westphal, Merold. "Prayer as the Posture of the Decentered Self." In *The Phenomenology of Prayer*, edited by B.E. Benson and N. Wirzba, 13–31. New York: Fordham University Press, 2005.

Yates, Christopher. *The Poetic Imagination in Heidegger and Schelling*. London and New York: Bloomsbury Academic, 2013.

Acknowledgments

Chapter 1: "The Meaning of Art." Not previously published in English. Published in Danish as "Meningen med kunst," *Billedkunstneren 1, marts 2014*, ed. Miriam Katz (Copenhagen: Billedkunstnernes Forbund, 2014), 20–21, and reprinted in Dorthe Jørgensen, *Nærvær og eftertanke: Mit pædagogiske laboratorium* (Skive: Wunderbuch, 2015), 148–151.

Chapter 2: "The Significance of Sensitivity." Not previously published in English. Published in Danish as "Fornemmelsens filosofi: Æstetik, fænomenologi og erfaringsmetafysik," *Filosofi og kunst*, eds. Ulla Thøgersen and Bjarne Troelsen (Aalborg: Aalborg University Press, 2012), 33–45.

Chapter 3: "Body and Prayer." Not previously published in English. Published in Danish as "Krop og bøn," *Kritisk forum for praktisk teologi 155*, eds. Jette Bendixen Rønkilde and Rikke Juul (Frederiksberg: Eksistensen, 2019), 62–70.

Chapter 4: "The Receptivity to Faith." Not previously published in English. Published in Danish as "Menneskets modtagelighed for tro," *Midt i en medietid: Digitalisering og medialisering i religion, filosofi og kunst*, eds. Kjeld Slot Nielsen and Sanne B. Thøisen (Frederiksberg: Eksistensen, 2020), 49–59.

Chapter 5: "Protestantism and Its Aesthetic Discontents." Previously published in *The Reformation of Philosophy: The Philosophical Legacy of the Reformation Reconsidered*, ed. Marius Timmann Mjaaland (Tübingen: Mohr Siebeck, 2020), 193–205. Presented orally in both Danish and English and with various titles at conferences in Oslo, Aarhus, and Copenhagen in 2016–2017.

Chapter 6: "The Metamorphosis of Beauty." Not previously published in English. Published in Danish as "Skær af guddommelighed: Skønhedens aktualitet i æstetikhistorisk perspektiv," *Passepartout: Skrifter for kunsthistorie 16*, ed. Peter Brix Søndergaard (Aarhus: Department of Art History, Aarhus University, 2000), 11–36. Revised for the present volume.

Chapter 7: "Experience, Metaphysics, and Immanent Transcendence." Previously published in *Truth and Experience: Between Phenomenology and Hermeneutics*, eds. Dorthe Jørgensen, Gaetano Chiurazzi, and Søren Tinning (Newcastle upon Tyne: Cambridge Scholars Publishing, 2015), 11–30. "Published with the permission of Cambridge Scholars Publishing" (requested remark).

Chapter 8: "Sensuousness and Transcendence." Previously published as "Sensoriness and Transcendence: On the Aesthetic Possibility of Experiencing Divinity," *Transcendence and Sensoriness: Perceptions, Revelation, and the Arts*, eds. Svein Aage Christoffersen et al. (Leiden: Brill Academic Publishers, 2015), 63–85.

Chapter 9: "The Philosophy of Imagination." Previously published in *Handbook of Imagination and Culture*, eds. Tania Zittoun and Vlad Petre Gläveanu (New York: Oxford University Press, 2017), 19–45.

Chapter 10: "The Intermediate World." Previously published as "The Intermediate World: A Key Concept in Beautiful Thinking," *Open Philosophy 1/1*, ed. Graham Harman (de Gruyter online, 2018; https://doi.org/10.1515/opphil-2018-0005), 50–58. Presented orally at the conference "In-Between" (Aarhus University, October 10–12, 2016).

Chapter 11: "The Aesthetics of Prayer." Previously not published in English. Published in Danish as "Bønnens æstetik" in Dorthe Jørgensen, *Den skønne tænkning: Veje til erfaringsmetafysik. Religionsfilosofisk udmøntet* (Aarhus: Aarhus University Press, 2014), 759–774.

The journal editors and publishers who have authorized me to reproduce previously published writings have my deep gratitude.

Imaginative Moods
© The Author and Aarhus University Press 2021
Cover: Camilla Jørgensen, Trefold
Layout and typesetting: Trefold
Publishing editor: Henrik Jensen
This book is typeset in Chronicle Text and printed on Munken Premium Cream 13, 100 g
Printed by Narayana Press, Denmark

Printed in Denmark 2021

ISBN 978 87 7219 105 8

Aarhus University Press
aarhusuniversitypress.dk

Published with the financial support of Aarhus University Research Foundation

All rights reserved. Except for the quotation of short passages for the purpose of criticism and review, no part of this publication may be reproduced, stored in a retrieval system, or transmitted, in any form or by any means, without the prior permission of the publisher.

International distributors

Oxbow Books Ltd., oxbowbooks.com
ISD, isdistribution.com